THE
HISTORY OF HORSE RACING
IN 100 OBJECTS

DEDICATION

To my mother and father, who told me about half of this stuff a long time ago

ACKNOWLEDGEMENTS

Michelle Grainger for being immaculately in charge; **Graham Dench** for elegance in editing; **Matt Limbert** for eloquence in design; **Liz Ampairee** for a great idea; **Edward Whitaker** for photographic wizardry; **David Cramphorn** for valour on the picture desk; **Nick Pulford** for the old days and a password; **Tim Cox** for profound and generous knowledge; **Sean Magee** for many good journeys in bad cars; **PF Sloan** for clarity; **David Ashforth** for the usual inspiration; **Botond Kovacs** for the Budapest connection; **Chica Herbert** for heat, light and cake; **Patricia Stewart** for that Arkle sparkle; **Clare Gabbett-Mulhallen** for usually being right.

RACING POST

THE
HISTORY OF
HORSE RACING
IN 100 OBJECTS

STEVE DENNIS

First published by Pitch Publishing on behalf of Racing Post, 2021

Pitch Publishing
A2 Yeoman Gate
Yeoman Way
Worthing
Sussex
BN13 3QZ

www.pitchpublishing.co.uk
info@pitchpublishing.co.uk
www.racingpost.com/shop

© 2021, Steve Dennis

Every effort has been made to trace the copyright. Any oversight will be rectified in future editions at the earliest opportunity by the publisher.

All rights reserved. No part of this book may be reproduced, sold or utilised in any form or transmitted in any form or by any means, electronic or mechanical, including photocopying, recording or by any information storage and retrieval system, without prior permission in writing from the Publisher.

A CIP catalogue record is available for this book
from the British Library.

ISBN 9781839500794

Typesetting and origination by Pitch Publishing

Printed and bound by Replika Press Pvt. Ltd.

CONTENTS

	INTRODUCTION	8
1.	FIRST PAST THE POST	10
2.	THE VERY STUFF OF ENGLAND	12
3.	STILL RACING AFTER ALL THESE YEARS	14
4.	THE SWIFTEST HORSE THIS BELL TO TAKE	16
5.	THE SPORT OF KINGS AND QUEENS	18
6.	FOUNDING FATHERS OF THE HORSE RACE	21
7.	DOING THINGS DIFFERENTLY	24
8.	A CLUB FOR RACING FANS	27
9.	STEEPLE TO STEEPLE	30
10.	CLIMBING UP INTO THE STANDS	32
11.	HELIOTROPE, CORNFLOWER, OLD GOLD	35
12.	AND THE REST NOWHERE	38
13.	SALE OF THE CENTURIES	41
14.	THE TOSS OF A COIN	44
15.	TO BE A THOROUGHBRED	47
16.	THE LIMEY ARISTOCRAT	50
17.	HATS, HORSES AND HIGH SOCIETY	52
18.	GOING ALONG FOR THE RIDE	55
19.	THE MOST FAMOUS FENCE IN THE WORLD	57
20.	A FOUR-YEAR-OLD NAMED MACCABEUS	60
21.	THE WHOLE WORLD WAS AT EPSOM	63
22.	WEIGHED IN, WEIGHED IN	65
23.	A CERTAIN WAY OF LIFE	67
24.	THE SPELL OF THE CUP	70
25.	THE AVENGER OF WATERLOO	73
26.	54	75
27.	A QUANTUM SHIFT	78
28.	MORE THAN THE HORSES	80
29.	BALLAD OF THE TIN MAN	83
30.	BLACK JOCKEYS ALL, AND ALL FORGOTTEN	86
31.	OUT ON HIS OWN	89

32.	A CELEBRATION OF LIFE	92
33.	DEEDS NOT WORDS	95
34.	THE PERFECT CLIMAX TO THE SEASON	98
35.	I GOTTA HORSE	101
36.	A GREATER LEVEL OF SAFETY	104
37.	BIG MAC, TOMMO AND THE NOBLE LORD	106
38.	A DEGREE IN OBSOLETE MATHS	109
39.	CHOICE	112
40.	A MILE A MINUTE	115
41.	FIRST, NUMBER …	118
42.	MORE THAN A HORSE RACE	121
43.	NON-TRIERS TO THE BACK	124
44.	PLACE IT ON LUCKY DAN	127
45.	SOME ENCHANTED EVENING	130
46.	STEVE'S BOYISH FACE	132
47.	GREATNESS IS FOREVER	135
48.	THE TEST OF TIME	138
49.	HE IS MOVING LIKE A TREMENDOUS MACHINE!	140
50.	ON THE MAP	144
51.	WELL DONE, GORDON	147
52.	THE JOLLY MADE A NOISE	150
53.	THAT'S RACING	153
54.	SHIBBOLETH	156
55.	YOU NEVER FORGET	159
56.	SOMETHING ALWAYS PRESENT	162
57.	LISTENING TO THE BLOWER	165
58.	SIC TRANSIT GLORIA MUNDI	167
59.	ARKLEARKLEARKLEARKLEARKLE	170
60.	A SAFETY NET HELD BY MANY HANDS	173
61.	A PRINCIPLE INVOLVED	175
62.	FOR THOSE ABOUT TO ROCK	178
63.	THE MAGIC NUMBER	180
64.	TO TEST THE BEST	183
65.	A FIVE-FOOT GIRAFFE	186
66.	ALL THESE FIRSTS	188
67.	THE WORD MADE FLESH	191

68.	WIT BY GILLETTE	194
69.	£4.75 A WEEK	197
70.	A NON-EXISTENT DYING AUNT	199
71.	THE GREATEST STORY EVER TOLD	202
72.	FOUR BROTHERS	205
73.	THE ANGRY BRIGADE	208
74.	SOMETHING OUT OF NOTHING	211
75.	THE SWEET-TOOTHED HORSE	214
76.	THE END AND THE MEANS	217
77.	LEGENDS IN THEIR LIFETIMES	220
78.	SEVEN-LETTER, SEVEN-FIGURE WORD	223
79.	TAKEN	226
80.	COME ON MY LOT!	229
81.	ALL ABOUT THE HORSES	232
82.	NO BLOODY GOOD	235
83.	FANTASY RACING	237
84.	THE MARE	240
85.	CARPET, SPANDEX AND RUBBER	243
86.	THE WILD ROMANCE OF LIFE	246
87.	ON THE SEVENTH DAY	249
88.	INTO THE VOID	252
89.	A YOUNG ITALIAN JOCKEY	255
90.	THE GREAT ACCUMULATOR	258
91.	UNDER THE SKIN	261
92.	DIGITAL REVOLUTION	263
93.	A TWINKLE IN HER EYE	265
94.	A FULL AND FULFILLING LIFE	267
95.	MY HORSE	270
96.	NOISE, COLOUR AND INTRIGUE	273
97.	PENETRATION AND SHEAR	276
98.	SHOW RATHER THAN TELL	279
99.	ALONE AT THE SUMMIT	281
100.	JUST THE GLORY OF A HORSE	284

INTRODUCTION

Horse racing is at bottom a thoroughly simple affair. The point has always been to find the fastest horse, the one who can beat the rest, and bet on that outcome with like-minded people holding slightly differing opinions. It is no more and no less, and its purity of intent has come through the last five centuries uncorrupted, which is more than you can say for the humans involved in it.

Over time we have adulterated this simplicity, added layer upon layer of veneer designed to complement it as well as complicate it, to improve it, refine it, expand it, although at heart it remains the same sport and retains the same spirit the first Elizabethans knew. So here, within these pages, are what might be called the instructions for horse racing, which when put together like jigsaw pieces result in a broad appreciation of the sport, the industry, the business, and, lest it be occasionally forgotten, the game, the entertainment, the thrill.

The writer Graham Greene divided his output into two genres, 'novels', which were serious works dealing with the human condition, and 'entertainments', which were thriller-type productions dealing a little less with the human condition, often only a very little less. This book falls into the 'entertainment' category; it is not an encyclopedia and should not be treated as such, although every attempt has been made to ensure scrupulous accuracy. A favourite disclaimer once assured the reader that 'all information may be incomplete or inaccurate', which is hard to beat for insouciance, but no book of this size can convey the entire grandeur of this grand old enterprise, at once trivial and vital, nor of the individuals within it.

History is written by the winners, so the pages are peopled with the sport's winners, great horses, great trainers, great jockeys, great innovators. The battles of history are fought by foot-soldiers whose lives too often end as merely footnotes, so room has been found for them too, the pioneers and pathfinders who suffered not always in silence so that those who followed them would not have to do the same.

Also included are technical and technological advances that have ushered racing from the 16th century into the embrace of the 21st century, although if a time traveller from King Charles's court materialised at a modern racecourse he or she would still recognise the sport essentially as their own. Some elements of racing are darkly marbled with wrongdoing and malpractice, and light has been cast on them. Other elements are delightfully comic, and their presence leavens these pages as they have leavened life itself.

Here too are the glorious names of famous and favourite horses, and hopefully your public and private champions appear in the text, with apologies at the ready in case they do not. It is uplifting to understand that horses can become the object of fervent, fierce adoration for men and women who may never have seen them in the flesh, but whose imagination has nevertheless been captivated by these majestic, magnificent animals.

This book has been written not for the expert but for the enthusiast, for the novice as much as for the knowledgeable, for the keen student rather than for the seen-it-all-before connoisseur. The primary purpose has been to initiate interest and knowledge rather than to reinforce it, to provide a window on the sport through which to climb and explore the territory beyond.

There are 100 chapters, only a hundred golden threads in such a rich and extensive tapestry, but these are the threads that hold the whole together. Hopefully there is something here for everyone, just as there is within the compass of horse racing itself.

1

The winning post.   Image © Edward Whitaker

FIRST PAST THE POST

Perhaps it is best to begin at the end.

The winning post signifies the end of the race, no more than a marker, but it defines everything that goes before and everything that comes after. A winning post is the end that justifies the meaning of competition.

People and horses have been making their way towards some form of finishing line since the emergence of the competitive instinct, a moment indefinable in the history of evolution but indelible in its story. My horse is faster than yours. No, mine is faster. All right. Race you. First one to that tree, house, stream is the winner, and then we'll know which horse is the best. And all the great ones, from Eclipse to Frankel, joined inextricably in blood and brilliance, have passed that test when it most mattered.

Fast forward through the millennia, across the line in the sand in front of the emperor's seat at the Circus Maximus, past the steeple of a church in an Irish village, all the way up to the stick surmounted by a red circle at your local racecourse. Its construction and its appearance barely matter – something as ubiquitous, as vital as a winning post has no mandated style or dimensions – but what it stands for matters immeasurably.

Here, function outstripped form a long time ago. In its early manifestations it would have been a wooden pole, cut from a tree on m'Lord's estate, oak, elm, ash, it didn't matter, hammered into the turf at a suitable viewing point. Truly, not much has changed since antiquity, and why would it? No one comes to see the winning post, it does not need to be decorative, a coat of paint every couple of years and a new one every ten years.

Much of the time it is simply something to support the mirror for the photo-finish camera, with a freshly mown strip of grass helping spectators to distinguish the winning line. At major meetings, the winning post can be just a small sliver of metal or wood at the centre of a vast advertising hoarding, almost lost in the corporate blizzard but its significance undimmed.

The frequently cited words of the great Italian trainer and breeder Federico Tesio – 'The thoroughbred exists because its selection has depended, not on experts, technicians, or zoologists, but on a piece of wood: the winning post of the Epsom Derby' – have lost a little of their accuracy but none of their thrust.

Tesio was speaking in the first half of the 20th century, and his aphorism rang true in his time. Nowadays there are winning posts all around the world that may lay claim to an equal or perhaps even greater role in underpinning the existence of the thoroughbred, but the sentiment sustains. The selection of the thoroughbred is still dependent on the one that reaches the winning post first.

It's not called the finishing post, because many may finish but only one can win. In racing, although not always in life, winning is everything. Those who reach the winning post too late lose the race and potentially their opportunity to influence the breed.

Or those who reach it too early. At certain racecourses – Longchamp and Sandown Park are the best examples – there are two winning posts, no more than a few metres apart, to account for certain vagaries in course topography and starting positions. Now and again a jockey blunders, mistaking the post being used for a particular race, and delivers what he or she believes to be a winning challenge for the wrong winning post.

The concept has found its way out of the sporting sphere, an acknowledgement of its importance. Elections are won on the 'first-past-the-post' system, completed projects have been 'got over the line', those who narrowly fail to reach their goal are 'pipped at the post'. The symbolism of the winning post is planted deep in the human psyche.

Strip it clean, shorn of all equipment and personnel save for two horses and two riders, and a race is still possible – but without a winning post there is nothing to distinguish it, nothing to lift it above a spot of exercise. The question has been asked uncountable times: which horse is the fastest? We look to the winning post, witness, prosecutor and judge all in one, and it tells us the answer.

2

Finishing line at the Kiplingcotes Derby.   Image © Alamy

THE VERY STUFF OF ENGLAND

It is the spring of 1519. King Henry VIII is happily married to his first wife, Catherine of Aragon. Ferdinand Magellan is busily preparing for the voyage later in the year that will become the first circumnavigation of the globe. Leonardo da Vinci has just a few weeks to live, Michelangelo is still basking in the praise for his Sistine Chapel ceiling. Gravity is a mystery, the sun goes around the earth, printed books are new-fangled nonsense and probably won't last.

And in the wolds of the East Riding of Yorkshire, not far from Beverley, on a chilly March morning, the Kiplingcotes Derby is run for the first time over four miles of open country. More than 500 years later, it is still being run. It is the oldest horse race in the world that is still held annually, and its numerous endearing eccentricities are the very stuff of England.

It was not called the Kiplingcotes Derby at the beginning, though. The appellation 'Derby', which has attached itself to races of every stripe, would not become common for at least another 300 years, as we shall see. It was called the Kiplingcotes Plate, and it would have been one of many similar contests taking place all over what would two centuries hence be designated Britain.

This race alone of them has survived war, extreme weather conditions and virulent disease. One of the least arcane rules of the race is that it must take place every year, otherwise it may never be run again. To circumvent this, in times of trouble, a lone local farmer leads a lone local horse from the stone starting post in Etton to the wooden winning post near Londesborough to ensure the race's future. The Kiplingcotes Derby, the ravens at the Tower of London, both must never be allowed to vanish.

What are the other rules? Ah, yes. Come through the looking glass and see. Anyone can take part. Just arrive with a horse.

Any number of horses may compete, as long as their riders report to the clerk of the course by 11am on the day of the race – always the third Thursday in March – with their £4.25 entry-money in hand. Some of the horses are former racers with their names changed to Sally, Bobby or the like, some are sturdy-legged hunters, some no more or less than Thelwellian family pets. The riders are an equally eclectic bunch.

Each rider must weigh at least ten stone. Those who are lighter must carry weights in their pockets to bring them up to the minimum. All are addressed before the race by the clerk, who instructs them in the ancient rule that 'any rider who layeth hold of any of the other riders or striketh any of them shall win no prize', and then all participants walk or trot the four-mile length of the course to the starting place.

The race takes place over country track and muddy field, and a furlong from the finish the course crosses the busy A614, where the clerk's aides stop the traffic both ways to allow the horses to clatter across the road. This is the first time the spectators, who largely gather around the clerk and the winning post, have seen anything of the race. Simply being there, though, is regarded as generous compensation for not knowing what the hell is going on.

The winning rider is awarded the trophy and £50. Uniquely, the rider of the runner-up pockets £4 from each entry fee and – if the field is large enough, and it usually is – often takes home more money than the winner. It makes little sense but it is part of the festivities which, after a period of dwindling interest, have become more popular and much better attended in recent years.

An hour, maybe two hours after the last of the stragglers has crossed the finishing line on the long lane that leads to Londesborough Wold Farm, there is little to suggest that anything out of the ordinary has happened here, save for the hoofprints in the mud. A little like Brigadoon, that mythical Scottish village that appears out of the gloaming every hundred years, the Kiplingcotes Derby comes to vivid thrilling life but briefly and then is gone, leaving no trace, for another year.

The race has endured for more than 500 years, the last sporting link to a time immemorial. May it last another 500 years.

3

Roman walls at Chester. *Image © Racing Post*

STILL RACING AFTER ALL THESE YEARS

Twenty years after the good gentlemen of Yorkshire had lit the seemingly eternal flame of Kiplingcotes, while Henry VIII was enjoying a short marital interregnum between Jane Seymour (third wife) and Anne of Cleves (fourth), as the sun faithfully orbited the earth, on the other side of the country another ancient pillar of the sport was ushered on to the stage. Football's loss was racing's gain when, in 1539, Chester racecourse staged its first meeting.

Chester is the oldest racecourse in the world, which is to say that it has the longest unbroken history of any extant racecourse. It is also the smallest racecourse in Britain, barely a mile round, almost circular, girdled by the River Dee and the remnants of the Roman city walls that provide a fine vantage point from which to watch the racing without paying a penny. Some of the best things in life are indeed free.

The meadows by the river had previously been the site of an infamous Shrove Tuesday football match, which was less an exposition of the beautiful game and more an excuse for a jolly good fight. In 1533 the city fathers, weary of the bloodshed and general bedlam, showed the footballers the red card and opened the way for racing to become the Shrove Tuesday sport of choice.

At the outset racing took place just once a year – like all racecourses of the time – on a feast day or holiday, but over the centuries the repertoire was expanded and by the middle of the 18th century the May meeting for which Chester is renowned had been inaugurated. The centrepiece of the May meeting is the Chester Cup, a handicap first run as the Tradesmen's Cup in 1824, while the Chester Vase and Cheshire Oaks are often relevant trials for the Derby and the Oaks at Epsom the following month.

Chester is the wide-margin winner when it comes to racecourse vintage. The first – officially recorded – race at Newmarket took place in 1622, while Ascot joined the fixture list in 1711. The wide-open acreage of The Curragh has probably played host to unofficial races since Brian Boru was a lad, but there is written record of racing taking place there in 1682.

France's oldest racecourse – it is stressed that these labels apply only to racecourses still in existence on their original site – is neither Longchamp nor Chantilly but little Laloubere, tucked into the lee of the Pyrenees, which first staged racing in 1809.

In Australia, 'Royal' Randwick in Sydney might be reckoned the old man of the party, having begun operations in 1833, but it was closed between 1840 and 1860 and the mantle therefore passes to Melbourne's mighty Flemington (1840). Both tracks are some way behind the oldest racecourse in the southern hemisphere, Champ De Mars in Port Louis, Mauritius, which flung wide its gates in 1812.

The oldest major racecourse in the US is sublime Saratoga in New York state (1864), although minor-league 'fairground circuit' Pleasanton in California began life six years earlier. Moreover, Fair Grounds in New Orleans staged racing for the first time in 1838, although it closed twice before becoming a permanent fixture in 1871. However, there is no quibble over the senior racecourse in Hong Kong, with the first meeting at glittering Happy Valley in 1846 occurring more than a century before the opening of sister track Sha Tin.

Chester is the grand old daddy of them all. It's apt that in a city of antiquity, founded by the Romans in the year 79, one of the sport's earliest footprints is still visible, still thriving, still racing after all these years.

4

The bells, the bells. *Image © Racing Post*

THE SWIFTEST HORSE THIS BELL TO TAKE

Lady Dacre is long dead but her name lives on, carefully engraved into the world's oldest sporting trophy, her gift to racing that has kept on giving since 1599.

The trophy comprises two little round bells, one gold and one silver, which are awarded – metaphorically, as the originals are a museum item, and another trophy is used instead – to the owner of the winner of the Carlisle Bell, run at (where else?) Carlisle every June.

Engraved on the golden bell, the larger of the two at approximately two and a half inches in diameter, are the words 'The Sweftes Horse Thes Bell To Tak For Mi Lade Daker Sake', and the old English needs no translation. The bell is believed to date from 1559; the silver bell bears the inscription 'HBMC 1599', which is thought to stand for Henry Baines, Mayor of Carlisle.

Who was Lady Dacre/Lade Daker? It is likely that she was Lady Elizabeth Dacre, mother of 11 children, wife of William Dacre, Third Baron of Gilsland and Greystoke, a prominent landowner and governor in north-west England. It is also likely that she gave the bell as a prize for the winner of a race on the annual feast day, and when a new, valuable race was inaugurated at Carlisle in 1599 the bell was evidently a sufficiently prestigious item to serve as both race name and trophy, along with the newer 'Baines' bell.

Trophies are an integral part of racing, with the post-race presentation ceremonies an opportunity for those who pay the bills to stand in the limelight, with trainers, jockeys and stable staff often receiving miniature versions of the original. The venerable Cup and Classic races generally supply an equally venerable gold or silver trophy for the owner, with the Gold Cup at Ascot, the Kentucky Derby and the Melbourne Cup particularly elegant examples of the genre.

Major races such as the Grand National, the Derby, the St Leger and those at the Breeders' Cup provide substantial trophies of a different but equally solid and satisfying form, and all the way down the racing pyramid beaming owners with excitedly tremulous hands are given something to hold as the camera clicks. Paintings, bronzes, glassware, photo frames and books – depending on the race sponsor's preference and pocket – are all commonly presented. The prize-money at this level of the sport is generally quickly spent on the next month's training fees, but a shiny something for the sideboard lasts forever.

The biggest trophies by size can often accompany the smallest races by value. The great silver cup for the amateur-ridden Foxhunter Chase at the Cheltenham Festival must be nearly 4ft high, and has been described by trainer Willie Mullins as 'the most magnificent trophy of the week'.

The amateur faction of the sport seems to deal in the most memorable trophies – point-to-point racing is short on prize-money but long on large silver cups, and often a bag or two of carrots for the winning horse. The Newmarket Town Plate, almost as eccentric as the Kiplingcotes Derby, almost as antediluvian as the Carlisle Bell, having been run since 1666 over a course used solely for this particular race, offers a box of Newmarket sausages and a voucher to a local clothes shop as part of the prize-giving.

The Carlisle Bell is not a big race nowadays, just an ordinary handicap over a few yards short of a mile, and its importance derives from its antiquity rather than its position in the racing calendar. The swiftest horse usually wins it, though; Lady Dacre would be pleased.

5

The royal crown. *Image © Getty*

THE SPORT OF KINGS AND QUEENS

It has always been the sport of kings and queens. After all, didn't Richard III stake his whole kingdom on a horse, and wasn't his subsequent defeat explained away by the want of a horseshoe nail? Excuses for beaten horses have become much more imaginative since 1485.

Before thoroughbreds existed, Henry VIII established a number of Royal Studs around the realm. A little further down the regnal line, James I was the first monarch to note the suitability of Newmarket Heath for field sports. He ordered the construction of a palace (which, much rebuilt and restored, later became Palace House, now the site of the National Horse Racing Museum) in the centre of the town and under his rule the first recorded race at Newmarket – a match for £100 between horses belonging to Lord Salisbury and the Marquess of Buckingham, with Salisbury's steed declared the winner – was run.

Charles I was also fond of Newmarket, but not with the same unbridled relish as his son Charles II, who was known as the Merry Monarch and gleaned a goodly part of that merriment from the races. He inaugurated the Town Plate at Newmarket and rode the winner of the race in 1671, and the Rowley Mile at the course – over which the 1,000 and 2,000 Guineas are run – earned its name from his favourite hack Old Rowley. The King also was given the nickname Old Rowley, as his libidinous nature and myriad offspring were said to resemble the activity of his stallion.

His niece Anne was never quite as merry but left an indelible mark on the sport she supported enthusiastically when, in 1711, on a ride through Windsor Forest, she emerged from the trees into a clearing near the village of Ascot and perceived it as a fine spot for horses to race. The first meeting at Ascot took place in August that year and the first race on the opening day of the modern Royal Ascot is the Queen Anne Stakes.

Not all 'racing monarchs' were great or good, though. George IV, of whom it was written that 'he would always prefer a girl and a bottle to politics and a sermon', making him a natural role model for a great many in racing, was embroiled in a famous scandal over the running of his horse Escape in October 1791.

At that time he was Prince of Wales, and Escape was regarded as one of the best horses in the land. However, he finished last of four at odds-on in a race at Newmarket, only the following day to reappear in a similar event and win easily at 5-1. The inference drawn by the public was that jockey Samuel Chifney had stopped the horse in the first race to obtain better odds in the second, and that the Prince of Wales was in on the scheme.

The stewards of the day believed the worst, and senior steward Sir Charles Bunbury (of whom more later) informed the Prince that if he continued to employ Chifney, 'no gentleman would start against him'. Rather than visit further disgrace on his jockey, the Prince sold his horses and gave up racing, although when he became King he renewed his affection for the sport.

Other residents of Buckingham Palace have gained considerable success on the Turf without attracting notoriety. Queen Victoria, though largely unamused by racing, bred fillies' Triple Crown winner La Fleche (1892) and the inaugural July Cup winner Springfield (1876) at the Hampton Court Stud. Her son Bertie, the future King Edward VII, was just as merry and had as much extra-curricular fun as Charles II and before ascending the throne owned homebred Triple Crown winner Diamond Jubilee (1900) and Grand National winner Ambush II (1900).

King George VI owned fillies' Triple Crown winner Sun Chariot (1942), but his greatest contribution to racing was through fostering the interest in the sport of his wife, Queen Elizabeth the Queen Mother, and their daughter Elizabeth II, whose passion for, knowledge of and influence within racing has had no equal among any of her crowned predecessors.

The Queen has owned and bred the winners of many major Flat races, including Dunfermline (1977 Oaks, St Leger), Highclere (1974

1,000 Guineas, Prix de Diane), Carrozza (1957 Oaks), Pall Mall (1958 2,000 Guineas), Aureole (1954 King George VI and Queen Elizabeth Stakes) and Estimate (2013 Gold Cup). The Queen Mother was devoted to the jumps, and owned many much-loved stalwarts including Special Cargo, hero of the indelible 1984 Whitbread Gold Cup, the enduring steeplechaser Game Spirit and Devon Loch, who the whole world knows as the unforgettable loser of the 1956 Grand National.

More than the big-race victories, though, the Queen's gift to horse racing has been as its figurehead. Her love for and devotion to the sport has endowed it with a legitimacy and favour that may otherwise have passed it by in the modern era. In a world bestrode and beset by abrupt perception rather than patient debate, it is not too facile to say that the Queen's unstinting support for racing has given those who might be indifferent or hostile to it pause for more considered thought. Colloquially, if the Queen is for it, it must be all right.

There are more major races around the world named in her honour than for anyone else, but the line of succession, in the racing sense, is uncertain. In his younger days Prince Charles rode in steeplechases and Princess Anne enjoyed success on the Flat, winning the ladies' race on Diamond Day at Ascot in 1987 aboard Ten No Trumps, but whether future generations of royalty will embrace the sport with the fervour the Queen has always shown is open to question.

6

The likeness of the Darley Arabian. Image © Alamy

FOUNDING FATHERS OF THE HORSE RACE

This far we have come without meeting the distinction of the thoroughbred as a specific breed. Up until this point, 'racehorses' were also work horses, farm horses, ordinary everyday horses whose pedigrees were dictated by convenience, by proximity, by chance. Three horses, whose names resonate in every jurisdiction of the world, at every stud farm, in the mind of every breeder, changed all that around the beginning of the 18th century.

The Byerley Turk, the Darley Arabian, the Godolphin Barb (also known as the Godolphin Arabian). It may not be strictly correct to say that absolutely every thoroughbred ever born can have its lineage traced back to this triumvirate – every blueblood in the Derby, every old soldier in a handicap at an Australian country track, every mud-covered gelding in a Sligo novice chase – for there were other contemporary stallions who have contributed to this broad genealogy, but these three are regarded as the founding fathers of the race, the horse race.

First came the Byerley Turk (probably foaled in 1678), who certainly lived life to the full. He was captured from the Turkish army in 1687 and brought to England, taking his name from his owner Captain Robert Byerley, who then rode him to war at the Battle of the Boyne two years later. A stud career in the north of England was due reward for the old warrior, and his influence took shape through his grandson Partner, grandsire of the prolific Herod.

In his hoofprints came the Darley Arabian (probably foaled in 1700). He was bought in Syria by Thomas Darley and shipped back to Yorkshire to stand at the family stud, where he sired Flying Childers, arguably the first great racehorse, and his brother Bartlet's Childers, great-grandsire of the magnificent Eclipse.

Bringing up the rear was the Godolphin Barb (probably foaled in 1724), who was brought from the Yemen via Paris to Derbyshire, from where he was purchased by Lord Godolphin and put to stud near Newmarket. He sired Cade, who sired Matchem, whose bloodline was unusually potent.

All three horses were small, elegant, lithe, tough creatures, light of bone and swift of foot, and their hot Arabian blood swiftly infused the traditional British stock with these most desirable characteristics. The begetting continued apace, and before long these three little horses were as those ancient grey-bearded Old Testament patriarchs whose issue had spread widely throughout the land. By 1753 they were all dead, yet what mattered most in them lived on.

More than 250 years later, a glance back through the male line of every pedigree inevitably ends with one of the same three names. However, inbreeding has always been a staple ingredient of the genetic soup, and over time one name began to appear much more frequently than the other two. One tap-root proved stronger, its branches bore more fruit, and that particular family tree belonged to the Darley Arabian.

The blood of the Darley Arabian, undiluted by the passage of time, has descended through the vital pipeline that leads from Bartlet's Childers via Eclipse, Waxy, Birdcatcher, Stockwell and Phalaris (foaled 1913), who changed the game at a stroke, creating the shape of modern bloodstock through his sons Pharos and Sickle.

Pharos sired Nearco, whose three-pronged assault on the stud books led via Nasrullah to multiple US champion sire Bold Ruler and thence to Secretariat and Seattle Slew; via Royal Charger to Turn-to and on to multiple Japanese champion sire Sunday Silence; via Nearctic to the unparalleled Northern Dancer, Sadler's Wells and Galileo in Europe. Sickle's grandson Polynesian sired the enormously influential Native Dancer, whose son Raise A Native produced the prolific Alydar and Mr Prospector in the US.

The offspring of this diminutive white-faced, white-footed horse have inherited the racing earth. Pedigree experts have calculated that around 95 per cent of the thoroughbreds alive today trace back to the Darley

Arabian, with that number increasing incrementally with every decade, while the other two lines are in danger of fading away altogether. Success breeds success, it's said, and the lines begun by the Byerley Turk and the Godolphin Barb have not bred sufficient success in the last 100 years, may be on the brink of becoming no more than evolutionary footnotes.

Through the revitalising effect of Phalaris, the influence of the Darley Arabian reigns supreme in modern thoroughbred genetics. In a century's time, writers may refer to him simply as the sole progenitor of the thoroughbred. Imagine: one little horse, and the whole world in his image.

7

Vital training equipment. Image © Author

DOING THINGS DIFFERENTLY

In such situations, it is usually hard to resist reaching for the now-hackneyed phrase from the novel The Go-Between: The past is a foreign country; they do things differently there. If author LP Hartley had received royalties for the use of just those 11 words he would never have needed to pick up his pen again.

But in racing's past they did do things differently, and nothing was done more differently in the 1600s, 1700s and early 1800s than the training of racehorses. Today's beasts are cosseted to the point of suffocation in comparison with their antique brethren in that foreign land of the past, and the fundamental reason for that is the way they were raced.

In racing's early eras, most races were run in four-mile heats, with a mere handful of runners, sometimes as few as two. There might be three heats of the same race run in an afternoon, and horses would be expected as a matter of course to gallop 12 miles in the span of a few hours. Modern racehorses wouldn't gallop as far as 12 miles in two weeks of training, and would take months to reach that distance on the racecourse.

Between heats, horses were removed to a shelter at each racecourse known as the Rubbing House for a little primitive physiotherapy. They were rubbed down, scraped free of sweat, swaddled in blankets to keep them warm and walked to keep them limber until such time as the next heat took place.

At Salisbury racecourse the old Rubbing House has recently been restored to Grade II Listed status. The original mortar was dated as pre-1706, which renders it a contemporary of the Salisbury Articles of 1654, a parchment now in the National Horse Racing Museum that sets out the conditions for the four-mile Salisbury City Bowl. Musketmen were stationed at every mile post and instructed to fire their guns as the horses passed them, to alert the crowd to their progress. In 1769 the race was won by the aforementioned Eclipse.

The City Bowl is still extant but is now a quotidian handicap run over a mile and three-quarters and the racecourse makes use of a commentator to keep the crowd informed rather than a small private militia. The past may be a foreign country but it's sometimes a grander, more exciting one.

There is an increasingly ramshackle example of a Rubbing House at the defunct racecourse on the High Moor of Middleham, which would also have been used during training while the mercifully short-lived method of conditioning known as the Yorkshire Sweats held sway.

This involved galloping horses daily for up to four miles while wrapped in two or three rugs, to provoke heavy sweating and thereby make them lighter and fitter. If this seems medically unusual, it should be remembered that at this time humans were regularly bled to remove 'bad humours' from the system and to treat disease. Perhaps the past wasn't quite so grand or exciting after all.

As time passed races were reduced in distance and training methods became more conventional. Instead of being worn to a raveling by galloping for four miles under blankets, horses were brought to a mid-level of fitness through roadwork, being trotted for weeks on the highways to build 'bone' and core strength before graduating to greater exertion on the gallops, and then not over long distances.

This process of evolutionary reduction reached its peak with the introduction of interval training, whereby horses are worked uphill for short distances in frequent repetition, usually on a surface such as woodchip or a proprietary sand-rubber composition. It is often the case that young horses only gallop on grass for the first time when they make their debut at the races, having done all their preparation on artificial gallops.

The name of the pioneer who first adopted this method of training is difficult to ascertain, with many claims outstanding, success having a hundred fathers and all that, but few would dispute that it was Martin Pipe who elevated the process into an art form. He was a jump trainer from the West Country, he was a revolutionary, he transformed the way racehorses were trained, and his reward was more than 4,000 winners, 15 championships between 1989 and 2005, and the sincere flattery of widespread imitation.

'I wanted the gallop to be in a straight line, five furlongs long, the horses cantered and galloped up and down – that turned out to be interval training,' he told the *Racing Post* in explanation of his methods.

'Getting there was all trial and error. The horses seemed to enjoy what they were asked to do, they love routine, love repetition. They had a break at the top of the strip and cantered back down – if you canter up something you have to canter back down because it makes you use the other set of muscles. Seems obvious, really. Just common sense.'

Common sense is a variable compound. To the trainers of the 18th century it was common sense to drive a horse to fitness by main force. If a child could be sent up a chimney, a horse could be galloped into the ground for its health, dammit. The shape of racing at the time encouraged this behaviour.

Now horses are coaxed to fitness without knowing that it's happening, an almost subliminal process of conditioning, and the modern shape of racing with shorter races, briefer bursts of considerable exertion, supports this method. Our forefathers, in their old-style hats and coats, would see the future as a foreign country, where they do things differently.

8

The Jockey Club in Newmarket. *Image © Racing Post*

A CLUB FOR RACING FANS

Like many things in life, the Jockey Club is not what it used to be. In the minds of the general public, such as they pay the subject any mind, the Jockey Club is the law, it runs horse racing. This was once true, but things have changed.

In 1993, the Jockey Club transferred its responsibilities for governance of the sport to the newly formed British Horseracing Board (BHB). It maintained responsibility for regulatory and disciplinary affairs, but in turn handed these over to the Horseracing Regulatory Authority (HRA) in 2006. The following year the BHB and HRA merged, in an amalgamation of acronyms, to form the British Horseracing Authority (BHA), which now performs the task of running racing that the Jockey Club had undertaken since 1750.

It all started in a pub, the Star and Garter tavern in Pall Mall, central London, and it had nothing to do with jockeys, for jockeys were several social strata below the aristocrats and gentlemen-about-town who came together to form their own private club, in the same respect that the Reform or the Garrick are private gentlemen's clubs. It was simply a club for racing fans, who could bicker and bet over cups of coffee and be with their own kind. 'Jockey' is merely an old word for horseman, which no doubt amused them in their begarlanded nobility.

Soon, the Jockey Club relocated itself to Newmarket, as that's where the horses were, built another coffee house at which to congregate, and this became the Jockey Club Rooms that now hold vast collections of racing art and arcana. The club grew, and because many of its members were very influential, held high rank and high office, it began to assume the status – almost by default – of an official body. It began to make rules for racing at Newmarket, and soon those rules were adopted by other racecourses in Britain and in time by racecourses around the world, in jurisdictions that set up their own versions of the Jockey Club based on the original model.

The Jockey Club became the lawman of racing. It contrived the rules, it ratified them, it enforced them. Its word was lapidary, it brooked no argument. Some of its most senior stewards – Sir Charles Bunbury, Lord George Bentinck, Admiral Henry Rous – were innovators and reformers who shaped the sport with the iron fist and the velvet glove, where appropriate.

Women, of course, were not invited. The Jockey Club was a boys' club, one, possibly two steps up in social awareness from a treehouse with a sign stuck to the door reading 'no gurls alowd'. It took more than 200 years of external cultural upheaval before the Jockey Club first elected a female member in 1977, whereupon it admitted three at once: Helen Johnson Houghton, Lady Halifax and Priscilla Hastings. Mrs Johnson Houghton had been shabbily treated by the Jockey Club, as shall be seen later.

With little other interruption, the Jockey Club successfully maintained its position as the head and figurehead of the sport until the growing commercial imperatives of the 21st century began, like Canute's incoming tide, to wash away the old certainties and privileges.

Before this, though, with a seer's prescience, the Club formed a vehicle called Racecourse Holdings Trust (RHT) in 1964 to purchase Cheltenham and save it from developers. Other racecourses – Warwick, Market Rasen, Haydock – soon congregated under the Trust's umbrella, coming in out of the hard rain of financial insecurity, and in this way was paved the Club's route towards its 21st-century reinvention.

The Club is now the biggest commercial operator in the sport, with the mandate to 'act for the long-term good of British racing in everything it does'. The RHT is now Jockey Club Racecourses with 15 venues, including Aintree, Epsom, Sandown and Exeter, in its ownership. The Club owns the National Stud in Newmarket; Jockey Club Estates oversees the gallops in Newmarket and Lambourn; Racing Welfare is the Club's charitable arm. And, to complete the circle, the Jockey Club once again has its headquarters in London, although this time not in a Pall Mall boozer.

The Jockey Club once controlled racing, and that imprint on the public consciousness is hard to erase. In an ongoing process of diversification, it now influences racing through commercial, intellectual and digital rights, which is not quite as pithy or catchy but almost as powerful, just as important. The more things change, the more they may stay the same.

9

A steeple, to race to. Image © Getty

STEEPLE TO STEEPLE

It is rare that two people get out of bed in the morning with the express intention of making history, but that is what – so the story goes – Cornelius O'Callaghan and Edmund Blake did in 1752, when on a wager they raced their horses from the steeple of St John's Church in Buttevant to the steeple of St Mary's Church in Doneraile, roughly four miles away through the fields of north County Cork. And so steeplechasing was born.

To suggest that this was the first race of its kind, though, that these two Irish huntsmen were the midwives of a brave new world, is to stretch credulity. The Buttevant-Doneraile race is certainly the first such event to have a written account, but one so sketchy that neither the identity of the winner nor the names of the horses were mentioned, which fosters the belief that when it took place this race was neither as important nor as ground-breaking as hindsight implies.

Hunting was a centuries-old pursuit even then and, given the competitive nature of its participants, it seems self-evident that other riders must have chased each other over stone wall, ditch and stream on their way to a clearly visible end-point. St John's in Buttevant was rebuilt in 1826 so the current steeple may not be the O'Callaghan-Blake version, and St Mary's in Doneraile now has a tower instead of a steeple. Nothing tangible remains but the mythology, which is usually enough. And so steeplechasing was validated.

Its growth was sporadic at first – possibly because it had always been present at a casual level, a steady hum in the background of life – and it wasn't until 1830 that the first organised steeplechase took place in Bedfordshire.

This was evidently the spur for increased interest, and the first edition of the Grand National was run at Aintree in 1836 or 1839, depending on one's faith in the reliability of kept records. The latter date is generally used, and that is certainly the year the race took hold of the public consciousness, a grip it has never relinquished. The National Hunt Committee was convened in 1866 to oversee this branch of the sport, thereby giving it the sobriquet of 'National Hunt' that it still informally retains, and it remained separately governed until the Jockey Club absorbed it in 1968.

Modern jump racing consists of steeplechasing (the big birch fences) and hurdling, and it is generally accepted – in Britain and Ireland – that its popularity exceeds that of Flat racing. This is primarily because of the extended careers of the horses involved, thus enabling a greater connection and affection for them, and the sense that it is possible to succeed without vast sums of money, that there are opportunities for the 'smaller man and woman' that don't exist in Flat racing.

The heartlands of jump racing are squarely in Britain and Ireland. France has a thriving jumping scene and has in recent years become the marketplace for trainers and owners on the left-hand side of the Channel, and in Czechia there is the famous and fearsome Velka Pardubicka, a marvellous spectacle that involves a section of ploughed field and daunting jumps, but elsewhere the sport is more thinly observed. It exists on minority terms in the US and Japan, and in Australia it barely survives owing to concerns over safety aspects.

The closest approximation to the days of Buttevant and Doneraile, however, can be found in point-to-point racing, a strictly amateur sport staged at weekends at courses in rural locations all over Britain and Ireland, with the emphasis firmly on fierce competition, inclusivity and pure fun as opposed to the worldly distractions of money and prestige. It can serve as a springboard to professionalism for promising riders and horses, and also as a soft landing for horses in their dotage.

Meetings are organised by the local Hunt, to which both riders and horses must be affiliated, and run by volunteers. No one races from steeple to steeple any more, but the ghosts of O'Callaghan and Blake would recognise the same spirit that moved them.

10

A grandstand view. Image © Getty

CLIMBING UP INTO THE STANDS

For those who spend their happiest hours at the racecourse, the grandstand becomes a second home. It isn't just something to keep the rain off, but instead a vantage point from which to marvel at great horses and great races; a waiting room for the few minutes it takes for bets won to lift the heart and bets lost to sink the spirit; a great communal confluence where unforgettable moments are shared with complete strangers who know as well as you do how much they mean.

This is the reason that when ancient, rickety grandstands are torn down and bright gleaming edifices erected in their place – as happened at Ascot in 2006, and Longchamp in 2018 – the initial reaction is disappointment and disdain and loss, as though a much-loved old armchair by the fire had been arbitrarily replaced by some awkward chrome-and-leather confection that defies the pursuit of comfort.

The first permanent grandstand at a racecourse, and moreover the first permanent grandstand at any sporting venue, was constructed at York and opened in 1756. Designed by local architect John Carr, it was a two-storey affair with a viewing platform on the roof and ample space within for racegoers to drink and socialise and view the sport.

It was a concept for which the racing world was perfectly ready, and imitations began to spring up at all points of the compass. Beverley, over the border in East Yorkshire, opened its grandstand in 1767. Ascot's first stand was built in 1793. Chester joined the grandstand club in 1819, Epsom's first grandstand was opened in time for the 1830 Derby, and Goodwood's was built the same year.

The only racecourse in Britain that doesn't have a grandstand is Bangor-on-Dee in north Wales, which opened for business in 1859 and has resisted the temptation to raise a grandstand ever since. Spectators stand instead on a grassy mound to watch the action, and hope fervently that the weather is favourable.

The inception of grandstands meant that demarcation became possible, the division of the viewing area at a racecourse into sections, to keep the upper classes away from the hoi polloi and to charge them more for that privilege. Patrons of the earliest grandstands evolved over time into the 'members' of a given racecourse, who pay a yearly subscription fee in return for an enamelled badge and privileges, enjoy the best facilities and the best view of the racing, generally being stationed by the winning post.

Casual racegoers may pay a premium to enter 'Members' or a lesser amount to go into the Tattersalls enclosure, where the right to roam freely about the racecourse is restricted. Even more casual racegoers may settle for the cheap seats of the Silver Ring, which is usually situated some way down the racecourse and provides no access to the parade ring or winner's enclosure.

All these enclosures and divisions are particularly British relics of an increasingly redundant social order. Racecourses in practically all other jurisdictions are far more relaxed in this regard, with general admission allowing nearly all racegoers to go where they please for a nominal sum, and only a small area reserved for those who for some reason feel the need to enjoy a more rarefied and expensive experience.

Certain grandstands are memorably emblematic of their site, such as the twin spires on the main clubhouse at Churchill Downs in the US or the seven-storey edifices tucked into the cityscape at Happy Valley in Hong Kong, but the most architecturally remarkable is at Meydan, in Dubai, which was opened in 2010 and is a mile in length, with capacity for 60,000 people. Ascot's vast grandstand could fit into it four times over.

It makes John Carr's grandstand look like a cupboard, but something so large and impersonal is unlikely to breed the affection engendered by the vast majority of grandstands around the world, a little ramshackle perhaps, in need of a lick of paint, but where every racegoer has a favourite place to stand or sit, to enjoy many happy afternoons and reminisce about happy afternoons of the past.

After the incomparable Secretariat had won the 1973 Belmont Stakes in truly otherworldly style, the celebrated sportswriter Hugh McIlvanney wrote: 'None of us can ever expect to see the like of that again. But let's go on climbing up into the stands, just in case.'

McIlvanney knew the homely potency of the grandstand, the place we go to shout and curse and cheer and roar and groan and sigh and then, with hope rising in our hearts once more, go there again half an hour later, a place of endless possibilities and limitless enjoyment.

11

The jockey's wardrobe. *Image © Edward Whitaker*

HELIOTROPE, CORNFLOWER, OLD GOLD

Red and yellow and pink and green, purple and orange and blue. Sing a rainbow. But don't forget flame and saffron and peach and sage, cyclamen, fuchsia and straw, for the world of jockeys' silks is a riot of colour, a dazzling kaleidoscopic delight.

In a sport full of largely mud-coloured horses, the vivid stripes and spots and diamonds and checks and stars worn by the jockeys have beguiled countless children on their first visit to the races, a shimmering symbol of the excitement inherent in racing. After the children become adults, certain sets of silks remain indivisible in the mind's eye with the horses who bore them to victory: the flaxen mane and tail of Generous with those dark green silks, Sea The Stars in startling sun-yellow, Brigadier Gerard's subtle cerise spots on violet, Slip Anchor running loose on the lead in the Derby with those bright apricot silks against the green grass.

Racehorse owners own the silks; jockeys merely dress up in them. Owners were not required to state their chosen designs until 1762, when 'the greater conveniency of distinguishing the horses in running' was desired. Most of the designs at this time were solid, single colours – the Earl of Waldegrave's 'deep red', the Duke of Grafton's 'sky blue' – and jockeys almost invariably wore black caps.

The plan may not have worked as well as expected. In the Racing Calendar of 1800, the Lords Sackville and Burford are both represented by 'white, black cap', the Marquis of Donegall and Mr Sitwell have selected 'all black', and Sir J. Shelley and Mr Howorth are down for 'orange'. It couldn't happen now.

Since then, almost up to the present day, an owner could register any colour, shade, hue or design he or she wanted as long as no one else had thought of it first. To open the *Benson & Hedges Book of Racing Colours*, first edition 1973, is to evoke WB Yeats's line about 'all the loveliness that has long faded from the world'.

There are around 9,000 designs listed there in full technicolour, more vivid and varied than any paint card, embracing the 159 tints and 22 jacket designs registered at Weatherbys, once the administrative arm of the Jockey Club and now of the British Horseracing Authority. Such largesse is no longer the case.

Owners in Britain are now restricted to just 18 colours, with all the fun ones – heliotrope, cornflower, old gold – proscribed, although owners are allowed to order off-menu (notably for offbeat designs, such as dartboard silks) if they are willing to pay a considerable premium for the privilege. Standardisation is the watchword of the bureaucrat, and commentators are no doubt relieved to not have to distinguish between cream, beige, buff and fawn at distance in murky conditions.

Owners in the US, Australia and Hong Kong appear to labour under no such restrictions. Watching racing in these jurisdictions is an exhilarating visual experience for it seems that anything goes in respect of colour and design – although for some reason 'navy blue' is prohibited in the US. No one seems to mind.

The word 'silks' has been used here as a placeholder, for familiarity's sake. The jackets and caps jockeys wear indeed used to be silk, for money was no object to the sky-blue Duke of Grafton and his ilk, but modern racing colours are made from polyester taffeta or the slightly sheenier nylon satin. Jacket buttons have largely been replaced by press studs, elasticated cuffs have superseded the loose cuffs around which Pat Eddery and Edward Hide wound rubber bands, and woollen jerseys, once de rigueur in jump racing to help fend off the cold, are all but extinct.

Colours can be a commodity, to be bought and sold. Sheikh Mohammed, seeking a distinctive look for his ground-breaking Godolphin venture, sought the old-money prestige and simplicity of the antique, solid, single colour designs. He wanted 'royal blue', but that design was registered to trainer Alan Bailey. Negotiations took place, and for what was reportedly a five-figure sum Sheikh Mohammed purchased the right to register the now world-renowned royal blue colours.

Owners may change their colours if they tire of them or believe they have brought nothing but bad luck. Sometimes they change by accident; Lord Derby's distinctive 'black, white cap' gained a white button when jockey Tommy Weston, racked with nerves before partnering Sansovino in the 1924 Derby, fumbled his white stock (scarf) through a buttonhole and rode so adorned. Sansovino won; the white button was surely lucky; Lord Derby changed his colours accordingly.

Whether a simple or complicated design, multi-coloured or plain, slate grey or kingfisher blue, the coloured jackets jockeys wear are the calling card of racing, its aesthetic essence, the very fabric of the sport.

12

Eclipse's skeleton. *Image © Getty*

AND THE REST NOWHERE

Dem bones, dem bones. Visitors to the Royal Veterinary College in Hertfordshire may come face to face with the earthly remains of the remarkable Eclipse, for here on display are the clean bones of the almost complete skeleton of one of the greatest horses in history.

When Eclipse died of colic in 1789, he was autopsied in an attempt to discover the reason for his superlative ability. It was found that he had a very large heart, which went a long way to explaining his athletic prowess, and thereafter his bones were reassembled and put on display as a curiosity. Later, his skeleton was periodically stripped down, transported around the country and rebuilt, with the consequence that along the way a few of the bones were lost and replaced by suitable bones from other horses. An inspection of the skeleton also reveals that his hooves are missing.

Eclipse (foaled 1764) was a true phenomenon of a horse. Born in the light and shade of a solar eclipse – naming him was a straightforward task – he was a surly individual with one long white sock, prone to galloping with his head low to the ground like a man looking for loose change in the street. He didn't begin his career until he was five – that was unexceptional for the era – but was odds-on for his debut after news of his private trial became public knowledge. He retired unbeaten and unextended in 18 races, many of them walkovers for such was his reputation and his brilliance that few owners wished to start their horses against him.

His name has echoed down the ages, not least for the phrase he unwittingly bequeathed to the language. His first race was the Noblemen and Gentlemen's Plate at Epsom in May 1769, a race run in four-mile heats, and following Eclipse's victory in the first heat the Irish gambler and lovable rogue-about-town Dennis O'Kelly bet that he could put the horses in the second heat in the correct finishing order. He called out 'Eclipse first, and the rest nowhere', and for that seemingly unlikely outcome he received good odds.

To be 'nowhere' meant finishing more than 240 yards (a measure known as a 'distance') behind the winner, and was a very rare occurrence. But rarer still was a horse like Eclipse, and he landed O'Kelly's bets with room to spare, distancing his rivals; O'Kelly later bought Eclipse with his winnings. The words 'so-and-so first, and the rest nowhere' have entered common parlance as an illustration of complete dominance, even though those who use them may never have heard of the racehorse.

When his career came to an end, through lack of competition as much as anything, Eclipse was markedly successful as a stallion. His most influential son was Potoooooooo (the horse was supposed to be named Potatoes, but his semi-literate groom scrawled his name on the stable door phonetically – Pot and eight Os – and it stuck) who helped extend the aforementioned golden thread of bloodlines that led from the Darley Arabian to Phalaris and then on into modern pedigree saturation.

He is assured of immortality within the pages of the record books, but a paragon of the Turf such as Eclipse naturally has commemorations aplenty. The Eclipse Stakes at Sandown Park is one of the most important Flat races of the season in Britain, and the annual Eclipse Awards in the US recognise the champions of the sport in categories that include the hugely prestigious Horse of the Year. And, of course, we can view his skeleton.

It may seem a little macabre to modern sensibilities but the occupants of the late 18th century were less fastidious, and it is certainly striking to see this great equine celebrity in his display case. Few other horses have been preserved in this way, although the skeletons of (aptly) Potoooooooo and 1933 Derby winner and multiple champion sire Hyperion are exhibited in the National Horse Racing Museum.

So there Eclipse stands, on tiptoe, on the tips of his pastern bones, for his hooves are missing. They were removed at some point post-autopsy and converted into inkwells, as slightly ghoulish keepsakes for racing aficionados. As is often the way, however, entrepreneurial zeal took wings, with the result that there appear to be five hoof-inkwells attributed to Eclipse in circulation. Hardly surprising, in that case, that he could run so fast.

13

Sold!   *Image © Getty*

SALE OF THE CENTURIES

So you want to buy a racehorse. You want to buy a champion. You have the money – well, you do at the moment, sir, but everyone knows that the best way to end up with a small fortune in racing is to start with a large one. Off to the sales with you, sir, and don't forget – caveat emptor.

    In the US, the place to go is Keeneland, in the bluegrass fields of Kentucky. In Australia, it's William Inglis & Son in Sydney. In Ireland,

Goffs is what you want, at Kill in County Kildare. The French buy their best horses at Arqana, in Deauville. In Britain, though, the name to look for is Tattersalls, and that has been the case for more than 250 years.

The asphalt jungle of Hyde Park Corner in London does not leap off the map as a fine spot to buy racehorses, but it was a much greener and quieter place when Richard Tattersall, former stud manager to the Duke of Kingston, set himself up as an auctioneer in 1766.

There had been sales of bloodstock on the site for some time, but Tattersall had influential contacts, a keen awareness of his craft and a lucky break when his main rival died two years later. Allied to that, Tattersall was a popular figure, of whom Charles Dickens wrote that 'he was free of the road, as no highwayman would molest him, and even a pickpocket returned his handkerchief, with compliments'.

Business – conducted twice a week, hunters, hacks and hounds – was good. Alongside the auction ring, Tattersall established two subscription rooms for the use of Jockey Club members, for the making of bets and settling them. Over time the 'Rooms' became synonymous with betting, and gave rise to the Tattersalls Committee – the apostrophe was lost along the way – that to this day adjudicates over disputes between punter and bookmaker.

In 1829, the unraced two-year-old Priam was sold for 1,000gns, thought to be the first four-figure sum paid for an untried horse, and went on to win the Derby the following year. Eight years later, Tattersall brought down the gavel on the first four-figure yearling. Prices continued to rise, and have never stopped. When the top-class two-year-old Vaguely Noble was sold at Tattersalls in December 1967 he fetched a world record price of 136,000gns. Nowadays that sum might represent no more than the opening bid for some majestically bred, regally related colt.

As the traffic outside the sale ring began to overpower the traffic going through it, the company – family-owned until 1942 – began to conduct sales at Park Paddocks in Newmarket as well as in London and at Doncaster. The last sales in London were held in 1939, and when the Park Paddocks site was refurbished in 1965 it steadily began to evolve into the most important sales complex in Europe. The Tattersalls October Book 1 sale features the best-bred yearlings in Britain and Ireland and, arguably, the world.

Bloodstock sales are heartily confusing for the novice, clutching his or her catalogue with its initially impenetrable lists of names and hoping that no one mistakes a nervous twitch for the final bid on a four-million-guinea yearling. Sales in Britain are still conducted in the archaic and defunct currency of guineas, a guinea being 21 shillings or, for younger readers,

£1.05. Guineas were used at auctions because the odd shilling (odd 5p) was easy to render unto the sales company as commission, and the tradition has never wavered.

There are many types of racehorses sold at auction: foals; yearlings, the core currency of the bloodstock sale; breeze-up two-year-olds who gallop – 'breeze' – pre-sale to demonstrate their desirability; horses-in-training who have the status of second-hand cars, a few dents and scratches but plenty of miles left in this six-year-old gelding; potential broodmares and mares in-foal; point-to-pointers; store horses who might make decent steeplechasers in five years' time; dispersals of stallions, mares and younger horses from stud farms that have closed or gone bankrupt or major owners who have died.

The most expensive horse ever sold at public auction is a colt named The Green Monkey, who cost his new owners $16 million as a breeze-up two-year-old in Florida in 2006, a price that is unlikely to be exceeded. The Green Monkey raced three times, failed to win, and earned a little more than $10,000 in place prize-money. As has been the case down the centuries, even before Richard Tattersall first cleared his throat and said 'selling now', buyer beware.

14

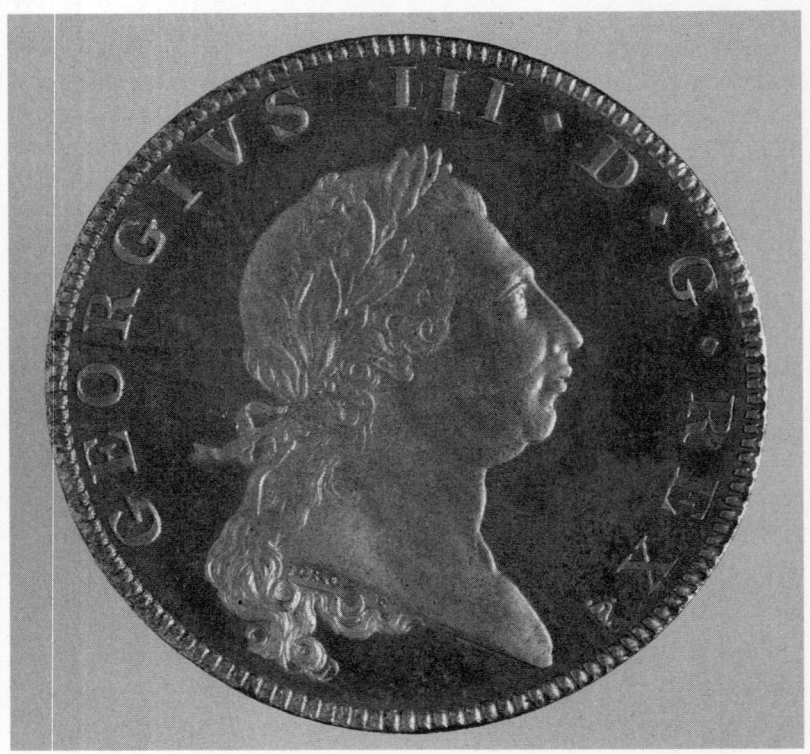

A pretty penny. Image © Getty

THE TOSS OF A COIN

Heads or tails? It is racing mythology, and like much mythology it may not have happened at all, but the image of the most celebrated horse race in the world being defined by the mere toss of a coin is an irresistible one. All the many Derbys in the world owe their name to the flip of a farthing, the spin of a golden sovereign.

In 1779, at a party near Epsom held by the 12th Earl of Derby to celebrate victory in the inaugural running of the Oaks with his filly Bridget, conversation turned to plans for a similar race for colts, to be held the following year. It was a popular concept, but every race needs a name. What to call this new race for three-year-olds to be run at Epsom in spring or early summer?

Diplomacy was important. Should the race be named after the party's host Lord Derby, or maybe after his friend Sir Charles Bunbury, the senior steward of the Jockey Club? According to social niceties, it would have been proper for the baronet Bunbury to defer to the senior peer Derby through rank if not through a guest's politeness, but legend has it that someone at the party fumbled in their pocket for a coin, drew it out, asked one of the men to call, tossed the coin and caught it.

There is no definitive record of whether it came down heads or tails, the face of George III or the reverse, but the details are secondary to the fact that the outcome meant the race would be named after Lord Derby. The first Derby Stakes was run over a mile at Epsom in May 1780 and won by a colt named Diomed – owned by Sir Charles Bunbury. Four years later the race distance was revised to a mile and a half; three years after that Lord Derby won his own race with Sir Peter Teazle; the rest is racing history.

The Derby is the most famous Flat race in the world. It is open to three-year-old colts and fillies, although fillies very rarely take part and none has won since Fifinella in 1916, and run at Epsom in early June. It is correctly known as 'The Derby', and not the 'Epsom Derby', because it is the original and no further identification or qualification is required. The list of Derby winners contains some of the greatest names in the sport's history, with Ormonde, Hyperion, Sea-Bird, Nijinsky, Mill Reef and Shergar just six names plucked randomly and subjectively from the roll of honour.

From Victorian times until the last decade of the 20th century, Derby day was a weekday (generally Wednesday) and attracted a vast exodus of racegoers from London and the surrounding area to revel in an unofficial holiday; Parliament used to adjourn to enable MPs to attend. The infield of the track – the Hill – is public land and annually drew such a vast and seething crowd to the sideshows, fortune-tellers and entertainments set up there that barely a blade of grass could be seen from the grandstands. The Derby no longer holds such a fascination for the public and the Hill is no longer the semi-lawless garden party it once was; there is plenty of grass to be seen there now.

The race itself is run over a wildly unconventional horseshoe-shaped switchback course that places as much emphasis on balance and agility as upon stamina. The sharp left-hand bend leading into the home straight is Tattenham Corner, which name has permeated the consciousness of the British public almost as surely as the name of the Derby itself, and even those who don't know one end of a horse from the other are familiar with the Derby.

Indeed, the whole world is familiar with the Derby, because in almost every racing jurisdiction the most prestigious race restricted to three-year-olds (but not exclusively) bears this name, a relic of both empire glory and the desire to manufacture instant tradition: the Irish Derby, the

Hong Kong Derby, the Kentucky Derby, the Deutsches Derby, the Derby Italiano, the Australian Derby and the Victoria Derby, the Indian Derby and countless more provincial affairs such as the Florida Derby and the Santa Anita Derby. And even donkeys have their Derby.

It is amusing to consider that, if the coin had fallen the other way, the Kentucky Bunbury would take place at Churchill Downs, and the Bunbury Italiano at the Capannelle in Rome. Sir Charles Bunbury is commemorated instead in the Bunbury Cup, a high-quality handicap run at Newmarket in July, and perhaps it is better that way.

The race that does not bear his name has captivated the racing world practically since its inception. It has been said – although it was probably apocryphal – that in the race's great gleaming heyday even the barefoot urchins loitering on street corners knew the name of that year's Derby winner.

That is incontrovertibly no longer the case, but for those who know and care the name of the Derby winner is the lodestar that guides their lives, the mnemonic that unerringly locates their younger selves in time and distance. There is powerful magic in it, like the trick of a coin made to disappear from view and then reappear in someone's hand, at a party, say, the head uppermost, or the tail.

15

Editions of the General Stud Book. *Courtesy of Weatherbys*

TO BE A THOROUGHBRED

To the untutored eye – even to the well-adapted eye – one horse can look very much like another horse. The assurance that a thoroughbred is who it is purported to be is central to racing and breeding, but in the early days of the sport that assurance was not always forthcoming.

The publication by James Weatherby of the Introduction to the General Stud Book in 1791 was the beginning of the task to rationalise and regulate the genealogy of racehorses or, as was declared at the time, 'to rid the Turf of the evil of false and inaccurate pedigrees'.

Racecourses had introduced the requirement for horses to be entered in races with a breeder's certificate under the breeder's hand. The practice of declaring a horse to be unfashionably bred to obtain favourable conditions in a race was rife, as was the reverse and more obvious problem, that of sellers proclaiming that a horse with a moderate pedigree was well bred in order to push up the price. Uncertainty is the mother of discord, so the information recorded in the *General Stud Book* was of considerable value and very soon it became the accepted authority.

The Introduction edition was a work in progress, given the lack of material with which Weatherby had to operate. The primary sources for his research were private stud records and the brief descriptions of race results, and records of matings were not comprehensive, particularly as there was at that time no requirement for racehorses to be named. That, remarkably, did not become necessary in Britain until 1946.

The *Stud Book* – published every four years – soon became not just a record of pedigrees but the list of members of a very exclusive club, and therefore the means to deny access to those without the right credentials. If a horse could not be traced back to one of the three aforementioned founding stallions (Byerley Turk, Darley Arabian, Godolphin Barb) on both sides of its pedigree, it would be excluded from the *Stud Book*, as would its progeny.

This situation reached a head when in 1913 the Jockey Club passed the Jersey Act, a local ordinance barring the registration of horses whose ancestors had not themselves been registered in an attempt to head off the influx of US-bred horses to Britain. Such horses were permitted to run in Britain, and the US-bred Durbar II won the Derby in 1914, but they were regarded as half-bred and barred from the *Stud Book*. The Jersey Act was not 'repealed' until 1949.

Towards the close of the 20th century, a considerable number of French-bred horses who were not registered in the French equivalent of the *Stud Book* began to run at the top level over jumps in Britain. They are known as AQPS horses (autre que pur sang; other than pure-blood) and were almost invariably the product of a thoroughbred sire and a non-thoroughbred dam. Grand National winners Mon Mome, Neptune Collonges and Pineau De Re were all AQPS non-thoroughbreds, as were King George VI Chase winners Nupsala, The Fellow, Algan and Edredon Bleu.

Over jumps, where the overwhelming majority of horses are geldings and of no purpose to the continuance of the breed, non-thoroughbreds may compete as long as they appear on the Weatherbys Non-Thoroughbred Register or on the AQPS register. On the Flat, only horses registered in one of the approximately 70 stud books approved by the International Stud Book Committee are permitted to race. The *General Stud Book* defines what it is to be a thoroughbred.

16

The Appomattox River, Diomed's resting place. *Image © Alamy*

THE LIMEY ARISTOCRAT

Scarcely had the American Revolutionary War drawn to its conclusion, with the British sent packing back across the Atlantic, than the victorious Yankees were welcoming with open arms one of the Limey aristocrats they had spent all those years defeating.

This blueblood, however, was a horse, and not just any horse. In 1780, Diomed had become the first winner of the Derby, but his reputation had suffered after a loss of form at the age of six, with defeats in his last half-dozen races uppermost in the minds of breeders. He had the pedigree to succeed at stud – he was a grandson of Herod – but he was only moderately effective and his fertility and consequent interest in him dwindled to the point where his owner Sir Charles Bunbury decided to cut his losses, selling him to a Mr Lamb and a Mr Younger for 50 guineas in 1798.

Shortly afterwards, James Weatherby brokered a deal to sell Diomed to American interests, despite his informing them that the stallion was 'a bad foal-getter'. Undeterred by the downbeat report, Colonel John Hoomes and John Tayloe III brought Diomed to the US, giving the fortunate Lamb and Younger a quick profit.

A 21-year-old stallion with a poor record and a reputation as a bad foal-getter is not the most tempting proposition for any breeder, but US breeders were desperate for an infusion of new blood and Diomed went into service straight off the boat, becoming arguably the first horse to cover mares on two continents in the same year. Stallions do this regularly in the modern era, shuttling between Europe and Australia to maximise the yield of a relatively short career, so Diomed might be said to be a pioneer twice over.

His arrival electrified the eastern seaboard of the US, and even before his first crop was born he was sold again, this time for a price believed to be six times that of his initial valuation.

The custom in those days was to travel the stallion from farm to farm to cover mares, as opposed to the modern convention of the stallion staying put and the mares visiting him. Diomed thus spent the next ten years of his life on the road, criss-crossing the state of Virginia, a travelling salesman with a girl in every village. Amazingly, his fertility recovered its former potency and his offspring were notable for their quality. He completely reinvented himself, and in so doing transformed the nascent US bloodstock industry.

His best son was Sir Archy, who won 18 of 21 races and became an influential stallion. Sir Archy's great-grandson Lexington was 16-time champion sire in the US and fathered a dynasty that was largely responsible for the imposition of the Jersey Act (previous chapter), as many of the mares he covered were unable to have their pedigrees traced to the requirements of the *General Stud Book* owing to details being lost or poorly recorded during the upheaval of the American Civil War.

Diomed died in April 1808, at the grand old age of 31. His obituarist may have dramatised a point in writing that 'There was almost as much mourning in the old colony at his demise as there was at the death of George Washington', but it is beyond doubt that Diomed had lit a flame in US thoroughbred breeding that would never go out.

The first US-bred horse to win the Derby was Iroquois, in 1881; in the colt's extended pedigree, the name of Diomed can be seen not once, but twice. The old patriarch was buried in a meadow near the Appomattox River, a corner of a foreign field that is forever England.

17

This way to the Royal Enclosure.   Image © Author

HATS, HORSES AND HIGH SOCIETY

Ascot has always been royal. It was 'discovered' by Queen Anne, and the site of the racecourse is Crown property, but to all observers from aficionados to anarchists the vast summer extravaganza of hats, horses and high society is the true, timeless manifestation of its Royal-ness.

The story of Royal Ascot, as might quite rightly be expected of something so firmly associated with the monarchy, is one of evolution not revolution. It did not arrive fully formed, like Champions Day at the same racecourse, but slowly took shape over the decades following the first running of the Gold Cup in 1807, which is generally accepted as the inauguration of the royal meeting. The race is simply known as the Gold Cup; the word 'Ascot' is not part of its official title.

The Gold Cup is the premier staying race in Britain and, by extension, the world, as few jurisdictions stage races over such marathon distances, particularly at the highest level. Its modern 'golden age' was from the mid-1970s to the early 1980s, when the great French-trained stayer Sagaro became the first to win the race three times, and popular champions Le

Moss and Ardross were dual winners. Yeats surpassed Sagaro's achievement when successful for the fourth time in 2009, but by then the race had lost some of its prestige in the eyes of horsemen owing to the increasing emphasis on speed at the expense of stamina in the bloodstock world.

Royal Ascot was a four-day festival (Tues-Fri) for much of its history, but was expanded to five days in 2002 with the incorporation of the Saturday card (formerly known as the Heath day). In recent years it has regularly attracted top-class horses from all around the world, with winners trained in the US, Hong Kong and notably Australia, the most celebrated of which was the remarkable and unbeaten sprinter Black Caviar, whose ultra-narrow victory in the 2012 Diamond Jubilee Stakes – after jockey Luke Nolen had eased the flying mare down too soon – left the entire racing world breathless.

In racing terms the meeting is an egalitarian affair, with plenty of handicaps mixed in with the top-level contests, and races over all distances from five furlongs to two and (almost) three-quarter miles. This latter is the distance of the Queen Alexandra Stakes, the longest Flat race in the calendar and a relatively uncompetitive curio that nowadays caters for horses well below the top class, but which was once the regular stage for the most popular horse in Royal Ascot history.

The gelding Brown Jack won at the royal meeting a record seven years running (1928-34), his first victory in the Ascot Stakes before six wins in the Queen Alexandra. His final success came at the venerable age of ten, and it was greeted with a colossal outpouring of delight from the normally staid Ascot crowd.

'Never will I forget the roar of the crowd as long as I live. Ascot or no Ascot, they went mad,' wrote the great jockey Steve Donoghue, Brown Jack's regular rider, in his autobiography. 'I have never seen so many hats flung in the air, and I have never heard such shrieks of joy. All my six Derby wins faded before the reception that awaited us.'

Brown Jack was a national hero. Anecdotal or apocryphal, the story goes that at every snarl-up on the way out of congested Ascot that evening the police stopped the traffic and waved his horsebox through.

For many, though, Royal Ascot is not about the horses, but about tradition, ceremony and fashion, the cornerstone of the season. Pre-racing 'tailgate' picnics are both lavishly boozy, especially in the owners' and trainers' car park, and impossibly grand (silver service in Car Park No.1), and the afternoon begins in earnest with the Royal Procession – introduced in 1825 by King George IV – in which the Queen and the extended royal family, including highly favoured guests, ride in horse-drawn carriages down the length of the straight mile course. The Royal Enclosure, that hallowed ground wherein no man or woman may set foot unless they have been invited, vetted and accepted, is another legacy of George IV, who ordered its construction in 1822.

The Royal Enclosure is fearsomely exclusive. The dress code is as inflexible as a new collar; gentlemen must wear morning dress with a black or grey top hat, while the requirements for ladies are manifold, falling under the description 'formal daywear' and including 'dresses and skirts of modest length', 'no strapless or off-the-shoulder tops, or uncovered midriffs', and a mandatory hat, although frankly what woman *wouldn't* wear a hat to Royal Ascot?

The social code is a little more malleable, although it's only since 1955 that divorcees have been permitted to wander the lawns, and the Enclosure is certainly more accessible than it was in the days when Lord Churchill was the royal representative (1901-34) and reputedly sorted applications into three trays: Certainly, Perhaps, and Certainly Not.

Those three descriptions might still stand in respect of modern attitudes to Royal Ascot. Some embrace it wholesale and with ecstatic squeaks, some raise a long-suffering eyebrow at the excesses of fashion and tradition and have eyes only for the horses, and some disdain it entirely, reckoning it the worst of excess and pomposity (an opinion possibly exacerbated by the singing of 'There'll Always Be An England' around the bandstand after the last race on each day).

Whether one goes there to see or be seen, though, Royal Ascot is undeniably the centrepiece of the British racing season, the glittering showcase that represents the best side of the sport to the outside world. Nothing – and nowhere – else is quite like it.

18

The modern horsebox. Image © Edward Whitaker

GOING ALONG FOR THE RIDE

Ingenuity deserves its reward. In the long and glorious history of punters attempting to get one over on the bookmakers, the story of Elis is a work of art.

Hardly anyone believed that Elis (foaled 1833) could win the 1836 St Leger. The only person who knew for a fact that Elis had a leading chance in the final Classic at Doncaster was his owner Lord George Bentinck, one of the pillars of the Jockey Club, a great reformer and – pertinently – a great innovator, and a man not averse to masterminding a betting coup with his less-than-hard-earned money. But, surely, there was little hope for Elis in the St Leger, despite the class and versatility he had shown earlier in the year when finishing runner-up in the 2,000 Guineas and the Goodwood Cup.

In those days, horses were walked from their stables to the racecourse in question in a leisurely fashion, to avoid unnecessary expense of energy. A week before the St Leger, Elis was still at home at the Goodwood stables of his trainer John Kent, and there was no way he could walk 250 miles to Doncaster in a week. Elis couldn't win; the bookmakers were happy to increase the odds, and Bentinck was happy to increase his stake.

With time ticking away, Bentinck revealed his masterstroke. He had constructed – or rather had had constructed; Lords didn't dirty their hands with hammer and nails – a carriage with a luxurious padded interior, a rudimentary horsebox, to be pulled by a team of horses with Elis (and a travelling companion) safely in the back, going along for the ride. The journey north took less than three days, and there was even time for Elis to stop along the way for a little exercise.

And so Elis, arriving late but refreshed at Doncaster races, was swiftly cut to second favourite by the bookmakers, but the damage had already been done in previous weeks at big prices. Elis was in front at halfway and never seriously pressed thereafter, winning by two lengths. Bentinck's grand plan had paid off – literally. A rough conversion of his winnings into current values produces a sum of well into seven figures.

The Elis coup was not the first time a horse had been transported – Eclipse was occasionally vanned from mare to mare in the course of his stud duties, and Sovereign travelled in a cart drawn by oxen from Worcestershire to Newmarket before meeting defeat in the Cesarewitch – but it was eyecatchingly successful and would have been merely the first of many similar ventures but for the speed in which technology began to transform life in the early Victorian era.

Before too many years had passed, the advent of the railway network made it a simple matter to transport horses from stables to racecourse and back again in speed and comfort. This new mode of travel had benefits for spectators, too, with 'raceday special' trains coming into service to take racegoers long distances around the country.

Almost a century after Elis's ground-breaking journey, a horse was shipped across the Atlantic for one specific race for the first time when the 1923 Derby winner Papyrus took on Kentucky Derby winner Zev in a match at Belmont Park.

Horses had previously been shipped from the US to Britain for a sustained programme – Prioress, the 1857 Cesarewitch winner, was the first US-bred-and-owned horse to win a race in England – but this was the first long-distance targeted in-and-out raid. Unfortunately, the brave undertaking underlined the old saw that it is better to travel hopefully than to arrive, as the effects of the voyage, allied to the completely alien conditions at Belmont Park, where the dirt surface was sloppy after heavy rain, militated against Papyrus, who was beaten by five lengths.

Trains, boats, and later planes. Horses circle the globe on a regular basis nowadays and when they do it is tempting to think of Elis, rattling along on the Great North Road, a horse being pulled by other horses, the wind in his mane, a strange gleam in his eyes, boldly going as no horse had gone before.

19

Becher's Brook, before recent changes. Image © Getty

THE MOST FAMOUS FENCE IN THE WORLD

Enduring fame arises in many forms: from glorious deeds, from changing the world for the better, from a moment of sublime inspiration. Captain Martin Becher simply fell off his horse and into a stream, and for this he will never be forgotten.

He had already earned a little temporary fame for winning what some consider the first running of the race that would eventually be known as the Grand National, in 1836 aboard The Duke, but that feat is often overlooked given the uncertainty over the race's authenticity. There were no such concerns three years later, in the race that is generally recognised as the first National.

Becher was riding a horse named Conrad, and was bowling along in the front rank when he came to a jump with a considerable drop on the landing side, and a brook running along the base of the fence. Here, Becher and Conrad parted company, and Becher landed in the water, where he ducked down to stay clear of the following horses. At the time he might have thought little of his early bath, but it piqued the public's imagination, and now the Captain's little mishap is immortalised in the name Becher's Brook, the most famous fence in the world.

The Grand National is, in turn, the most famous race in the world. It captured the public imagination like no other race and continues to do so, and its annual renewal at Aintree in early April is part of the collective sporting memory, a communal experience. The great old race contrives to produce a 'story' surrounding the winning horse almost every year, and few are the racing enthusiasts who did not have their interest sparked by a small bet on the National, before watching it on television at home with the family and becoming swept along by the race's drama and grandeur.

The elements of the race are as familiar as the days of the week: Becher's Brook, the Melling Road, the Chair, Valentine's, the Canal Turn, the Elbow, the big green fences coated with spruce branches, the enormous field of horses (maximum 40), the 30 fences, the four-and-a half-mile marathon distance (see below), the compelling, ever-changing narrative of the race's ten-minute duration, the gripping uncertainty that begins to resolve itself only as the leaders turn back towards the grandstands with two fences to jump, the neverending run-in over which fortunes can change in a matter of strides.

The Grand National has always been different. Over the years it has changed in numerous ways, and there are many who say that the race is not what it was, that its character and its soul have been lost amid those changes, but the Grand National has always been a race of its time.

Concern over the stiffness of the fences was addressed in 1961, when the fearsome upright 'walls' were sloped on the take-off side to make them more forgiving. As fears over the safety of the horses increased through the modern era, prompted by the very public nature of any fatalities, further alterations were made.

Those big National fences are now constructed with a softer inner core, the drops on the landing sides have been phased out, the distance of the race has been cut by a furlong and a half to quell the headlong rush to the first fence that saw a disproportionate number of fallers because they were going too fast to land safely.

Even the brook into which Becher tumbled has been covered over. Welfare is now rightly paramount, and although the National is no longer the dauntingly searching test it once was it still retains the capacity to exhilarate and enthral.

Several of the great Aintree stories and occasions find a place later in these pages, but there are plenty to go around. In 1901 the race was run in a snowstorm, and the winner Grudon had butter packed into his hooves to prevent the snow packing within his shoes. Tipperary Tim was the sole finisher in 1928, winning at 100-1. Six years later the exceptional Golden Miller became the only horse to win the National and the Cheltenham Gold Cup in the same year. Still fresh in the memory is the 1997 'bomb scare' National, won by Lord Gyllene after the course was evacuated and the race delayed for 48 hours.

The Duke of Alburquerque, a Spanish nobleman with an apparent indifference to pain and an obsessive desire to ride in the National, was a regular feature in the race between 1952 and 1976, and an equally regular feature in the local hospitals the following day with a broken bone here or there. At long last, in 1974, the 55-year-old Duke completed the course for the first time aboard his beloved Nereo, in eighth place. Three years later, the Jockey Club refused him a riding permit.

That was the unsettling era of the 'last Nationals', the hourglass forever running out on the race's future, with Aintree perennially under threat from developers. The course was eventually rescued by the Jockey Club, its purchase funded partly through public donations.

Dick Saunders, at 48 the oldest winning jockey, carved his niche aboard Grittar in 1982, the same year that Geraldine Rees became the first female jockey to complete the course, a distant last of eight on the weary Cheers. Twelve months earlier, the National had been won by Aldaniti, ridden by Bob Champion.

In 1979, Champion had been diagnosed with testicular cancer and Aldaniti had broken down so badly that it seemed he would have to be put down. The two invalids recovered slowly, regained their strength, returned to action, and on a sunny afternoon at Aintree they combined for the most emotional, most miraculous victory imaginable.

The great power of the Grand National, more than any other race, is to bestow widespread, enduring fame upon its chosen few. Becher would surely have reckoned that worth getting wet for.

20

Justice for all.   *Image © Getty*

A FOUR-YEAR-OLD NAMED MACCABEUS

Sometimes, as the time-honoured cry of exasperation has it, the game's not straight. Horse racing is often regarded as being a seamy, seedy pursuit, prone to corruption, to wrongdoing, dirty deeds on a grand scale. And sometimes that's true.

In 1844, Running Rein won the Derby. Or did he? That question – and the answer 'No' – underpins one of the greatest scandals in the sport's history, for the horse believed to be Running Rein was not the three-year-old Running Rein at all but a four-year-old named Maccabeus.

The plot was three years in the making, and had its genesis in the greed of gambling-club owner Abraham Levi Goodman, who was the living antithesis of nominative determinism. Goodman bought both horses in 1841, and later campaigned the older, stronger Maccabeus under the name of Running Rein in two-year-old races, winning at Newmarket and arousing suspicion but no retribution from the authorities.

The precedent having been set, Maccabeus was entered for the Derby in the name of Running Rein and duly outran his younger, less mature rivals, landing bets worth reportedly £50,000 for Goodman. Before the Derby, however, a letter was handed to the Epsom stewards requesting them to examine Maccabeus/Running Rein's teeth, as it would be obvious from their appearance that the horse in question was four, not three. This was not done, the stewards declaring in a rather mealy mouthed manner that only if the horse won would an inquiry follow.

Maccabeus/Running Rein won; the owner of the runner-up Orlando was encouraged to object to the outcome and then took legal action against Goodman. In court, the judge demanded that the Derby winner be produced so that he could be examined, and when this did not happen he awarded the race to Orlando by default.

'If gentlemen condescend to race with blackguards, they must condescend to expect to be cheated,' said the judge in his summing up, a phrase that has passed into racing folklore. The 1844 Derby was rotten to the core: another runner, Leander, was discovered to be at least six years old, and the favourite and second-favourite The Ugly Buck and Ratan were nobbled.

The practice of switching one horse for another was not new in 1844 and it has been employed periodically ever since. In 1953, at Bath, a good horse in Santa Amaro was switched for a moderate one in Francasal in order to land a coup in a seller, the lowest grade of race.

As is almost always the case, the good horse, the ringer, won the race. That's usually the easy bit. The conspirators had hatched an elaborate plan that involved employing a man to climb a ladder and cut the phone wires into Bath racecourse, and then betting heavily with off-course bookmakers secure in the knowledge that they couldn't lay those wagers off into the betting ring and shorten the starting price – because the phone lines had been cut. It was a sharp idea but the deception was discovered and the miscreants received jail sentences instead of winnings.

It was a similar story with the two-year-old Flockton Grey at Leicester in 1982, who scuppered every vestige of the plan's subtlety when trouncing his rivals by 20 lengths, alerting all and sundry to potential wrongdoing. The horse was actually three-year-old Good Hand.

The celebrated case of Gay Future was slightly different. The real, talented Gay Future won the intended race at Cartmel in 1974, but a nondescript animal had been registered with that identity and the name appeared in the newspapers and racecards against a horse with no form.

That was one half of construction magnate Tony Murphy's plot. The other was to couple Gay Future in doubles and trebles with two horses of little ability, bets that bookmakers would gleefully take. The two makeweights would then be withdrawn at the races for ostensibly legitimate reasons, meaning that all the bets would become singles on Gay Future, and a great deal of money would be won.

Everything went marvellously, until a reporter phoned the yard of trainer Tony Collins to ask about the two non-runners, and was told by a stablehand that the horses hadn't left their field all day. This minor fact betrayed the intentions behind the doubles and trebles, and Murphy and Collins were warned off for ten years apiece.

There is a pleasing ingenuity behind the Gay Future sting that made many observers wish that they'd got away with it. Top of the list for chutzpah, though, are the anonymous masterminds who adopted the startlingly simple stratagem of inventing an entire race meeting and betting on all the winners.

In 1898, someone calling himself G. Martin sent a racecard for a meeting in Cornwall called Trodmore Hunt to *The Sportsman* newspaper in London, which was grateful for the information and printed the card. In those days, the cards for obscure minor meetings were often carried in the press, so no one gave Trodmore Hunt a second thought.

The following day, G. Martin sent in the results. What a helpful chap, thought *The Sportsman*, and printed them too. The day after that, *The Sporting Life* copied the results, but with a small error. They reported that Reaper had won at 5-2, whereas *The Sportsman* had the horse winning at 5-1. Bookmakers, having taken bets on Reaper as well as all the other winners, enquired as to which was correct, questions were asked, and answers came there none – the whole thing was a brilliant hoax.

The culprits were never discovered. But for a misprint, they'd have got clean away with it, and with all the money. Corruption is rightly, universally condemned, but you have to take your hat off to the Trodmore Hunt gang.

21

Packing them in at Cheltenham. Image © Racing Post/Edward Whitaker

THE WHOLE WORLD WAS AT EPSOM

Crowd figures are notoriously tricky to confirm with confidence, unless the old aphorism about three being a crowd is taken into account. That goes double for events in the sepia-tinted past, but it seems highly likely that the world record attendance at a race meeting belongs to Derby day at Epsom, although an exact figure is impossible to ascertain.

It depends how much credence is placed on estimates, and the nature of the viewing areas of Epsom, where colossal crowds once congregated in the free-to-enter public area of the Hill, make generalisations the logical step. Where should we begin?

In 1829 – the year of Frederick – *The Times* reported that 'the whole world was at Epsom yesterday'. That appears unlikely, although sometimes, when waiting at the bar at a busy racecourse in high summer, it can seem a little like that. A decade or so later, Charles Dickens reckoned that the population of Epsom's green acres on Derby day 'may be counted in the millions'.

Hyperbole aside, is it nevertheless possible that a million people were present when Morston won the Derby in 1973, as estimated by the BBC? Was the figure of 250,000 in attendance in 1920, Spion Kop's year, a 'record' as reported in *The Times*, or simply an attempt to address levels of magnitude without paying too much attention to precision? Was the 'something like 150,000' reported in 1864, the year of Blair Athol, a product of accuracy or a weary newspaperman plucking a number from the ether? The 'something like' may give it away.

Estimates of 500,000 in attendance on Derby day are relatively commonplace up to the mid-1980s, but with no ticketing or other paper record of spectators wandering across common land, and the relative impossibility of gauging crowd numbers by sight alone, it is wise to build in a substantial margin of error.

The reported crowd of 150,000 on the Knavesmire in York to watch the Great Match of May 1851, in which The Flying Dutchman defeated Voltigeur, may have some basis in fact, but the Knavesmire is also public land and the figure can only be the sketchiest of estimates. What is undoubtedly true is that such numbers dwarf those of the present day.

In 2019, the ticketed attendance on Derby day watching Anthony Van Dyck prevail was 36,000, with perhaps a similar number looking on from the sadly depleted Hill. On Gold Cup day at the Cheltenham Festival the attendance is approximately 70,000, and there is little room for manoeuvre in those packed grandstands. Gold Cup day at Royal Ascot draws a similar number, with Grand National day at Aintree attracting closer to 75,000.

Elsewhere around the world, six-figure attendance for the major events is commonplace. A little more than 170,000 squeezed into Churchill Downs to watch American Pharoah win the 2015 Kentucky Derby, while the record at roomy Flemington, in Melbourne, is 130,000.

At the other end of the spectrum, figures compiled by the Horserace Betting Levy Board illustrate a landscape familiar to all racegoers who patronise the smaller racecourses in midweek, when the crowd – especially at all-weather meetings during the winter – stretches the definition of the word to its snapping point.

The average attendance at British racecourses in 2019 was 3,895, while a more forensic examination of the statistics lays bare the realities in the lower reaches of the sport. The average attendance at those all-weather meetings in February 2019 was just 502, which may yet come as a surprise to grizzled veterans of wintry days at the likes of Wolverhampton or Kempton, when horses sometimes seem to outnumber spectators, when three feels very much like a crowd.

22

Lead weights carried in the saddle. *Image © Edward Whitaker*

WEIGHED IN, WEIGHED IN

It's one of the small things at a racecourse that few people ever see, but without which the day's sport would be unable to function. Roundish, grey, palm-sized, weighing a pound or fractions thereof: a piece of lead.

When a jockey weighs 8st 3lb and his mount is set to carry 8st 6lb, three of those little lumps of lead are slipped into the pockets of the weightcloth that sits underneath the numbercloth, beneath the saddle. The jockey's weight is then checked by the clerk of the scales, and he or she is 'weighed out'. After the race, the jockey must 'weigh in' at the same weight, so the weight is checked again and, if satisfactory, the jockey is 'weighed in'. An announcement is made over the public address system when the riders of the winner and the placed horses have passed this second check – 'weighed in, weighed in' – and the result becomes official.

Modernity has reached the weighing in/out process, and jockeys now stand on digital scales and their weight is clearly displayed. Before electronics, an apparatus akin to bathroom scales was used, with the jockeys seated while a pointer oscillated over the correct weight, and before that jockeys used to sit on one side of the sort of balance found in Mrs Beeton's kitchen while weights were placed on the other side. In Britain, the maximum weight in Flat racing is 10st 7lb and in jump racing 12st 7lb, although in practice these limits are very rarely reached.

Now and again, the process goes awry. It can happen that a jockey's weightcloth slips from beneath the saddle during a race, and should that occur the horse is automatically disqualified. Sometimes a jockey inexplicably and unforgivably fails to weigh in, whether distracted or simply absent-minded, and the horse is automatically disqualified and the rider fined and suspended.

It has also been known for a jockey seeking to gain an unfair advantage to remove some of the lead before the race, hand it to an accomplice, ride in the race at a lighter weight than advertised, and then collect the lead and replace it before weighing in. There is a way around every system, usually paved with bad intentions.

In some races, such as the Derby, the Champion Hurdle, or a race for maidens, horses carry weight according to the specific conditions of a particular contest. In handicaps – the Grand National, the Cambridgeshire, the Melbourne Cup – a horse's weight is calculated by a team of official handicappers employed by the governing body and based on recent form.

The process of handicapping is designed to give each horse an equal chance of winning, despite various grievances loudly aired by trainers and owners, and these races generally attract more runners as a result. The first race ever framed in this way was the Oatlands Handicap, run at Ascot in 1790 and won by Seagull.

Another factor in the amount a horse must carry is the weight-for-age scale. The first evidence of this being used dates from 1727 and a table in the first-ever form book, but the modern WFA scale is the work of the aforementioned Admiral Henry Rous, who in 1851 refined the system that is still in use today.

Essentially, the WFA scale gives immature three-year-olds a concession when competing against more mature four-year-olds (and older). This concession varies with race distance and position in the calendar. In late April, over a mile and a quarter, a three-year-old receives 17lb from its elders to help with levelling the playing field. As the year progresses and the three-year-old matures, its concession is steadily reduced. In early October, over a mile and a quarter, the same three-year-old receives just 4lb from its elders. Most major all-aged races – the Breeders' Cup Classic, the Champion Stakes, the Prix de l'Arc de Triomphe – are weight-for-age races.

There can be several reasons behind a horse being asked to carry 9st in a given race. The conditions of the race may dictate it, or the opinion of the handicapper, or the intricacies of the weight-for-age scale, or the sex allowance for fillies and mares, or a combination of these. To ask is one thing, to ensure it another. That's the job of those little pieces of lead, unseen, unheralded, indispensable.

23

Racing's greatest daily.   Image © Author

A CERTAIN WAY OF LIFE

Horse racing is, for a minority sport, incredibly well served by the media in all forms, print, broadcast and digital, something those within it occasionally forget. Racing is televised daily by terrestrial and satellite channels, there is a profusion of websites, professional and amateur, devoted to the sport, a number of glossy magazines appear monthly or bi-monthly, and the *Racing Post* remains its stalwart daily paper.

Mainstream newspapers and publications have also played a role in bringing fine journalism and sparkling prose from the racing press room to the masses. The sublime John Oaksey captivated with every word in *Horse & Hound*; Richard Baerlein provided readers of *The Guardian* with erudition, insight and plenty of winners, a task later ably shouldered by Greg Wood and Chris Cook; Alan Lee decorated daily the pages of *The Times* for many years and the lyrical Chris McGrath gave similar service to *The Independent*.

Such important coverage has sadly dwindled to a trickle, with racing coverage cut wafer-thin or dispensed with altogether as all aspects of print media struggle to retain their relevance and market share in the altered landscape of the digital age.

Newspapers come and go, and *The Sporting Life* has gone, but in its luminous prime it was an institution. If any newspaper could be described as totemic it was the *Life*, for it stood for far more than just the place to find out what was running that day and what had won the day before.

The Sporting Life, first published in 1859, was a shibboleth for a certain type of person, a certain way of life. If a character in a film or on television was portrayed reading *The Sporting Life*, the implication was immediate that here was someone a little raffish, a bit wide, likely in possession of a heart of gold underneath that slightly grubby shirt but not the sort of chap – and it was always a man, even though women read the *Life* too, even the Queen Mother – you'd lend a fiver to, or want your daughter hanging around.

This was most unfair. Most readers of *The Sporting Life* were blameless individuals, guilty of no more than a mild obsession with Sir Gordon Richards or Lester Piggott and a passion for idiosyncratic pagination, but semiotics is a powerful force.

It was the paper in the margins of which the frequently unwell writer Jeffrey Bernard worked out his bar bill, its pages hinted at the beguiling olfactory combination of cigar smoke and horse liniment, it peeped cheekily from the jacket pockets of Arthur Daley, Sid James and Robbie Box. In a faintly disapproving world, to unfurl its enormous broadsheet dimensions on a commuter train full of stuffy *Times* and *Telegraph* readers was a badge of honour, an act of pride.

In the beginning, the *Life* cost a penny and was published twice a week. In 1883 it became a daily (except Sunday, naturally), soon absorbed its London analogue *Bell's Life*, and embarked upon a competitive rivalry with its northern counterpart *The Sporting Chronicle* (first published 1871, closed 1983). The *Life* saw off the weekly *The Pink 'Un*, more formally known as *The Sporting Times* (first published 1865, closed 1932), and *The Sportsman* (1865-1924), and when the *Chronicle* stopped its presses it had the field to itself, but only briefly.

In April 1986, with the financial backing of Sheikh Mohammed and fuelled by the inspiration of Brough Scott and Graham Rock, the *Racing Post* was published for the first time, with the technological leap forward of a colour photograph on the front page. Its cover price was a benevolent 25p, half the price of the *Life*, whose infamous owner Robert Maxwell immediately began a price war to see off the new opposition.

The new tabloid newspaper polarised the market. It was never as fierce as City-United, Roundhead-Cavalier, but those who liked the cutting-edge production of the *Post* and the winning tips of Diomed and Spotlight tended to be not the same people who preferred the traditional outlook of the *Life*, Monty Court and Jack Logan and the winning tips of Augur and Man on the Spot.

Over time, and following a few heavy financial setbacks, notably the losses of the Top Cees libel trial and the contract to supply betting shops with display editions for their walls, the *Life* began to founder and its last edition was published in May 1998.

The *Racing Post* settled easily into the role of newspaper of record and, with just a momentary challenge from another newspaper called *The Sportsman*, which lasted a mere seven months in 2006, still provides its readership with a welcome daily diet of the good stuff that sustains, nourishes. It may never be visual shorthand for an entire culture, but perhaps that's for the best.

24

Melbourne's empty streets on Cup day. Image © Getty

THE SPELL OF THE CUP

The Melbourne Cup is more than a horse race, it is a national institution, an international institution. It's a race that does not confer champion status upon its winner, that is run over a distance that largely excludes the best horses of the day, that has struggled with its identity in recent years, but somehow the Cup rises above all these things as brightly as the sun.

In a society fond of nicknames, the Melbourne Cup is known as 'the race that stops a nation', a description of the quietness that falls over the country on the first Tuesday in November, when businesses close for the day and traffic thins out in the streets because everyone is obsessed with the Cup. Melbourne is an eerie place on the big day, full of echoes and empty pie shops, as the spell of the Cup falls over it.

It's been that way practically since the inaugural running in 1861, won by Archer, who won it again the following year. Four years later the local authorities declared Cup day a half-holiday, giving official sanction to the idea. In this respect it resembles the Derby, which was an unofficial public holiday in its Victorian heyday when vast crowds treated it as a day out. The public affection for the Derby has waned considerably since those heady days, but the fervour for the Cup is still mighty.

The race is a two-mile handicap run at wide, sweeping Flemington with a maximum field of 24. It has been won 12 times by revered trainer Bart Cummings (the Cups King) and by many of the great horses of Australian history, including the magnificent Carbine, who carried 10st 5lb to victory in 1890, Rising Fast (1954), the only horse to win the great triple of Caulfield Cup, Cox Plate and Melbourne Cup in the same year, Rain Lover (1968, 1969), Might And Power (1997) and the marvellous mare Makybe Diva (2003, 2004, 2005), the only triple winner of the Cup.

High above all these in the pantheon, though, out on his own for esteem and performance, is the unequivocally great Phar Lap, the one true icon of Australian racing, its household god. Phar Lap (foaled 1926), humbly bred in New Zealand and given a name that translates as 'lightning', won the Melbourne Cup in 1930 as the shortest-priced favourite ever, but his cultural impact goes far beyond the simple status of big-race winner. Phar Lap is Phar Lap, mate. You wouldn't understand.

He was a huge chestnut gelding with the nickname Big Red – a pet name he shared with Man O'War and Secretariat – and was trained by Harry Telford. Part of the mystique surrounding Phar Lap was his remarkable ability, for he won 37 of his 51 races including the Cox Plate (twice), the Australian Derby and the Victoria Derby as well as the Cup, but his key to the lock of folk-hero status was his supernatural consistency.

At a time when Australians and New Zealanders were beginning to experience the crushing weight of the Great Depression, Phar Lap shone through the grey days like a beacon. Between April 1930 and November 1931 he ran in 35 races and won all but three of them, finishing runner-up on two occasions. He was the one thing the public could rely on, a few dollars on Phar Lap wouldn't win you much given the odds but you'd win all right. He gave people something to feel good about.

Desperate bookmakers hired gunmen to shoot at him after he had finished exercise on the morning of the Melbourne Stakes in 1930, but they missed and in the afternoon he won, as usual. A more effective way of stopping him was to load him with weight, and even Phar Lap couldn't win the 1931 Cup under 10st 10lb, the heaviest weight ever allotted in the race, his last outing in Australia.

After that he and his groom Tommy Woodcock – the pair were devoted to each other – were shipped Stateside for the Agua Caliente Handicap at Tijuana, Mexico, the richest race in the world at that time and a race Phar Lap won with ease. Less than three weeks later he was dead, the cause believed to be arsenic poisoning, although there is an alternative case for a stress-based condition. Australia mourned, believing its hero had been murdered; it still mourns.

The sharp increase in international competition during the 1980s drew the Melbourne Cup into a wider embrace, and in 1993 the Irish horse Vintage Crop, trained by Dermot Weld and ridden by Mick Kinane, became the first northern-hemisphere winner of the race, a watershed moment for the whole sport. Nine years later Weld won again with Media Puzzle, and since then horses trained in Japan, France, Germany, Britain and Ireland have won the race and been placed numerous times.

This overseas dominance led to a crisis of confidence in Australia, where horses are bred for speed rather than stamina, and where these days a considerable number of Cup runners are former European stayers imported by local owners and trainers. There were calls for international competition to be restricted, but common sense prevailed in order to maintain the Cup's prestige on a global level, and it continues to be a major draw for northern-hemisphere-trained horses, a race that now stops more than one nation.

The Melbourne Cup is bigger than the sum of its parts, though, big enough to overcome its internal strife. Cup day is usually sunny, a six-figure crowd disports itself tipsily on the Flemington lawns, and for a brief moment everyone comes together to watch a horse race. It is a collective experience, a collective triumph.

25

Gladiateur, at Longchamp. Image © Getty

THE AVENGER OF WATERLOO

Revenge is sweet, even if it takes 50 years. The Battle of Waterloo in 1815 was a profound defeat for France and the last flourish for Napoleon Bonaparte. As the Little Emperor rode away from the ruins of the battlefield on his faithful grey charger Marengo, he could never have imagined that one day, years hence, another horse would settle the account for la belle France.

Gladiateur (foaled 1862) had the name for it, and the physique. A big, strapping beast with a voracious appetite for a test of stamina, he was trained in Britain by Tom Jennings snr and ridden by the short-sighted Lancastrian Harry Grimshaw, but everything else about him was French to the coeur. He showed little at two, his strength not yet come to him, but the following season he grew into a titan.

He was victorious in the 2,000 Guineas, the Derby and the St Leger, becoming only the second horse to win the Triple Crown, and in so doing went a long way towards banishing the complacent notion that Britain was the supreme racing nation of the world.

Before his St Leger triumph, he travelled home to Longchamp for the Grand Prix de Paris, then the most valuable and prestigious race in the country. He won by three lengths, prompting the local newspapers of the day to christen him – with no little hyperbole – as The Avenger of Waterloo, and his significance to the burgeoning French racing and breeding industry should not be underestimated. Apres lui, le deluge.

As a four-year-old, Gladiateur won the Gold Cup at Royal Ascot by 40 lengths after having been 300 yards behind the leader at one stage, although there were admittedly only three runners in the race. He was a failure at stud, but the memory of his great avenging deeds is preserved in a lifesize bronze statue that stands in a prominent position at Longchamp.

How do we best remember our champions, and keep the memories of them fresh? Racing tends to be good at public commemoration, swift and generous with its repayments to those who have served it so well. The number of horses who have had statues raised to them at racecourses is considerable. It would be near-impossible to compile an exhaustive list, but practically every major racecourse and many minor tracks have statues of their heroes and ours on site.

Yeats prowls the parade ring at Ascot, a short distance from Frankel and Motivator. Phar Lap is immortalised at Flemington. Secretariat runs full tilt across the Belmont Park parade ring. Kincsem stands outside the grandstand at Kincsem Park in Budapest. A snowy Desert Orchid shares the parade ring at Kempton Park with Kauto Star. Red Rum can be found in his spiritual home of Aintree.

Double Trigger is at Doncaster, Hurricane Fly and Snow Fairy are at Leopardstown, Persian Punch, Brigadier Gerard and Eclipse are at Newmarket, Zenyatta at Santa Anita, Generous at Epsom, Vintage Crop and Ridgewood Pearl at The Curragh, Silent Witness at Sha Tin, and there are no fewer than four at Cheltenham: Arkle, Golden Miller, Best Mate and Dawn Run.

There are other methods of commemoration beyond bronze and plinth. Many horses have races named after them, a pertinent example being the Prix Gladiateur. The names of others adorn racecourse bars – all the bars at Ascot are named after horses, Nijinsky, Swain, Mill Reef, Dancing Brave etc – and a handful of country pubs. Thoroughfares, too: in Belfast there are several streets named after Derby winners, and reportedly more than 250 roadways in the US bear the name of Secretariat.

We have read about the skeletons of Eclipse and Hyperion, but at trainer Sir Mark Prescott's Newmarket yard hangs the flayed hide of the great champion sire St Simon. A mile across town, in the display window of Gibson Saddlers, stands the stuffed body of 1880 Derby runner-up Robert The Devil, his nose rubbed smooth by generations of fond hands. His entry on Wikipedia asserts that he was stuffed after his death, which seems more humane than the alternative.

26

Some horses have pets.   Image © Getty

54

Fifty-four races, 54 wins. The story of the indefatigable, invincible, immortal Kincsem is a long one, full of interesting diversions, but the starkness of her career statistics is her lasting monument. No horse in history has come even halfway close to emulating her unbeaten record.

The pride of Hungary then and now, Kincsem (foaled 1874) raced for four seasons in seven countries, regularly running three or four times a month, criss-crossing Europe by train, making every stop a winning one. In slight mitigation, eight of her victories were walkovers because she had frightened away the opposition, and she rarely faced more than four rivals in her races, but her dominance then and resonance now is undisputed.

Kincsem's name means 'my treasure' in Hungarian, but she looked no more than fool's gold before she raced. She was a long, narrow, chestnut filly of unprepossessing appearance, and when breeder Erno de Blaskovich offered her for sale she was rejected, so he put her into training with expatriate Englishman Robert Hesp. It was the best decision he ever made.

She won ten races in ten different cities at two and 17 races at three, including the Austrian Derby, Hungarian St Leger and the Grosser Preis von Baden (her first of three wins in the race), but her four-year-old campaign defined her brilliance on a wider scale, with success in the Goodwood Cup and Grand Prix de Deauville among 15 victories. Before travelling to England she won seven races in 27 days, in Bratislava, Budapest and Vienna, and then had two months away from the track while training at Newmarket and Goodwood.

The depth of the opposition faced by Kincsem in what was then the Austro-Hungarian empire is open to debate, but her two rivals at Goodwood were of high quality. The favourite Pageant had won the Chester Cup and would win the Doncaster Cup, while Lady Golightly had the Yorkshire Oaks and Nassau Stakes to her name. The sceptical English bookmakers priced Kincsem as the outsider of the three, and it was the only race in which she was not odds-on during her career.

The market looked perceptive half a mile from home and it was only in the closing stages that Kincsem asserted herself over Pageant, with a typically hard ride from regular jockey Elijah Madden seeing her home by two lengths. The sporting press marvelled at her prowess while casting a cold eye over Madden's use of the whip, which must indeed have been considerable to attract such attention in that less compassionate era.

She defeated the French Guineas winner Fontainebleau by half a length in a strong field at Deauville, but then a month later, at Baden-Baden, she came within a whisker of losing her unbeaten record when dead-heating for the Grosser Preis. The custom of the time was to stage a run-off, and in this a weary Kincsem prevailed by five lengths. She proved as effective as ever at five, winning a dozen races, and was retired to stud the following season.

Anecdotage surrounds the legend of Kincsem like a perfumed cloud. Her two boon companions were apparently a stable boy called Frankie, who adopted the surname Kincsem, and a black-and-white cat named Csalogany (nightingale, in Hungarian), whose existence is verified by Jozsef Hesp, the great-great-grandson of her trainer Robert.

The story goes that when Kincsem had disembarked from the ship that brought her from England to France after the Goodwood Cup, she refused to board a waiting train because Csalogany was nowhere to be found. For two hours Kincsem planted herself and would not move, calling constantly for her friend, until Csalogany came trotting up and leapt on the mare's back, whereupon Kincsem calmly boarded the train.

Many racehorses develop relationships with other animals. The brilliant steeplechaser Remittance Man was a worrier, so shared his box with a calming sheep named Nobby. Grand National winner Foinavon was devoted to Susie the snow-white nanny goat, while the great US folk hero Seabiscuit had quite the superstar's entourage of Pumpkin the cow pony, a dog named Pocatell and a spider monkey called Jo Jo. The unlikely foursome reportedly all slept together in the same stall.

Pebbles, 'England's superfilly', fell in love with stablemate Come On The Blues. 'They spend hours looking at each other,' said trainer Clive Brittain. 'Their relationship is like a happy marriage.'

If Kincsem had not retired unbeaten, she would still take high rank in the annals of the Turf, but the cachet of invincibility is a potent one. Very few horses, apart from those whose careers are compromised at an early stage through retirement or injury, maintain an unblemished record.

Kincsem's 54 is more than twice as many as the next on the list, the 25 of outstanding Australian sprinter Black Caviar, with relative nonentity Peppers Pride, who raced solely in the state of New Mexico and went unbeaten in 19 races, third in the all-time standings ahead of many equine paragons such as Eclipse, Ormonde, Ribot and Frankel.

Other horses have won more races than Kincsem. The record is the 137 races won by Puerto Rican legend Galgo Jr in the 1930s, while the British record is held by the mare Catherina, who won 79 times in the 1830s, but they were both beaten many times. In defying all-comers, over the course of four long seasons, at 13 racecourses in seven countries, Kincsem set a statistical standard that surely will never be surpassed.

Her statue stands outside the grandstand at the racecourse that bears her name, Kincsem Park in Budapest. On racedays, there are sometimes bunches of flowers left on the plinth, in continued remembrance and recognition of this most extraordinary mare. Kincsem was perfection itself.

27

Sandown Park, the first enclosed racecourse.   Image © Edward Whitaker

A QUANTUM SHIFT

It might have been a lunatic asylum. On busy summer Saturday afternoons it can seem as though it might nevertheless be one, but the unlikely blueprint to turn Sandown Park into a racecourse instead represented a sea-change in the sport.

Before Sandown emerged fully formed from the suburbs, racecourses had not evolved far from their origins on common land. Racecourses were born of suitable locations, not made, and when the requisite area of land in genteel Esher came up for development the idea of a racecourse was a poor third choice behind a lunatic asylum and a small 'new town'. As punters know well, though, outsiders of three are by no means forlorn hopes, and the energy and radical vision of racecourse manager-elect Hwfa Williams – plus his connections to the future Edward VII – won the day.

The first meeting at Sandown Park took place in April 1875, and at a stroke the old mould was broken. Sandown was not only the first purpose-built racecourse in Britain but the first enclosed racecourse, girdled by fencing all the way around. This was crucial, for it meant that every racegoer had to pay a fee – it was at least half a crown at the outset, although it's a little more than 30p these days – to enter the racecourse, a quantum shift in the world of sporting entertainment.

The idea behind it was firstly and most obviously to make money, but the secondary motive was to ward off the rowdier elements and make Sandown a racecourse with an exclusive club-like atmosphere, with the intention of providing a habitat in which women would feel safe and welcome. Now, being well-heeled is certainly no guarantee of being well-behaved, to which anyone who has seen the idle aristocracy at play can attest, but the notion appealed to late Victorian society.

One diarist noted, 'Sandown is a place where a man could take his ladies without any fear of their hearing coarse language or witnessing uncouth behaviour,' which of course is a perfect summary of the behaviour at every racecourse, everywhere.

The 'Club' concept was a revolutionary innovation but an immediate success. Four years later, the Club had 1,800 members. Another factor in play here was the proximity of the course to the railway. London was 20 minutes away by train, engineering works permitting, and a gate leading directly from the platform, down a lane, and into the racecourse was eminently convenient. Sandown became a leisure destination, to use an unfortunate phrase, and its future was assured.

Williams had laid the course out for Flat and jump racing, and in 1886 the inaugural running of the Eclipse Stakes, Sandown's most prestigious race of the season, was won by Bendigo. The prize fund for the race was £10,000, making it the most valuable in Britain, worth twice as much as the Derby. The Eclipse has been won by many of the greatest names in the sport, including Ballymoss, Mill Reef, Brigadier Gerard, Dancing Brave, Nashwan, Daylami and Sea The Stars.

Over jumps, Sandown has evolved into one of the premier venues in the world, with the two-mile Tingle Creek Chase – named after a brilliantly fast, much-loved chaser of the 1970s – the centrepiece of its winter season. The three fences nearest to the railway line have become known, unsurprisingly, as the Railway Fences, and are in closer proximity to each other than any fences on any other racecourse, making for a unique and exacting test of jumping.

The 'Park course' template laid down by Williams at Sandown, of a custom-built and enclosed arena, has been copied and standardised by every new racecourse to open its doors thereafter, with notable examples including nearby Kempton Park (1878), the now defunct Hurst Park (1890), Lingfield Park (1890) and Haydock Park (1899). Between the medieval and the modern, Sandown was the pivot.

A mint julep. Cheers! Image © Getty

MORE THAN THE HORSES

It's the greatest two minutes in sport. It's also decadent and depraved. It's also a run for the roses. The Kentucky Derby may not quite be all things to all men, but it is still the greatest and most prestigious race in the US, the most bound by tradition, the race that connects more people to racing than any other.

The Derby (pronounced Durby; two nations separated by a common language), held at Churchill Downs in Kentucky on the first Saturday in May, was run for the first time in 1875. It's for three-year-old colts and fillies, although only three fillies have won it, the most recent being the striking grey Winning Colors in 1988.

It owes its genesis and its name to the race run at Epsom, for after Colonel Meriwether Lewis Clark attended the 1872 Derby (the Darby; two nations etc) he was inspired to create a similar contest back home, and built the racecourse at Churchill Downs, just outside the city of Louisville, to stage it. When Aristides won the inaugural running he did so over a mile and a half, as at Epsom, but in 1896 the race distance was cut to a mile and a quarter, the classic US distance, and the race's identity began to take shape.

As would be expected, many of the all-time great US horses – and by common extension the world's greatest – have won the Kentucky Derby, and its position as the first leg of the coveted Triple Crown series gives it a mystique that endures in the psyche of racing devotees and once-a-year fans alike. Secretariat, very possibly the greatest of them all, holds the track record for the race, and other winners whose name and fame stretch beyond the racetrack include Spectacular Bid, Affirmed, Seattle Slew, Northern Dancer, Swaps and Citation.

There is more to Kentucky Derby day than the horses, though. The day's traditions are as much part of the Derby experience as trying to pick the winner, and are fiercely defended from those who prefer to treat the day as a high-class series of horse races. The 'official' drink of the Kentucky Derby is the mint julep, a sugary concoction that gets its kick from Kentucky bourbon, served in souvenir glasses.

While the field for the Derby parades in front of the grandstand, the entire crowd combines in a rendition of the Derby song 'My Old Kentucky Home', the antebellum slave-song tearjerker (especially if too many mint juleps have been taken) written by Stephen Foster, who also gave the world 'Oh! Susanna' and 'Camptown Races', with the latter surely a far more entertaining candidate for a racetrack sing-song. Even the many thousands of the great unwashed crammed into the track infield – as febrile a spot as the Hill at Epsom – raise their glasses and voices in sentimental accord.

The infield was made famous (infamous) by an article written in 1970 by Hunter S. Thompson, in typically haphazard first-person style, in which he recounted a day spent among the drunks and debauchees and encapsulated it in the memorable phrase 'decadent and depraved'. Thompson would know.

The finishing touch to the day is the blanket of red roses that is draped across the neck and withers of the race winner, more than 500 blooms in all, and possibly the last thing a sweating, race-weary horse needs, but it all adds to the colour and the gaiety and the occasion for the largest crowd in racing; attendances of more than 150,000 are an annual occurrence.

Back to the horses. The Kentucky Derby has known its share of controversy, with disqualified winners such as Maximum Security in 2019 and Dancer's Image in 1968, legendary jockey Bill Shoemaker misjudging the finish line on Gallant Man in 1957, standing up in the saddle and losing the race by a nose, and jockeys Don Meade and Herb Fisher fighting each other with whips and fists during the closing stages in 1933, when Brokers Tip beat Head Play by a nose.

The Derby is no longer the most valuable race of the US season and its pre-eminence in a purely racing sense has been diluted by the emergence of the end-of-year Breeders' Cup races, but its place in the public consciousness is secure. The first four months of every year are devoted to country-wide trials and preparations for the Derby, and all roads lead to Churchill Downs where, under the famous twin spires of the grandstand, one three-year-old colt will cross the line in front and begin the rest of his life as a celebrity.

Like several other races of similar standing – the Grand National, Derby, Melbourne Cup – the Kentucky Derby is a little bit more than a race, a little more than the sum of its parts. To be in the historic grandstand, breath minty from an excess of juleps, among a hundred thousand people putting their hearts and souls into the singing of a sentimental song while a champion waits to be crowned within the headlong span of two minutes, is to be part of one of the greatest occasions in racing.

29

The end for Fred Archer. Image © Getty

BALLAD OF THE TIN MAN

It was in the drawer of the nightstand, where the chamber pots were kept. It was the work of a second to grasp it, to put the barrel in his mouth, to pull the trigger. Fred Archer, out of his mind with illness, malnutrition, worry and sorrow, killed himself on 8 November 1886. He was only 29.

Archer was the greatest jockey of the Victorian era, and is still regarded without murmur as one of the all-time greats of the saddle. The records he set are records no more, but he was so far ahead of his contemporaries that his achievements still resonate in the modern era.

In a career that began when he was a boy of 12, he was champion jockey 13 years running (1874-86), winning 2,748 races at an astounding strike-rate of 34 per cent. His tally of winners puts him eighth all-time on the list of British Flat jockeys, with those above and directly below him enjoying much longer careers – decades, even – than that afforded to Archer.

It was said of him that he would have been a much happier man had he been five inches shorter – Archer was 5ft 10in tall, and with riding weights considerably lower than they are today he spent his entire life starving himself for his art. He pared himself almost to transparency on a diet stretching to half an orange and a mouthful of champagne per day, washed down with a vicious purgative known as Archer's Mixture, and even then could barely tip the scales at 8st 7lb. Little wonder that in the best-known image of him, his eyes peer luminously from a wasted, melancholy face.

The rewards, though, were abundant. He won the Derby five times, the St Leger six times, the 2,000 Guineas and Oaks four times apiece, and landed the Grand Prix de Paris – then the most prestigious race in France – on three occasions. Perhaps his apotheosis in the saddle came in the 1880 Derby, which he won on the brilliant Bend Or.

Three weeks before the Derby, Archer was riding work on Newmarket Heath aboard the unsympathetically named Muley Edris. Archer was hard on his horses, had been hard on Muley Edris in his races, and the four-year-old had not forgotten this. When he dismounted, Muley Edris bowled him over, knelt on his chest and began to savage him with his teeth. By the time help arrived and his malign assailant had been pushed away, Archer's right arm was in a bad way.

He had been bitten through to the bone and he was still in great pain on Derby day, but with an iron brace supporting his useless arm – and despite dropping his whip two furlongs out – he coaxed and coerced Bend Or to victory by a head from Robert The Devil.

His presence by then had long moved beyond the confines of the racecourse and into the public domain. His name was common parlance, and even now one might ask the apocryphal 'man in the street' about jockeys and mention of Fred Archer is not unknown, among the usual citations of Piggott and Dettori and McCoy. He was also a wealthy man – he was nicknamed the 'Tin Man' for his purported avarice and love of 'tin' (money) – but his private privations and his personal anguish left little room for happiness in his life.

Even when he married his beloved Nellie in 1883 in a ceremony that was described by the newspapers of the day as the 'celebrity wedding of the decade', his joy was short-lived. Almost exactly a year later their son William died shortly after being born, and later in 1884 Nellie herself died in childbirth, although their daughter, also Nellie, survived.

'Poor Nellie – she was my glory, my pride, my life, my all,' he said. 'She was taken from me at the very moment that my happiness did really seem to me to be so great and complete as to leave nothing else in this world that I could wish for.'

Though his heart was broken his brilliance remained intact, and the following year Archer set his record seasonal tally of 246 winners and won four of the five British Classics, but the demands on his spirit and his strength were growing too much to bear. In 1886 he won the Derby and St Leger on the unbeaten Ormonde, probably the greatest horse he ever rode, but the end was nigh. The combination of severe wasting and a chill caught at Lewes racecourse in early November that turned into typhoid fever sent him finally to his bed, where he lay in the death-grip of delirium and distress.

The coroner's report revealed what one might have expected, that 'the deceased shot himself whilst in a state of unsound mind, the weak state and high fever having disordered his brain to such an extent as to leave no doubt that he was insane at the time he committed the rash act'.

Archer was patently suffering from long-standing depression and was perennially in a state of chronic hunger. Nowadays these aspects of acute mental and physical distress would be recognised as relatively common. Depression is an acceptable self-diagnosis in today's society and help is readily available, although young men and women in sport and in racing are still finding themselves adrift beyond the limits of their hope, and taking what seems to them to be the only way out.

Poor Fred Archer was lost and alone. History, though, would always be his friend. Insane or, perhaps, just intolerably weary of life, Archer summoned up the last of his strength, got out of bed, and opened the drawer of the nightstand.

30

Willie Simms, champion Black jockey.   *Image © Alamy*

BLACK JOCKEYS ALL, AND ALL FORGOTTEN

Who was Willie Simms? It sounds like one of Bob Dylan's early songs, and the rebuke characteristic of his protest anthems is apt. Who was Billy Walker? Who was Jimmy Winkfield? Alonzo Clayton? Oliver Lewis?

Once upon a time these gentlemen were big-race jockeys, household names, men of renown. Why aren't they remembered now? They were African-Americans, and their stories have been largely whitewashed out of racing's history books.

In the first Kentucky Derby, 13 of the 15 riders were black. The race was won by Aristides, ridden by Oliver Lewis, an African-American, and black jockeys won more than half of the next 27 Kentucky Derbys. In 1902, Jimmy Winkfield won the Derby for the second time, the last time a black jockey was victorious in America's greatest race. They dominated the sport for a generation, and then vanished. Not too much imagination is required to work out why.

Before the American Civil War, many jockeys in the US – certainly in the South – were slaves, and it was only natural that they be employed to ride in races aboard the horses they looked after at home. After the war, and emancipation, the best of those young black jockeys were free to move north and ride on the lucrative city circuits. The good times did not last long.

The Jim Crow laws enforcing racial segregation were upheld nationwide in 1896, when the US Supreme Court enacted the 'separate but equal' doctrine. Fewer owners wanted to employ a black jockey, recession and anti-gambling legislation reduced opportunities as well, and rough riding by white jockeys against black jockeys began to go unpunished. Black jockeys began to disappear from view, and that beginning soon became the end. One African-American jockey rode in the 1911 Kentucky Derby, another in the 1921 Derby. The next black jockey to ride in the Derby was Marlon St Julien, in 2000.

At such a remove, it is hard to appreciate the prolonged impact black jockeys had on the sport. Isaac Murphy won three Kentucky Derbys (1884, 1890, 1891) and more than one-third of all his rides were winners, a phenomenal, Fred Archer-esque strike-rate. He died in 1896, before the full effect of Jim Crow came to bear on the African-American jockey colony, and his name now adorns an award given by the National Turf Writers Association to the rider with the highest winning percentage each year.

Billy Walker won the Derby in 1877; George Lewis in 1880; Babe Hurd in 1882; Erskine Henderson in 1885; Isaac Lewis in 1887; Alonzo Clayton in 1892, at 15 the youngest jockey ever to win the race; James Perkins in 1895; Willie Simms in 1896 and 1898. Black jockeys all. Simms is also a part of British racing history, although that too has been forgotten.

In 1895 Simms became the first African-American jockey to win a race in Britain, his four victories a small addendum to a career that included two championships and a landslide of big-race wins, notably the Preakness and Belmont Stakes.

Jimmy Winkfield, the last name on the Derby-winning list, led an extraordinary life. He left the US in 1904 and rode with great success in Poland and Russia, where they called him the 'Black Maestro'. When the two Revolutions of 1917 brought such bourgeois pursuits as racing to a halt, Winkfield helped lead 250 thoroughbreds to safety on a 1,100-mile trek from Odessa, via Bucharest, to Warsaw.

He then moved to Paris and resumed his riding career, and on retirement took out a training licence until the Nazis requisitioned his yard. Winkfield returned to the US, where he found the prejudices that had led to his original flight still intact, still waiting for him. In 1961 he was invited to a reception in a Louisville hotel during Kentucky Derby week, but was refused entry at the front door because of the colour of his skin.

The world is a slightly different place now. Deshawn Parker became the first African-American jockey to be champion (by races won) in the US since James Perkins when he topped the lists in 2010 and 2011, but there have been very few black jockeys riding regularly in Britain. Compton Rodrigues (born in Guyana) won plenty of races in the 1970s and early 1980s, and Royston Ffrench, champion apprentice in 1997, is of Jamaican descent.

The first and only black jockey to win a Classic in Britain is Sean Levey, who was born in the country formerly known as Swaziland and won the 2018 1,000 Guineas on Billesdon Brook. His victories at the top level include the Queen Elizabeth II Stakes and Sun Chariot Stakes, and it is a racing certainty that his achievements will not be forgotten.

No one will say 'who was Sean Levey?'. If only the same could be said for Willie Simms, Jimmy Winkfield and their comrades.

31

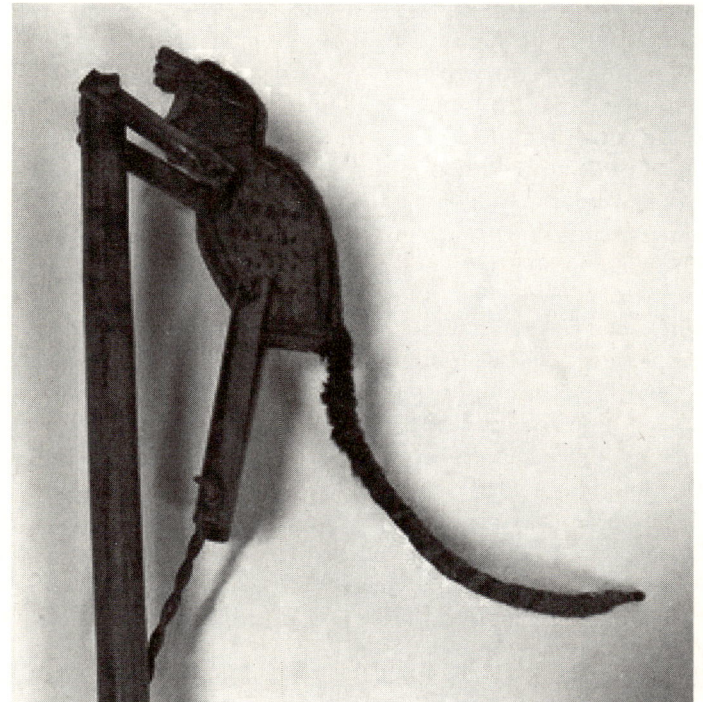

The original monkey up a stick. *Courtesy of Manchester Art Gallery*

OUT ON HIS OWN

James 'Tod' Sloan died from cirrhosis of the liver in 1933, at the age of 59, but his legacy is ongoing, enduring. Few people can have had such a lasting impact in three vastly different fields as did Sloan. He was famous for being by himself, for being an American, for changing the face of British horse racing.

All that fame derives from his career as a jockey, which was as brief as a firework but just as brilliant. Before Tod Sloan, whose nickname derives from a childhood insult (they called him Toad, which he hastily adapted, as well he might), all jockeys rode 'long', their stirrups dangling low. It was a stance that had not evolved since days of antiquity, the province of cavalrymen and huntsmen, as a brief glance at Victorian sporting art will confirm.

Nowadays, jockeys ride 'short', their stirrups pulled up high, their backs flat, bodies folded hairpin-style, streamlined and aerodynamic. Tod Sloan is the man responsible for that.

As is very often the case, Sloan was not an inventor but an innovator, adapting someone else's idea with resounding success and bolting his name to it. Willie Simms – see previous chapter – first brought this crouching style to Britain in 1895, but Sloan, who had risen to the top of the rankings on the east coast of the US, popularised it when he began to ride in Britain from 1897, short visits at first and then taking up residence two years later.

The locals naturally had to denigrate the new style by terming it the 'monkey crouch', describing Sloan as the 'monkey up a stick' of the popular contemporary child's toy, but as the winners mounted up – he won five races in an afternoon at Newmarket in September 1898, and 108 races the following year – they had to concede that the crouching, cocksure Sloan was on to something big.

His preference to ride from the front, honed by his experience on US tracks, threw into disarray the general slow-quick British style and also proved enormously effective. His profile, his reputation and his bank account rose exponentially, as did his opinion of himself. He took to smoking foot-long cigars in the parade ring, nettling the peerage.

His important wins in Britain included the 1899 1,000 Guineas, on Sibola, and the 1900 Gold Cup, on Merman, who was owned by Lillie Langtry, the famous actress and serial mistress. This was the social world in which Sloan now moved, and he revelled in it while it lasted, which wasn't long.

Sloan was suspected of involvement in a betting scandal and the following year the Jockey Club, possibly eager for the chance to cut the uppity little Yank down to size, denied him a licence. This action was reciprocated by the US authorities and Sloan's career was over. His lasting influence was only just beginning.

His name entered the language through Cockney rhyming slang: to be on one's own, to be on one's Tod Sloan, to be by yourself, on your tod. Moreover, whenever anyone sings that ebullient patriotic standard that goes 'I'm a Yankee Doodle Dandy, a Yankee Doodle do or die', they are unknowingly referring directly to Sloan.

The song is titled 'The Yankee Doodle Boy', it was written for the 1904 musical Little Johnny Jones, about a brash American jockey who goes to England to ride in the Derby, and Sloan was the very recognisable model for Johnny Jones. As the lyric states, 'Yankee Doodle came to London, just to ride the ponies'.

Now everyone who rides the 'ponies' on the racecourse adopts a slightly modified version of Sloan's groundbreaking, trendsetting crouch, which was so successful that the old-style method of riding 'long' disappeared practically overnight. Jockeys now perch almost on the horse's withers with only a toe in the stirrup iron, an exhibition of core strength and balance that helps conserve a horse's energy for the business of running fast, rather than for carrying a human's weight.

They made fun of Sloan, now they imitate him; he was ahead of his time, out on his own at the forefront of innovation, on his tod.

32

Cleeve Hill, overlooking Cheltenham.   *Image © Racing Post*

A CELEBRATION OF LIFE

The Cheltenham Festival is a vast, sprawling, four-day Godzilla of a meeting that dominates the landscape of jump racing as surely as a California redwood dominates a grove of once-mighty oaks. It is difficult to rationalise that something so enormous could grow from a tiny seed, and likewise the Festival was once no more than a minor character on the racing stage.

It began as a two-day affair in 1911 under the title of the National Hunt meeting, the centrepiece of which was the four-mile National Hunt Chase (first run in 1860), then second only to the Grand National in terms of prestige. The dozen races included three selling races and a bumper, and the meeting was considered a big success, a feather in the cap of clerk of the course Frederick Cathcart, regarded as the 'father of Cheltenham' and its greatest servant.

In 1923 the meeting was expanded to three days, and the following year Red Splash won the inaugural running of the Cheltenham Gold Cup, at the time regarded as no more than a convenient trial for the Grand National. The Champion Hurdle was added to the schedule in 1927, and by then the meeting had a shape that would be familiar to the modern racegoer, although there was no implication that the Gold Cup and Champion Hurdle were championship races; that cachet was not attached until the 1950s.

The word 'festival' was not applied to Cheltenham even at that stage, unless the Cheltenham Literature Festival is taken into account. The March meeting was known as the National Hunt meeting, Tuesday to Thursday, 18 races, and it is this sepia/rose-tinted model people reach for when muttering about the Festival having grown unsatisfactorily large and unwieldy.

Anything as successful as the Cheltenham Festival cannot be expected to stand still, however, and in 2005 new races were introduced and a fourth day incorporated. More races have since been added, and every year the prospect of a fifth day is mooted, to a chorus fairly divided between hoots of derision at the inevitability of the meeting's dilution and calls for common sense about the inevitability of financial imperatives.

Considering that the Cheltenham Festival is now indisputably the highlight of the jumping year, a racing institution, a commercial behemoth, it attracts more than its fair share of criticism, notably for the implication that the meeting overwhelms the rest of the season, that its importance undermines the importance of other big races, that there is a broad sense that nothing matters except the Cheltenham Festival. These are not unfounded complaints, but the tangible glories of the Festival far outweigh its perceived downsides.

These four days in spring are as much a celebration of life, of the sport as a whole, as they are a demonstration of racing excellence. The anticipation of the build-up is breathless, the appreciation of the nerve-tingling action is profound, and the memories last forever.

The great good-natured invasion of the Irish provides a friendly rivalry upon which to renew many once-a-year acquaintances, and it is not an exaggeration that many racegoers save a little money every week, squirrelling away a few pounds and euros, so that when the winds of March set every heart a-dance there is plenty in the pot with which to bet on their heroes.

Heroes is not too strong a word. The men, women and horses who perform at Cheltenham become the subjects of an almost religious devotion, their names recited like a catechism, their deeds magnified with every passing year. There could not be room here for them all, but simply typing their names is pleasure: Arkle and Golden Miller; Kauto Star and Denman; Winter, Dickinson and Francome; Walsh, McCoy and Mullins; Night Nurse and Monksfield; Istabraq and Moscow Flyer; Willie Wumpkins and Danoli; Henderson, Nicholls and O'Neill; Badsworth Boy and Dawn Run; Desert Orchid and Sprinter Sacre.

On the Tuesday and Wednesday races are staged on the Old Course, built more for speed. On Thursday and Friday the action switches to the New Course, with its emphasis on stamina. One or two of the races struggle for a sense of belonging and the natural flux of sponsors' names can occasionally be distracting, while the sheer volume of people – crowds average 65,000 – can make the essential processes of buying a drink, having a bet and finding a toilet harder work than desirable.

But if the jumping year is a jumble of many fine things, the promise of the Cheltenham Festival is the golden thread that binds all together. As the runners for the first race of the meeting mill around at the start, the yearlong frenzy of anticipation reaches boiling point.

When the tape rises and the horses break away, a great exhalation of release and relief and sheer happiness rolls like a cloud from the grandstands across the great green amphitheatre of dreams that lies in the benevolent shadow of Cleeve Hill. The Cheltenham Festival is certainly not perfect, but in an imperfect world it comes as close to nirvana as most of its innumerable army of adherents are ever likely to know.

Emily Davison's unused return ticket. *Image © Alamy*

DEEDS NOT WORDS

Emily Davison stood in the sunshine amid the Derby day throng at Tattenham Corner, waiting for the right moment. As the leading horses swept past, she slipped under the running rail, into the path of the chasing group, into the pages of history.

Davison's actions, and subsequent death, belong to social history as well as racing history. She became a martyr for her cause, a symbol of defiance, but left behind a tangle of conjecture about her motives and her final moments. The King's horse, the maverick suffragette, the watching world: the 1913 Derby will never be forgotten.

At that time, women were not permitted to vote (neither were 40 per cent of men). The suffrage movement sought emancipation, adopted a militant stance in order to achieve its goal, and Davison was one of its more radical members, a firebrand activist whose actions led to imprisonment and cruel treatment on several occasions. She was a brave and intelligent woman, but had become dangerously unpredictable and had fallen out of favour with the Women's Social and Political Union when she caught a train to Epsom.

Later, afterwards, when her belongings were searched, the return half of the train ticket was discovered, along with a pass for a WSPU event that evening. It seems implausible that Davison, 40, had martyrdom on her mind. It is almost certain that her intentions were to stop the race, or at least one of the horses, brandish a flag in the purple, white and green colours of the WSPU, and thereby draw attention to her cause while at the same time enabling her return to the mainstream of the movement.

She emerged on to the track after the first group of horses had passed, was narrowly avoided by two others, and was then knocked to the ground by one of the stragglers. It was Anmer, owned by King George V, but Davison certainly did not intentionally select the King's horse.

Given her location, she could have had no inkling of the progress of the race or the position of the individual horses. It was a fluke, pure luck, pure gold for publicity purposes, but Davison had no time to appreciate that nuance.

In newsreel footage she can be seen, with one hand clearly holding something that might be a rolled-up flag, raising her arms either to grab at the horse's bridle or in shock at the rapidly unwinding chain of events, before Anmer, travelling at around 35mph, cannons into her. Horse, jockey and suffragette went crashing to the turf.

Anmer and jockey Herbert Jones were unscathed, but Davison was knocked cold, sustained severe internal injuries, and died in hospital four days later without regaining consciousness. The coroner's stated cause of death was 'fracture of the base of the skull'.

In a footnote, although it almost deserves a chapter of its own, the outcome of the 1913 Derby was intensely dramatic. A rough race was won by the hot favourite Craganour, but he was disqualified after an inquiry based as much upon the personal animosity between senior steward Eustace Loder (who had bred Craganour) and the horse's owner Charles Bower Ismay as on any foul play in-running, and the race awarded to 100-1 outsider Aboyeur. Moreover, the third horse to finish, Day Comet, was not seen by the judge and was eventually placed fifth.

Davison was arguably of greater assistance to the WSPU in death than she was in life. The WSPU had lost a renegade and gained a talisman, despite widespread Establishment disdain such as that expressed in a telegram sent by Queen Mary to Herbert Jones, in which she wrote of 'the abominable conduct of a brutal, lunatic woman'.

Her funeral cortege was followed through the streets of London by 6,000 suffragettes, and the public lined the route to pay their respects in even greater numbers. Davison's funeral drew 30,000 mourners, and her headstone was inscribed with the motto of the WSPU: 'Deeds Not Words'.

War broke out the following year, and the contribution made by women, allied to the efforts of the suffrage movement, led to changes in legislation. In 1928, the Representation of the People Act enfranchised all women and all men over the age of 21.

Davison didn't live to cast a vote, but her actions on Derby day were a highly visible contribution to the cause, and her place in the pantheon of women's rights, and in history, is unimpeachable. Deeds not words; a fine sentiment to live by and, in Davison's case, to die for.

34

France's racing monument. *Image © Getty*

THE PERFECT CLIMAX TO THE SEASON

Some races are born great, like the Breeders' Cup Classic. Some slowly achieve greatness, like the Cheltenham Gold Cup. And some have greatness thrust upon them, like the Prix de l'Arc de Triomphe. Europe's premier Flat race had no option but to succeed, given the circumstances of its birth.

With France and the rest of Europe beginning to emerge from the horrors of the First World War, the Societe d'Encouragement wanted to create a new marquee race to give the industry a boost, a weight-for-age contest to complement the established Prix du Conseil Municipal, which had a penalty structure. The new race needed a name; it might have been called the Prix la Victoire, but instead the decision was made to call it after the great monument on the Champs-Elysees that had been the site of a victory parade by the armed forces the previous year.

How could the race fail, given the poignancy of its name and the sincerity of its intentions? The inaugural running in 1920 was won by the perfectly named Comrade, trained in Newmarket by Peter Gilpin and owned by the Count de Saint-Alary, an entente tres cordiale and an auspicious beginning for a race that would become one of the most international races in the calendar.

Incidentally, Count Evremond de Saint-Alary was not only a renowned breeder but a man whose passions were easily roused. In June 1896 he challenged a journalist who had criticised one of his horses to a duel with swords, avenging his horse's honour with a swift (but non-fatal) victory. Such a refreshing attitude would certainly add a little piquancy to the life of modern racing hacks . . .

The Arc, for three-year-olds and up, run over a mile and a half at Longchamp – or ParisLongchamp as its recent rebranding suggests, although that may take a decade or three to catch on – in the autumnal beauty of the Bois de Boulogne, retains its great importance partly through its position as the most valuable race in Europe and partly through its position in the calendar, the early October date making it the perfect climax to the European season.

As a result, many of the finest horses in history have won the race. The incomparable Sea-Bird, the greatest French horse ever, won by a comfortable six lengths in 1965 from a truly cosmopolitan field containing champions from France, Ireland, the US and Russia. Sea-Bird was unfashionably bred, and his dam Sicalade was unsentimentally sold to a butcher for the equivalent of £100 before he had raced.

The greatest Italian horse in history, Ribot, won two Arcs, the second by an official margin of six lengths that was more like eight or nine, judged on photographic evidence. Other dual winners include the Irish-trained Alleged and the fillies Corrida, Treve and Enable, while champions such as Mill Reef, Allez France, All Along, Peintre Celebre, Montjeu and Sea The Stars gild the roll of honour.

Arguably the most dramatic and memorable of Arcs was the 1986 iteration, when a field containing 11 Group 1 winners was dismantled by the electrifying finishing burst of Dancing Brave. His rider Pat Eddery nervelessly delayed his challenge until a furlong and a half from the line, whereupon the brilliant colt flashed past a dozen horses to win by an easy length and a half in race-record time.

The race has also been a personal triumph for three generations of the Head family, who can claim ten winners between them. William Head trained two Arc winners, his son Alec trained four, and Alec's daughter Criquette trained three, while her brother Freddy rode the winner on four occasions, three of those being for a family member. Their finest hour came with Three Troikas in 1979: trained by Criquette, ridden by Freddy, and owned by their mother Ghislaine.

Perhaps it is fair to say that the French are not the most enthusiastic of racegoers, instead preferring to watch the action from the cosy camaraderie of a boulevard cafe, in front of a television with a cognac and a handful of pari-mutuel tickets. Even the big days do not attract the level of interest that would be evident further afield, with the possible exception of the Prix de Diane at Chantilly in high summer, where attendance is boosted by the day serving as a showcase for the latest haute couture.

For the Arc, though, they do emerge blinking into the soft autumn air of Paris, although the influx of visitors from Britain and, more recently, from Japan, if that nation provides a runner with a leading chance, may outnumber the locals even then. Their sudden appearance in their thousands, though, must say something fundamental about the prestige and the glamour and the historic appeal of the Prix de l'Arc de Triomphe.

The marketing gurus sell the great occasion with the slogan 'It's not a race, it's a monument'. Clever wordplay, for sure, and right on the money. The Prix de l'Arc de Triomphe is a monument to the magnificence of the thoroughbred, a living monument to the sentiments of its origin.

35

A feather fit for a Prince. Image © Alamy

I GOTTA HORSE

He had a horse.

That was the first thing everyone learned about Ras Prince Monolulu, the most exotic creature ever to appear on a British racecourse. Later, they learned that he wasn't an Abyssinian prince at all, just an ordinary man, an extraordinary man. But the first thing people knew about him, apart from the fact that they'd never seen anything like him in their lives, was that he had a horse. He told them.

'I gotta horse! I gotta horse! I gotta horse to beat the fav-our-ite!'

The cry echoed around racecourses from the 1920s to the 1950s, unforgettable to anyone who heard it. Prince Monolulu was a tipster, a showman, a little bit of a conman, the most famous black man in Britain, a national treasure. His effect on society was seismic.

He wore a headdress stuffed with ostrich feathers, he wore dazzling jackets and waistcoats and always carried a large umbrella, his huckster's patter was mesmerising. He sold tips in little brown envelopes for five shillings or maybe ten, whispering 'if you tell anyone, the horse will lose', tipping every horse in the race so there was always someone who could say that Prince Monolulu had the winner. Win or lose, though, people loved him.

His real name was Peter Carl Mackay, and he was born in the US Virgin Islands, in the Caribbean, in 1881. He came to Britain at around the age of 20, spent the next decade roaming Europe as a sort of itinerant entertainer, was interned in Germany during the First World War, and then returned to Britain to make his name and his fortune.

The latter came from his support of 1920 Derby winner Spion Kop – he won £8,000, which might have set another person up for life, but Prince Monolulu spent it all and more along the way. His name, and his fame, was all his own work.

'God made the bees, the bees make the honey, the soldier does the dirty work and the bookie takes the money. Don't back the fav-our-ite, the outsider always wins. And when you win – roast beef, two veg, Yorkshire pudding, whisky and soda. God save the King! I gotta horse!'

His irresistible magnetism made him a permanent fixture on the Pathé newsreels of Epsom and Ascot, the first black man to appear on the BBC. Here was this tall, charismatic, bewitching middle-aged man in multi-coloured raiment, standing at the centre of a drably dressed racecourse crowd who couldn't take their eyes off him. On Sundays, or when the races didn't promise much, he could be found at Petticoat Lane market or Hyde Park Corner, near his home in central London, surrounded by people, putting on a show. For many, he was the first black man that they'd ever seen.

'Black man for luck!' he often shouted, and although it wasn't a particularly lucky time to be a black man or a black woman, Prince Monolulu was rarely regarded with anything other than awe and affection, even when (as happened quite often) he was being taken in charge by a policeman for using unseemly language and sent before a judge. His fines mounted up, but there were always people willing to buy another of those little brown envelopes. He always conveyed an air of mystique and mischief, even when he couldn't have felt like it.

It is sometimes difficult to know where the truth ends and the myth begins, for Prince Monolulu constructed his own mythology, embellishing wildly as the opportunity arose, his autobiography entitled I Gotta Horse (what else?) not entirely non-fiction. He may have had six wives but probably had three, notably the actress Nellie Adkins. Their wedding photograph hangs in the National Portrait Gallery, the groom far more elaborately dressed than the bride.

Even his death, in February 1965, was shrouded in the improbable. The story – in a biography of writer Jeffrey Bernard – goes that Prince Monolulu was in hospital, where Bernard visited him to conduct an interview, bringing a box of Black Magic chocolates. The Prince asked for a chocolate, Bernard put a strawberry cream in his mouth, and Prince Monolulu choked to death.

Like everything in Prince Monolulu's life, it sounds unlikely enough to be true. That was the magic of the man who embodied the racecourse experience between the wars, the face and voice of the sport, a Prince among men. I gotta horse! *I gotta horse!*

The modern skullcap.   *Image © Edward Whitaker*

A GREATER LEVEL OF SAFETY

As usual, the problem was only addressed when it was too late, too late specifically for Captain Geoffrey 'Tuppy' Bennett. Safety issues are often examined on a reactive rather than a proactive basis, and protective equipment for jockeys was no exception.

Bennett was something of a celebrity after riding Sergeant Murphy to victory in the 1923 Grand National, but nine months later he took a heavy fall at Wolverhampton, in which he was kicked in the head and never regained consciousness, dying two weeks later. As was the custom of the time, he was wearing nothing more protective on his head than a silk cap. His death prompted a revision of the regulations, and from the following October skullcaps were declared mandatory for all riders in steeplechases and hurdles.

These covered the top of the skull and no more, with no protection at the back of the head or behind the ears, but at least it was something to take the initial impact of the fall. However, as seen in a photo of Aubrey Brabazon taking the final fence in the 1950 Cheltenham Gold Cup on three-time winner Cottage Rake, a slight, sweet smile adorning his face but no chinstrap in sight, they were little more than a cosmetic measure.

No such rule applied to Flat jockeys until September 1956, when an edict from the Jockey Club brought Britain into line with Ireland, where skullcaps had been introduced four months earlier. Perhaps the move resulted from the sight of the great French jockey Roger Poincelet winning the King George VI and Queen Elizabeth Stakes at Ascot bareheaded, aboard Vimy in 1955.

Newsreel footage shows Poincelet's white cap hanging by its ribbons around his neck, his luxuriant hair rippling in the breeze, and by the time he returned to unsaddle he was cap in hand, so to speak. Poincelet evidently had an issue with headwear at Ascot, as the same thing had happened in the King George the previous year when he was runner-up on Vamos.

By 1968, Lester Piggott was wearing a chinstrap when riding Sir Ivor to a majestic victory in the Derby, but no headgear at all when he exercised the colt the day before the race. Photographs of horses being schooled over fences with their riders simply wearing a flat cap turned back to front are common in that era, but it would not be permitted today.

In 1986, body protectors (sleeveless, a reinforced waistcoat) became compulsory for jockeys in Britain and Ireland, although they were of a homespun quality compared to modern values. Ten years later, a directive ordered that helmets – no longer skullcaps – should conform to European standards of safety, and five years after that body protectors were also standardised.

The wearing of helmets and body protectors to the recognised industry standard, last updated in 2018, is mandatory both on the racecourse and on the home gallops. Gumshields may be the next item of safety equipment required to be worn by jockeys, although some already use them.

Body protectors are padded with heavy-duty foam and are not guaranteed to protect against serious injury, although soft-tissue injuries are greatly reduced. Helmets, made from fibreglass with a thick expanded polystyrene lining, now cover the back of the head and there is substantial padding behind the ears, measures that provide greater protection in falls.

Modern apparel might have saved Tuppy Bennett, although there is no form of safety gear that can exclude the possibility of serious injury, or worse. Racing's brave men and women know the risks, but at least they are far better equipped for them than their predecessors.

37

What time is the racing on? Image © Getty

BIG MAC, TOMMO AND THE NOBLE LORD

Life is an unending process of one generation taking for granted everything that beguiled the previous generation with its novelty. Today it's straightforward to watch racing online and on television practically 24 hours a day, following the sun west from Australia, Japan and Hong Kong, via South Africa, France and Britain, to the east coast of the US and thence to the west coast, with no more than a brief hiatus to collect the thoughts and cross the international date line before the action in Sydney begins again.

In May 1925, the flame that lit the fuse that would eventually explode into such unremarked-upon blanket coverage flickered into life with the first live radio broadcast of a horse race. As they did with the moon, the Americans got there first.

The victory of Flying Ebony in the Kentucky Derby was broadcast on three stations out of Chicago and Louisville, and around five million tuned in. Later that year, a little over 30,000 residents of the state of Victoria turned on their radios to hear Windbag win the Melbourne Cup. Two years later, the BBC joined the club with the first live broadcast of the Grand National, won by Sprig, and then the Derby, won by Call Boy.

Horse racing is a very visual sport, with the magnificent horses, the dazzling silks, the green fields, the intensity of competition, perfect for television even in the antique days of black and white pictures. In 1931, the first remote outside television broadcast in the world beamed back images of Cameronian winning the Derby; although the Derby had been filmed since 1896, it had only been shown in cinemas after the event.

The broadcast was primitive, indistinct and only available to a very small number of people, but a line can easily be drawn from this pioneering moment all the way through to Serpentine winning the 2020 Derby under the full glare of the ITV Racing cameras, via John Rickman's deferential trilby, Julian Wilson's patrician demeanour, and a wild-eyed John McCririck shouting about 'Burlington Bertie'.

After the Second World War, racing on television became a more regular, better regulated experience. The BBC screened racing from Sandown in 1948 and Ascot in 1951, its reach increasing under the guidance of Peter Dimmock; the Kentucky Derby was shown live to local subscribers in 1949 and then nationwide in 1952; the Melbourne Cup was broadcast live from 1960.

In the same year, BBC viewers were treated to an afternoon's sport from Aintree on Grand National day, although the BBC was embarrassingly coy in regard to talking about betting, fearful that such a move would – like the glimpse of a stockinged ankle to a Victorian gentleman – cause an uncontrollable frenzy of debauchery in its audience. The presenters, wise to the public's desire for information, got round this problem with pseudo-innocent comments such as 'ah, there's X, everyone's *favourite*' and 'yes, here's Y, everyone's *second favourite*'.

Thus began the process of welcoming strangers into the racing nation's living rooms, people who very quickly became much-loved friends. On the BBC it was Julian Wilson and John Hanmer, a little bit of Jimmy Lindley and the velveteen voice of Peter O'Sullevan. Over on ITV it was John Rickman and Brough Scott, a spot of Raleigh Gilbert and John Penney, and the mellifluous tones of John Oaksey.

When ITV ceded coverage to the new Channel 4 in 1984, the new faces in the gallery included John McCririck, a buffoon on the outside but a needle-sharp journalist on the inside, former champion jump jockey John Francome, whose amiable Wiltshire burr allowed him to get away with verbally sailing pretty close to the wind, Derek 'Big Fella' Thompson, a man never, ever lost for words, and the more cerebral, analytical Jim McGrath.

Everyone had nicknames – the Noble Lord, the Greatest Jockey, Tommo, Big Mac – and the atmosphere was far more convivial than it was three buttons away on the BBC. Viewers tuned in for the humans as well as the horses, the high-water mark of Saturday-afternoon camaraderie. In 2017 – five years after the BBC had discarded the sport – ITV replaced Channel 4 as the sole terrestrial racing broadcaster in Britain, renewing its old covenant with the sport.

As mentioned earlier, horse racing in Britain and Ireland is extraordinarily lucky with the exposure it receives through broadcast media, while other minority sports are pushed to the fringes or out of sight altogether. Two satellite channels cover every race meeting for the die-hards, and ITV turns on the populist approach for the traditional Saturday double-header and the big midweek festivals.

Once it was one race a year, then maybe four a week. Now we count our blessings, change the channel, open up a new browser. Somewhere, anywhere, any time of the night or morning, another race is being broadcast to the world.

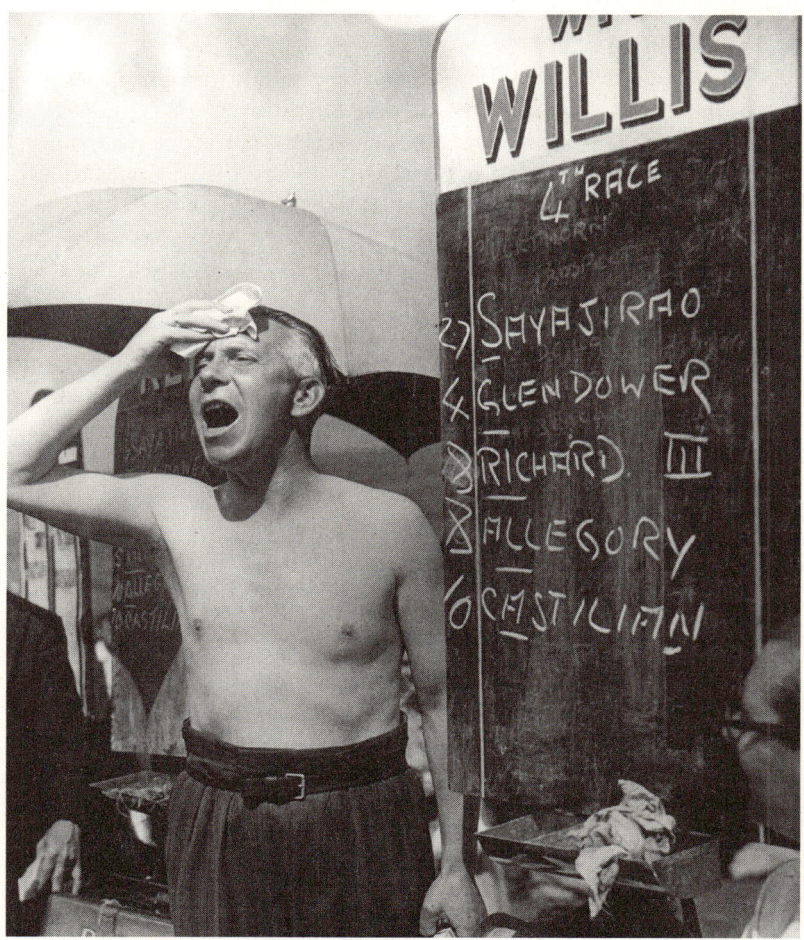
Losing your shirt at the races.   Image © Getty

A DEGREE IN OBSOLETE MATHS

The story of the bookmaker's little boy is well known. In class one morning, his teacher said, 'Come on then, Timmy, can you count from one to ten?' Timmy stood up, blushing, and looked around at his classmates. 'Yes, miss. One, 5-4, 11-8, 6-4, 13-8, 7-4, 15-8, Two, 9-4, 5-2 . . .'

The betting market and starting prices (SP) are mother's milk for those who know the secret, and a bewildering array of meaningless numbers for those who don't. An SP of 2-1 is mercifully accessible – you bet one, you get back two, plus your initial one – but what and why is 85-40, or 100-30? It's all a lot easier if you were born in the 1950s, like the art of letter-writing.

Starting prices have always been the product of observation and compromise and used to be defined by the odds available in the on-course market, agreed by members of the SP Executive, which included the *Racing Post* and the Press Association. Very broadly speaking, if ten bookmakers were offering 4-1 about Wrecking Crew and five bookmakers were offering 5-1, Wrecking Crew's starting price would be returned at 4-1, it being more representative of the odds available when the race started.

This SP was then transmitted to the wider world of betting shops, credit firms and online resources. Recently, though, owing to the absence of bookmakers (and practically everyone else) from racecourses, SPs have been defined by the off-course market made by bookmakers online, and this method, overseen by the Starting Price Regulatory Commission, will be the main driver of SPs even when bookmakers return to the racecourse, although the prices laid on-course will still be taken into account.

What must now be considered the old method of returning SPs was standardised in 1926 when, for the confidence of the off-course market (all punters who are not at the racecourse), reporters from the *Sporting Life* and the *Sporting Chronicle* began to undertake this important role. Those betting at the racecourse were simply 'on' at whatever price was available when the bet was struck, so if a wager was placed at 3-1 and the odds of the horse in question later drifted out to an SP of 7-1, the on-course punter was paid out at 3-1 and the off-course punter at 7-1. Disappointment in betting may not solely be confined to those whose horses lose.

The appearance of the prices themselves is arcane, being based on pre-decimal currency. To truly master the betting market, one must remember that in every £1 there used to be four crowns, eight half-crowns, ten florins, 20 shillings, 40 shiny sixpences, 80 threepenny bits and 240 pennies. This is now entirely useless information, unless you want to bet on Wrecking Crew.

If Wrecking Crew is 11-4, and you bet a quid, it means you are invisibly betting four crowns to win 11. If the colt is 13-8, you have the equivalent of eight half-crowns to win 13. 85-40? Forty shiny sixpences to win 85, which is a return of just over £2. 100-30? An old-style quid and a half to win a fiver. The stake is always returned on winning bets.

It is not simple, and there is an educated school of thought that suggests in a decimal age, decimal odds should be used, as in practice on the online betting exchanges: 6-1 in decimal odds is 7, 11-4 is 3.75 and so on. With decimal odds, the unit stake is always included in the price, and a degree in obsolete maths is not required; with traditional odds the unit stake is not, and it is.

This is only an issue in Britain and Ireland as all other jurisdictions use decimal odds, and as tradition is almost as hard to erase as prejudice, the pre-decimal odds will continue to be used, at the very least alongside their decimal brethren.

The longest-priced winner ever in Britain and Ireland was the 300-1 presumed no-hoper He Knows No Fear, at Leopardstown in August 2020. Over jumps, the record is 250-1, when Equinoctial won at Kelso in November 1990.

The general assumption that betting at odds-on, where the profit is less than the initial stake (2-5, bet five to win two, collect seven), is relatively risk-free is misguided and disproved on a daily basis. Former trainer Barry Hills, as shrewd at betting as he was at the day job, once said: 'Never bet odds-on. If you could buy money they would sell it at a shop down the road.'

Tree Of Liberty matched the jump record when beaten at 1-20 (bet 20 to win one, collect 21) at Ludlow in March 2018, but the overall record for shortest-priced loser belongs to Royal Forest, who was 1-25 when runner-up at Ascot in September 1948.

At least the horse's backers had a run for their money – the previous year, 1-20 chance Glendower whipped round at the start of a two-horse race and unseated jockey Gordon Richards. One well-known punter of the time had a standing arrangement with a bookmaker to back Richards's best-fancied mount of the day to win him £1,000. Twenty grand up in smoke, and in 1947 that was rather a lot of half-crowns, shillings and shiny sixpences.

39

Tote betting tickets. Image © Edward Whitaker

CHOICE

There is something about the Tote that forever falls between two stools, something fundamentally unconvincing while at the same time enormously popular. It was intended to be a financial saviour of racing, but it hasn't been; it was intended to be an alternative to the bookmakers, but it fulfils this role only in a minor key; it can be an unsatisfactory betting medium, but everyone has used it at one time or another and its place in racing culture is unassailable.

The Tote was introduced to British racecourses in July 1929, when the totalisator machines began operating at Newmarket and Carlisle. The concept was immediately popular, and by the end of the year the new system had been rolled out at 22 racecourses, but right from the start the Tote was not functioning as intended.

Jockey Club senior steward Lord Hamilton of Dalzell, the driving force behind the new initiative, wanted the Tote to be run by racing, specifically the Jockey Club, but instead control was transferred to a new body, the Racecourse Betting Control Board, which was responsible to the government. This led to the Tote becoming only a contributor to the funding of racing rather than the sole or primary source of income, as is the case in numerous jurisdictions around the world, notably France, the US, Japan and Hong Kong.

Totalisator betting is pool betting, in which some of the pool is used to cover costs, some is returned to racing, and the greater part returned to punters as winnings. As an alternative to traditional fixed-odds bookmakers, the Tote has advantages and disadvantages. In a role as an accessible, low-volume entry point for inexperienced racegoers, the Tote reigns supreme. Stakes can be small, the method of placing a bet is uncomplicated, and each-way betting or place-only betting is commonplace.

The disadvantages of the Tote are that large bets skew the pool disproportionately, so serious gamblers do not use it, and liquidity is compromised as a result. Pre-race, the pool system naturally provides only a guide to the final dividend, which can be off-putting, and as a broad rule the dividends payable on short-priced horses are often smaller than they would have been with a fixed-odds bookmaker, although as a result outsiders can often be much better value.

Where the Tote succeeds unconditionally is in its combination bets, notably the Jackpot and the Placepot, as well as forecast bets (first two), trifecta bets (first three) and the Scoop6, which was once a money-spinning highlight of televised racing but has recently retreated from the limelight. The Placepot – select a horse to be placed in each of the first six races at any meeting – is arguably the most popular bet of all, frequently providing entertainment throughout the afternoon and a substantial payout at the end of it.

However, the pivotal moment that prevented the Tote becoming everything it was intended to be was the legalisation of betting shops in 1961 (of which more later). In general, British and Irish punters prefer fixed-odds betting to pool betting, and the increased opportunity afforded by high-street betting shops was a vast and enduring setback for the Tote. What the Tote does provide is choice, which punters in France etc do not have, but unfortunately for the Tote most punters choose the alternative.

The thorny topic of a Tote monopoly frequently arises, as the pool betting monopoly in jurisdictions around the world, where all profits are reinvested in the sport and consequently prize-money is considerably higher than in Britain, is an unbridled success, but it will never happen. There may have been an opportunity in 1961 for a different path, but it was never a realistic option and the shape of betting in Britain and Ireland is now too firmly entrenched to allow for such a sea-change.

The Tote is now in private hands, having been sold first to bookmaker Fred Done in 2011 and then to an alliance known as the UK Tote Group in 2019. It still serves British racing admirably, both in a financial sense and as a familiar, trusted resource at racecourses, but it is only a minor presence in the betting landscape, a long way from the lavish hopes entertained at its genesis.

40

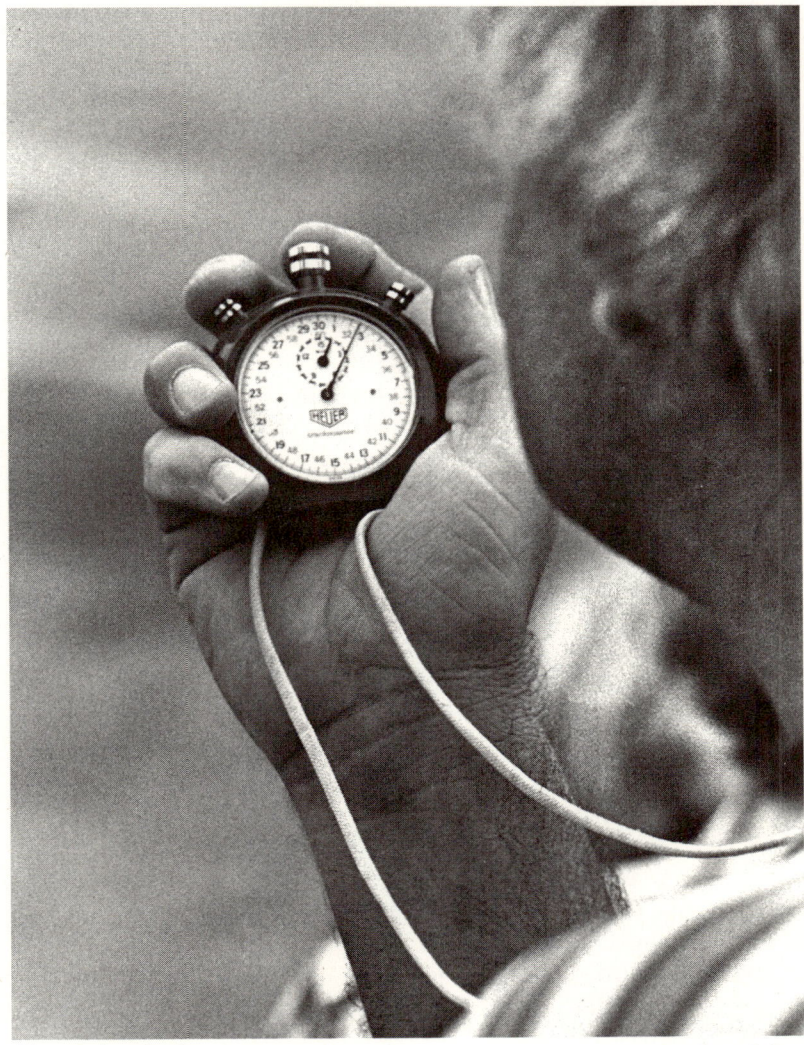

He went how fast?   Image © Getty

A MILE A MINUTE

Who is the fastest horse ever? It's an important question, because speed is the most prized asset in the modern thoroughbred. The answer may come as a surprise.

In 1721, the superlative Flying Childers, considered one of the first great racehorses, won a four-mile race at Newmarket in six minutes and 40 seconds, during the course of which he was timed to be travelling at a mile a minute. Hold on to that thought. Flying Childers reportedly hit a speed of 60mph; not so much Flying Childers as Rocket-Powered Childers.

This is patently nonsense. No horse in the modern era has ever been timed at under a minute and a half for a mile. The fastest sprinters in the world do not come close to 60mph; the lightning-quick Battaash averaged roughly 40mph when winning the King George Stakes at Goodwood in 2019, assisted by the downhill nature of the track. Flying Childers could shift, evidently, but there is no way he could cover even short distances at mile-a-minute pace, unless he fell down a well.

Understandably, accuracy was a problem with the earliest timing of races, which began in earnest in the 1880s. The issue was not permanently addressed until electrical timing was used for the first time in 1931, at Hawthorne, near Chicago, which operated through the runners breaking a beam of light connected to a timing mechanism. Newmarket was the first racecourse in Britain to introduce electrical timing, in 1952, but many racecourses persisted with hand-timing for years, which tends to involve a slow reaction time to the start and anticipation of the finish, knocking off tiny fractions at both ends, leading to artificially fast times.

The fastest time for five furlongs in Britain, the equivalent of the 100m dash in athletics, was long attributed to Indigenous, who was hand-timed at 53.6sec at Epsom in 1960. Epsom's five-furlong course is downhill all the way until near the finish where it rises slightly, assisting the setting of speed records, but the stopwatch that froze Indigenous in time was calibrated only in fifths of a second. The record more properly belongs to Stone Of Folca, who covered the distance in an electrically timed 53.69sec in 2012.

Speed records are more venerated in the US than in Britain. The time set by Secretariat when winning the 1973 Kentucky Derby is of particular interest, as he ran each quarter-mile faster than the one before. Normal horses slow down towards the conclusion of a race, whatever the visual impression, but there was nothing normal about Secretariat. His time of 2m 24sec for the mile-and-a-half Belmont Stakes had an impact akin to Roger Bannister's four-minute mile. 'Two-twenty-four flat. I don't believe it. Impossible,' wrote Kent Hollingsworth, editor of the magazine *Blood-Horse*. 'But I saw it. I can't breathe. He won by a sixteenth of a mile. I saw it. I have to believe it.'

As jockey Ron Turcotte reined Secretariat to a halt, outrider Jim Dailey came to meet him, as outlined in William Nack's fine biography of the horse.

'How fast you go?' said Dailey.
'Two-twenty-four,' said Turcotte.
'You're crazy.'
'I'm telling you.'
'It can't be.'

As a glorious footnote, Secretariat's performance in the Belmont was so otherworldly that even as he was being restrained by Turcotte after the line, slowing down from a headlong gallop, he unofficially broke the world record for a mile and five furlongs. Secretariat aside, the majority of track records are not set by the best horses, owing more to circumstance – very fast ground, a tailwind, a close finish, the pace throughout the race – than pure ability.

Race times in isolation, though, are not particularly relevant, unless they hint at the truly extraordinary. The point of horse racing is to win the race, not necessarily to run a fast time. If a horse is winning easily, the jockey will not ask for further effort simply to try to set a record time, and there are no awards for breaking the course record. The evidence of the clock is more pertinent to those seeking to understand how a race was won, rather than which horse won it.

Sectional timing has belatedly made its way into British racing and is a potent weapon for a certain type of punter, a more cerebral, less instinctive punter. It is now straightforward to break down a horse's performance into bitesized pieces, furlong by furlong, to note where in the race the pace changed, whether the horse was using its energy efficiently, whether a beaten horse ran too fast early, or not fast enough late.

This can then be used to form a more accurate picture of a horse's capabilities than that gained by eye, and that brings us back to where we came in. Sectional timing was unavailable at Newmarket in October 1721, but perhaps that's for the best. As they say, never let the facts get in the way of a good story.

41

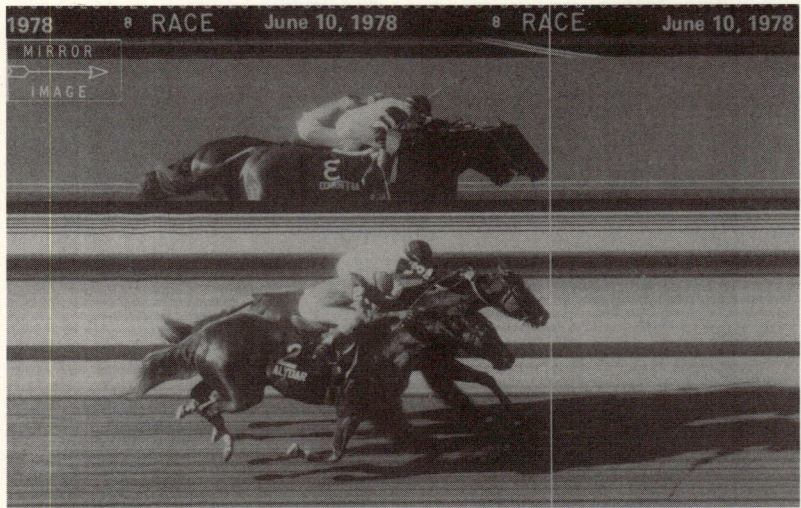

An official photo-finish print.   Image © Getty

FIRST, NUMBER...

It was Bing Crosby's idea; not just a pretty voice. The photo-finish camera owes its implementation to the man who brought us a trillion White Christmases.

Crosby loved racing so much that he built his own racecourse at Del Mar, in southern California, and recorded the song that is played there on every raceday, 'Where The Turf Meets The Surf'. For opening day in July 1937, Crosby recruited an engineer at Paramount Pictures, Lorenzo Del Riccio, to install his innovative circular flow camera to record the race finishes. The camera was an instant success, because it gave clarity where before there was opacity, it gave winners where before there were dead-heats. Crosby had hit the right note, as ever.

It took ten years for the photo-finish camera to cross the Atlantic. The first time it was used on a British racecourse was to split Parhelion and Salubrious in the Great Metropolitan Handicap at Epsom in April 1947. Two years later, the first Classic to be decided by a photo-finish was the 2,000 Guineas, in which Nimbus beat Abernant by a short head.

The photo-finish apparatus, which in Britain is regulated by RaceTech, the technological arm of the Racecourse Association, consists of two cameras and a mirror attached to the winning post on the far side of the course from the grandstand. One camera covers the whole width of the track and the other focuses on the mirror, providing the reverse image should one horse's nose be obscured by the other.

Before digital technology was employed, there was often a lengthy wait, perhaps several minutes, for the outcome of the photo-finish to be announced, a deliciously agonising period of hope and uncertainty that as it stretched on made it appear more likely that the judge would declare a dead-heat. Then the public address system would strike up with 'here is the result of the photograph', and the entire racecourse would fall silent. 'First, number . . .'

The photo print would be displayed at the course, so the disgruntled could see for themselves. Now the result is announced within seconds, before the horses have galloped out, the winning margin decided by so many pixels, the shortest official verdict a nose.

Before the advent of the photo-finish camera, dead-heats were common. They are now more or less collector's items, with the triple dead-heat in the 1956 Hotham Handicap at Flemington high on the 'wow' list, while the dead-heat between Ya Malak and Coastal Bluff in the 1997 Nunthorpe Stakes at York enabled Alex Greaves (aboard Ya Malak) to become the first woman to ride a Group 1 winner in Britain. Egregious blunders were equally frequent.

In the 1913 2,000 Guineas, Louvois was declared the winner from Craganour by a short head, despite most people present believing that Craganour had won by at least half a length. A month later in the Derby – 1913 was not a good year for racecourse judges, or indeed for Craganour, who was disqualified after passing the post first in this race – Day Comet finished third, but the judge missed him entirely and placed him fifth. Insight won the 1927 Cambridgeshire fair and square, but the judge placed him third.

It is hard not to feel sympathy for the pre-camera judge, given the near-impossibility of ascertaining which of two horses running at 35mph on either side of the course had a sliver of a nose in front of the other, with no replay for assistance, blink and you miss it, blink and you miss the winner. With the new technology, mistakes were almost eliminated, except for those deriving from human error.

At Cheltenham in November 2020, a dead-heat was called between Elle Est Belle and Ishkhara Lady when there was a convincing case that the latter had prevailed. It was the last race of the day, visibility was poor, and the image provided by the camera was indistinct, so the judge felt unable to split the pair.

At least the wrong winner was not called, an error to which judge Jane Stickels was particularly prone. She declared the wrong winner four times between 1994 and 2006, correcting herself within minutes but too late to prevent widespread confusion and the incorrect settling of bets, earning herself the nickname 'Calamity Jane' and costing bookmakers millions of pounds in dual payouts.

This sort of thing is, thankfully, exceedingly rare. The photo-finish camera is such an efficient, integral part of the sport that it is difficult to imagine life without it. A dead-heat in a major race is unsatisfactory, unwelcome, for the purpose of a race is to arrive at a winner, not a compromise. Thankfully, races such as the 2006 Derby, when Sir Percy beat Dragon Dancer by a short head, with the third horse a head away and another short head back to the fourth, are now routinely dissected by the disinterested eye of the camera, the result made plain in short order. Nothing to make a song and dance about, as Bing might have said.

42

It's a match! A versus B. *Image © Getty*

MORE THAN A HORSE RACE

Match. Fight. Duel. Black pieces against the white. Red corner, blue corner. Goalkeeper, penalty-taker. The purest definition of sport, a situation shorn of everything but simplicity and imperative. It happens very rarely in horse racing, but when it does the prospect grips like a vice.

An organised match race, a showdown, your horse against mine, winner takes all. May the best horse win, and may it be mine. It has to be planned, otherwise it's merely a poorly attended contest. It has to involve two great horses, or else where's the compulsion? And it has to have some overt edge to it, so the importance of Horse A doling out a hiding to Horse B, or vice-versa, becomes all-consuming. Let battle commence, and all that.

In the earliest days of the sport the match-race was a common occurrence. Lord East had beef with Marquess West, so they ran it off with horses instead of the old ten paces, turn and fire. Perhaps there was a bet involved, like Blake and O'Callaghan between Buttevant and Doneraile. As competition increased, as the racing calendar developed a structure, races became more well-subscribed and the match became a relic of the past. Its rarity became its potency.

More than 100,000 people were on the Knavesmire in 1851 to watch the Great Match between Voltigeur and The Flying Dutchman, two Derby winners who had met before, so there was a grudge to work out. The Flying Dutchman won by a length, settling the score.

In July 1975, the incredible Ruffian faced Kentucky Derby winner Foolish Pleasure in a match at Belmont Park. The big, black, burly Ruffian was unbeaten in ten races, had led every step of the way in all ten, and in an era flavoured by the Billie Jean King/Bobby Riggs 'battle of the sexes', this great filly was favourite to beat the colt.

It was not a race but a tragedy. Ruffian was in front, as ever, when she broke her right foreleg just before halfway. The joy went out of the day in an instant. Vets worked to save her, but she was a volatile patient and thrashed around madly post-op, undoing the surgeons' efforts. She was put down, and buried in the Belmont infield, facing the winning line.

Another compelling occasion was the duel between Cheltenham Gold Cup winner Dawn Run and Queen Mother Champion Chase winner Buck House, female against male, at Punchestown in April 1986. The two-mile trip suited Buck House better but the public's heroine Dawn Run was too strong, winning by two and a half lengths. The memory is lit from within with a poignancy, for before the summer was out both horses were dead, Dawn Run in a fall, Buck House from colic.

There has been nothing since, excluding the ridiculous mismatch between So Careful and Klute at Haydock in 1988; Klute was a half-bred, a pet, on a fool's errand, and was unceremoniously beaten out of sight. In 2000, there was a will to contrive a match between two outstanding champions in Dubai Millennium and Montjeu, and Sheikh Mohammed, owner of the former, suggested that each camp put up $6 million for a purse. Best-laid plans, and all that; a day after that announcement, Dubai Millennium fractured a leg on the gallops and was retired.

The match everyone knows, though, whether from the book, the film, or a healthy fascination with racing history, is the race between

Seabiscuit and War Admiral at Pimlico in November 1938. The match had been months in the making, with each camp issuing demand and counter-demand, and the sense of anticipation as the big day neared was electrifying. The two horses were polar opposites, perfect match rivals.

War Admiral was racing royalty, bred in the purple, winner of the Triple Crown. Seabiscuit was a tough cookie, a nuggety little horse who came from obscurity and along the way developed into 'America's horse', one of the greatest public favourites in history. With the Second World War on the horizon and the effects of the Great Depression still shackling the country, this was more than a horse race, it was something to lift the spirits of an entire nation.

There was, too, a dash of chicanery to sweeten the pot. War Admiral's connections stipulated that the race must be started by bell, in those days before starting stalls (see next chapter). It was unorthodox, but would assist the fast starter War Admiral, and in a match it is very often the case that the horse who leads early stays in front. Seabiscuit's trainer Tom Smith worked him with the unfamiliar bell every day, building in him an almost Pavlovian response to its clamour. His jockey George 'Iceman' Woolf walked the track the night before and located a firmer strip of dirt a few feet off the rail, which would suit Seabiscuit, who had already won a match that year, a rough-ridden affair against Ligaroti three months earlier at Del Mar.

Raceday, a bright Tuesday in November. Forty thousand crammed into Pimlico, 40 million listened to the radio broadcast, including President Roosevelt, who kept a cabinet meeting waiting while he listened to the race. 'People who never saw a horse race in their lives are taking sides,' wrote Dave Boone in the *San Francisco Chronicle*. Everyone had the most unshakeable confidence in 'their' horse. War Admiral was the hot favourite, Seabiscuit the plucky underdog. There could never be another race like it.

Seabiscuit started faster than War Admiral, took the lead, Woolf angling towards that prized strip of ground. The pair raced neck and neck down the backstretch, made the far turn in lockstep, and then as they entered the home stretch the strength in Seabiscuit suddenly broke the will of War Admiral, and the beloved Biscuit drew off to win by four lengths, track record time. A nation that had held its breath, exhaled.

43

A good place to start. Image © Edward Whitaker

NON-TRIERS TO THE BACK

Never mind what the old song almost says, it's just as much about how you start as how you finish. This wasn't the attitude in racing until well into the 20th century, with the starting procedure mired in chaos and ineptitude and dissatisfaction.

    Mechanisation would solve all the problems, but that wouldn't come along in its most efficient form until 1939. Before then, it was a bunfight. For the small fields of the 1700s and early 1800s, this was not an insuperable problem, although hardly efficient. The next technological leap forward arrived in the 1820s, when a flag start came into operation. A gentleman with another flag was stationed a little way down the track to alert the starter to false starts, but this was no sinecure.

    In the 1840 Oaks, for example, there were 15 false starts and a delay of approximately an hour before Crucifix reached the winning post first. The 1863 Derby involved 32 false starts and another hour's delay. This delinquency persisted until the first mechanical starting gates were introduced, initially in Australia before arriving in Britain in 1897.

    This gate evolved into a five-strand mechanism behind which the horses lined up across the track, and then, at the press of a button, the gate shot up to allow the horses to pass beneath. A comparable method of starting is still in place in jump racing, where the relative length of races apparently makes it less important to be scrupulous about a level start.

Now that horses had something to line up against, the process became less stressful for humans and animals alike. A story that is hopefully not apocryphal involves a particular starter's instructions to jockeys – 'all right jockeys, triers to the front, non-triers to the back'. Another starter always used to check with perennial champion jockey Gordon Richards before he let the field go. One day Richards was having problems, calling 'no sir, no sir,' whereupon fellow jockey Harry Wragg called out 'yes sir' and the starter reflexively pressed the button, giving Wragg a flying start at the expense of his great rival.

These shenanigans were on borrowed time. In 1939, starter Clay Puett unveiled the first set of electric starting stalls at Lansdowne Park in Vancouver. They were an immediate and unqualified success, and within a year every major racecourse in the US was using them. Puett's innovative design, with individual compartments and v-shaped front gates, was quickly copied worldwide and is still in use today, with only minor variations on the original.

It took a long time for the concept to be adopted in Britain, though, where the first race run from stalls was a five-furlong contest for two-year-olds at Newmarket in July 1965, won by Track Spare. Only four more races were started from stalls that year, an inexplicably slow take-up of an already proven system. The Derby was first run from stalls in 1967, and it wasn't until the early 1980s that every racecourse in Britain was equipped with a set of electrical starting stalls.

Horses are loaded into their predetermined stall by a dedicated army of stalls-handlers, who lead, coax, push and shove each half-ton of horse into place, sometimes almost lifting bodily, but gently, the recalcitrant ones. If some horses can be hard to get in, others become impossible to get out.

High-profile cases include Percy's Lass, later the dam of 2006 Derby winner Sir Percy, who stood stock-still as the stalls opened for the Princess of Wales's Stakes at Newmarket in 1988, declining ever so politely to race. It was a one-off decision; she started normally in subsequent races, but simply didn't fancy it that day. The 2009 Oaks and Irish Oaks winner Sariska was similarly uninterested in the Yorkshire Oaks and Prix Vermeille, and was retired as a result. What is it they say about leading a horse to water?

In the US the apparatus is known as 'the gate'; in Australia it's called the 'barrier'; in Britain it's 'stalls'. Modern stalls – the familiar green and white ones used in Britain are manufactured by Australian company Steriline – are constructed in sections of ten and are extremely reliable, although malfunctions are not unknown.

The gates are held closed at the front by spring-loaded latches wired to an electrical circuit, and on rare occasions one compartment can open fractionally before or after the others, or not at all. The freakishly fast Hungarian sprinter Overdose was denied victory in the 2008 Prix de l'Abbaye at Longchamp when the race was declared void after a rival's stall failed to open. So much has changed for the better at the start, but the potential for chaos and dissatisfaction can never be eradicated.

44

Hollywood's most famous winner. *Image © Getty*

PLACE IT ON LUCKY DAN

Oh, The Pie, The Pie! Velvet Brown won the Grand National, we saw it happen on many a Sunday afternoon. What a pity she was disqualified, not for being a 12-year-old girl, as most people believe, but for not weighing in. Blatant disregard for the correct procedure. Probably a lengthy suspension.

Racing has been well served by Hollywood and the silver screen, in volume if not in verisimilitude. *National Velvet* (1944) is a classic of the girl-with-a-pony genre, with Elizabeth Taylor winning a horse in a raffle and riding him to victory in the big race at Aintree, although it is quite a strange National. There are plenty of fallers, but the field never seems to diminish, and at one point the horses run right-handed with a mountain in the background, but as they say it's the sport that counts, and *National Velvet* is part of the British collective memory.

It's not as funny as *A Day At The Races* (1937), though, in which the Marx Brothers and a horse named Hi-Hat thwart the diabolical JD Morgan's scheme to close down their friend's sanatorium and replace it with a casino. Groucho is a vet called Hugo Z. Hackenbush, is pretending to be a doctor, and the usual mayhem ensues. 'Take one of these every half-mile and call me if there's any change,' he says, giving a pill to a horse. Get your Tootsie-Frootsie ice-cream! Get your Tootsie-Frootsie ice-cream!

Derby Day (1952) uses the Classic race as a backdrop to a dramatic day in the lives of four very different people, all heading to Epsom for very different reasons. The action on the track can't be faulted, as it's footage of the 1949 Derby, won by Nimbus. It's a little more genteel than *Brighton Rock* (1947), an adaptation of the Graham Greene novel that features Richard Attenborough as psychopathic gangster Pinkie Brown, who gets more than a close shave from the equally villainous Colleoni as the razor gangs fight among the bookmakers at Brighton racecourse.

Brighton Rock isn't a racing film but leans satisfactorily on the sport, as does the magnificent *The Sting* (1973), an all-time great ensemble movie in which Paul Newman and Robert Redford (Gondorff and Hooker) conspire to con Robert Shaw (Doyle Lonnegan) in 1930s Chicago, to a backdrop of jaunty Scott Joplin ragtime. The final scene in a betting parlour, where Lonnegan gets his come-uppance, is a masterpiece of misdirection. 'I said *place it* on Lucky Dan. That horse is gonna run second!'

Biopics of great horses have done well at the box office, with *Seabiscuit* (2003), *Secretariat* (2010) and *Phar Lap* (1983), all horses already discussed in previous chapters, at the head of the field. Of course they get the studio treatment, and of course the action portrayed on the track is eye-rollingly inauthentic – in *Secretariat*, the climactic Belmont Stakes sequence features 'Penny Chenery' calling out 'Let him run, Ronnie,' when in reality Secretariat was moving like a runaway train and Chenery was worried he was going much too fast – but they deliver a satisfactory emotional payload and make cinemagoers think hard about racing for an hour and a half.

Arkle (Pat Taaffe) leads Mill House over the last in the 1964 Cheltenham Gold Cup, on his way to becoming the greatest steeplechaser in history.
Image © Racing Post

Night Nurse (Paddy Broderick) clear of his rivals in the 1976 Champion Hurdle, his first of two victories in the race. Image © Racing Post

Frankel (Tom Queally) demolishes the field with an astonishing performance to win the 2011 2,000 Guineas.
Image © Racing Post

Sir Henry Cecil, trainer of Frankel and so many great horses, at his inimitably elegant best at Deauville in 2011.
Image © Racing Post

Barney Curley, the genius behind the Yellow Sam coup of 1975, and of several subsequent vast and successful gambles. Image © Racing Post

Shergar (Walter Swinburn) wins the 1981 Derby by ten lengths, a record winning margin. Image © Getty

Seabiscuit (George Woolf) leads War Admiral (Charles Kurtsinger) in the early stages of their match race at Pimlico in 1938. *Image © Getty*

Secretariat (Ron Turcotte) in all his majesty, on his way to victory in the 1973 Kentucky Derby. *Image © Getty*

Subzero, Australia's greatest equine benefactor with his friend and keeper Graham Salisbury, licks the Melbourne Cup he won in 1992. Image © Getty

Nijinsky (Lester Piggott) beats Meadowville in the 1970 St Leger to claim the final leg of his Triple Crown. Image © Racing Post/Mark Cranham

Phar Lap (Jim Pike) in full flight, all four feet off the ground as he wins the 1929 AJC Derby at Randwick. Image © Getty

1990 Cheltenham Gold Cup winner Norton's Coin with owner/trainer Sirrell Griffiths (flat cap). Image © Racing Post/Mark Cranham

Dawn Run and Jonjo O'Neill going to post before adding the 1986 Cheltenham Gold Cup to her victory in the 1984 Champion Hurdle. Image © Racing Post/Mark Cranham

Kauto Star (left), winner of the 2007 and 2009 Cheltenham Gold Cup, with stablemate Denman, winner of the 2008 Cheltenham Gold Cup, and trainer Paul Nicholls. Image © Getty

Northern Dancer, probably the most influential stallion in racing history, at Windfields Farm in 1965.
Image © Getty

Red Rum, three-time Grand National winner, chats to trainer Ginger McCain, winner of four Grand Nationals. Image © Getty

Jenny Pitman, the first woman to train a Grand National winner, with her Aintree hero Corbiere in 1983.
Image © Getty

The bewitching racecourse tipster Prince Monolulu, telling the ladies that he's gotta horse at Epsom in 1954. Image © Getty

Fred Archer, one of Britain's greatest jockeys, champion 13 years running between 1874 and 1886.
Image © Getty

Lester Piggott, racing legend and outstanding big-race jockey, at home in Newmarket with wife Susan and daughters Maureen and Tracy. Image © Getty

Dick Francis, who didn't win the 1956 Grand National on Devon Loch, shakes hands with triple Champion Hurdle winner Persian War. Image © Getty

Florence Nagle, the first woman to be granted a training licence, at her West Sussex yard in 1966. Image © Getty

AP McCoy, champion jump jockey 20 times and winner of more than 4,300 races, trades the racecourse for the golf course. Image © Racing Post/Edward Whitaker

Emily Davison, the firebrand suffragette whose activism led to her death at Epsom on Derby day in 1913.
Image © Getty

Miss Emilie Davison.
Instantané pris quelques jours avant l'incident d'Epsom.

Frankie Dettori, winner of seven races in one day at Ascot in 1996, the model of Italian style and panache in the royal blue of Godolphin.
Image © Racing Post/ Edward Whitaker

Phil Bull, polymath, innovator and founder of ratings service Timeform, with his ever-present cigar.

Meriel Tufnell, the first woman to ride a winner in Britain, celebrates after her pioneering success on Scorched Earth in 1972. Image © Getty

Martin Pipe, the revolutionary who changed the way horses were trained, with jockey Peter Scudamore after yet another winner. Image © Racing Post/Edward Whitaker

Vincent O'Brien, probably the greatest trainer in history, at home in 1957 with wife Jacqueline, daughters Elizabeth and Susan, and baby son David.
Image © Getty

Sir Gordon Richards, champion jockey 26 times and winner of a British record 4,870 races, in relaxed mood with wife Margaret. Image © Getty

Michael Dickinson, silly boy, training genius, mastermind of the historic Famous Five of the 1983 Cheltenham Gold Cup.
Image © Racing Post

Kincsem, the Hungarian mare who was never beaten in a 54-race career between 1876 and 1879.

Dark Horse (2015), a documentary-drama about Welsh National winner Dream Alliance, is from the same school, strumming on the heartstrings to good effect. If a proper weepie is required, though, then *Champions* (1983) is the film. It tells the colossally uplifting true story of cancer-patient jockey Bob Champion (played by John Hurt) and his crippled horse Aldaniti as they recover to win the Grand National. The portrayal of the racing action leaves a little to be desired, but the sweeping soundtrack is a three-handkerchief job and Aldaniti plays himself to a tee.

Others worth watching include *The Rainbow Jacket* (1954), repeated viewings of which apparently galvanised five-time champion Willie Carson to become a jockey, and *The Rocking-Horse Winner* (1949), an adaptation of a DH Lawrence short story and therefore a little edgier than, say, *National Velvet*.

One that should not be missed, however, on a purely subjective basis, is the wonderful *Let It Ride* (1989). Set at gorgeous Hialeah (now closed down) and starring Richard Dreyfuss, Jennifer Tilly and Robbie Coltrane, it's about Dreyfuss's character Trotter enjoying the sort of afternoon at the track that everyone dreams of. A cast hamming it up like Triple Crown winners, whip-song dialogue, Fugue For Tinhorns. 'Why are they cheering? Because I'm having a Very Good Day!'

45

The sun sets on racing.   Image © Getty

SOME ENCHANTED EVENING

Five o'clock comes at last, the phone back in its cradle, the computer keyboard pushed away, work done for the day, spring slipping seamlessly into summer outside the window. Don't go home, go racing. Evening meetings are bliss, the antidote to a hectic day, a cure for care.

The installation of floodlights at some racecourses, at Newcastle, Wolverhampton, Kempton, Southwell, Chelmsford City, means that evening racing continues all year round, even through the bleak midwinter, the all-weather tracks keeping the wheels of betting commerce turning, and there is of course a certain pleasure to be gleaned from an icy night, a few stars twinkling beyond the floodlights, a cloud of warm air huffed from the winner's nostrils. Some enchanted summer evening, though, a cold drink, a lambent cast to the fading light, the sense of winning a little back in the game of life; that's more like it.

In Britain, it all started at Hamilton Park in July 1947, a Friday night, contrived to make a weekend of the visit of King George VI and the future Elizabeth II the following day, and a bold experiment in race-planning that has passed the test of time with flying colours. Eight years later the now sadly defunct Alexandra Park in north London staged its first evening meeting, something that quickly became an irresistible attraction for the city's workforce, Monday nights at the Ally Pally, the racecourse that looked like a frying pan.

More than 12,000 turned up for that first night card, were still queuing to get in after the first race, and although the racecourse closed in 1970 there are still plenty of old-timers whose eyes mist over at the thought of the good old days, the good old nights.

The baton of Monday night entertainment for Londoners passed to Windsor, where the flame still burns brightly. Most of the meetings at the figure-of-eight circuit take place on Monday evenings, and although the quality of racing is rarely high the meetings are hugely popular. Racegoers may take a boat down the Thames from the railway station to the racecourse, an idyllic way to beat the traffic.

Only three or four British racecourses do not stage evening meetings, Ascot being one of the few exceptions, and the most prestigious night card of the season is held at Sandown in May. For those who work in racing, the resumption of regular evening racing in April can be a blessing or a curse.

It once enabled jockeys to increase their workload and thereby their income, riding here in the afternoon and then, after what is almost certainly a hair-raising drive across country, although the upper echelon of riders often travel by helicopter or light aeroplane, there in the evening, although this practice has recently been suspended. For stable staff, though, evening meetings present a problem, with horseboxes often not returning home until midnight or later from racecourses where the last race was scheduled for 9.30pm, making it a very late night followed by the habitual very early morning start.

The most striking venue for night racing is Happy Valley in Hong Kong, a racecourse almost miraculously set down in the middle of the urban jungle and surrounded by tower blocks and skyscrapers. It's a breathtaking setting, and a race meeting there is a visual extravaganza, the light show from around the circuit almost outshining the action on the track.

The energy of the frantic Happy Valley meetings is far removed from the evening meetings in Britain, which are of a far more languid, languorous design, providing a contrast with the busyness of the day and enabling people who would not otherwise be in a position to go racing to appreciate the delights of the sport, a different type of crowd for whom handicap ratings, value bets and big names mean nothing at all, and that's quite all right.

Sometimes racecourses stage live concerts after the last race, to make a proper night of it, to extend the feeling of escape. Evening meetings are special. Loosen the tie, slip out of the heels, breathe deeply. Every half an hour the horses go by; life is good.

46

Hmm. Steve Donoghue or Gordon Richards . . . Image © Getty

STEVE'S BOYISH FACE

Women make up 50 per cent of the adult household and, it's been said, 100 per cent of the brains, so no one should be surprised when once a year, possibly twice, their collective power is enough to move not mountains but markets.

The word 'housewife' may now be viewed by some as pejorative, but in the first half of the 20th century it was simply descriptive of a role. In those days betting off-course was a hole-in-corner sort of thing, a clandestine affair of street bookmakers and unseemliness, but twice a year, in early April and early June, the mainstream newspapers would start making a fuss about the Grand National and the Derby, and the runners and riders would soon become common knowledge.

Sweepstakes were subscribed to, small talk on the doorstep or in the corner shop turned to the chances of this horse or that. There was no time or inclination to become submerged in the nuances of form. The Grand National was a pinsticker's race anyway, unless one of the names leapt from the page, but the Derby was different. The Derby was more accessible, and it involved celebrity jockeys, whose renown made them headline news. Housewives absorbed this intriguing information, and acted accordingly. Sixpence or a shilling out of the housekeeping was a tempting prospect for a little bet, just for interest's sake, of course.

The first jockey to wear the mantle of housewives' choice was the hugely popular Steve Donoghue, whose name had entered the language anyway as a term of friendly encouragement. 'Come on Steve!' they shouted at the racecourse, and 'come on Steve!' became shorthand for asking someone to get a move on. Donoghue was a household name, ten-time champion jockey, and more pertinently won six Derbys between 1915 and 1925. To the public, he was utterly reliable, and to the vast sorority of housewives he was their Derby choice.

When Donoghue retired he was replaced in all affections by Gordon Richards, the most successful jockey in British history in terms of championships and winners, and of whom people said 'Gordon always tries'. Trying was not enough in the Derby, though, as Richards let his housewives down 28 times before redemption finally arrived in the shape of Pinza, in 1953.

The expected flood of small bets on whatever Richards was riding in the Derby enabled bookmakers to price his mount accordingly, as even if the horse was cut to shorter odds than its form entitled it to be, it would be supported regardless. This tactic was applied even more stringently with Lester Piggott, the next and by far the most effective housewives' choice with nine Derby winners between 1954 and 1983. As soon as Piggott's Derby horse was established, its price was cut regardless of its chances in preparation for the tide of unsophisticated faith that would inevitably materialise.

After Piggott it was Steve Cauthen, the young, handsome, wholesome-looking American with the type of Southern charm that sets hearts aflutter, and the housewives' annual flutter was thereby assured. The 'Kentucky Kid' won the Derby twice, on Slip Anchor (1985) and Reference Point (1987), both hot favourites, and although Cauthen's strike-rate was not as high as Piggott's, his smile was infinitely more appealing. 'Housewives seem to like Steve's boyish face,' a bookmaker's spokesman told *Sports Illustrated* magazine.

Cauthen gave way to Frankie Dettori, whose Italian good looks arguably surpassed even Cauthen's 'boyish face'. Dettori has always been box-office, has always been a public figure, the go-to guy when people who know nothing about racing need to broach the subject. His cheeky-chappie persona, his apparently bottomless reserves of bonhomie, his superlative ability, all these things combined to make him the obvious choice for anyone wanting a Derby bet without working too hard at it.

Two victories at Epsom, on Authorized (2007) and Golden Horn (2015), cemented his position as the housewives' choice, but when Dettori eventually retires there is no obvious candidate to take his place, no charismatic, enigmatic, romantic heir to the line of succession. Surely someone will emerge from the pack; housewives of Britain, the nation looks to you for inspiration.

The undisputed.   Image © Racing Post

GREATNESS IS FOREVER

There are always arguments in sport about who is the best, the best ever. Cruyff or Pele? Maradona or Messi? Federer, Nadal or Djokovic? Senna, Schumacher or Hamilton? They pass the time agreeably, but there is no possibility of a definitive answer. There are no arguments, however, about the identity of the best trainer. The verdict is unanimous: Vincent O'Brien.

The quiet man from County Cork reached the top of his profession in jump racing and then, a few years later, did the same on the Flat. O'Brien trained Champion Hurdle winners, Cheltenham Gold Cup winners, Grand National winners, Derby winners and Prix de l'Arc de Triomphe winners. A list of his best horses would stretch out of the door and halfway down the street, and his achievements are unlikely ever to be equalled. O'Brien stands alone, at the top.

He was born in 1917, and first put his foot over the threshold of public attention at the age of 27 when landing an audacious double in the Irish Cambridgeshire and Cesarewitch. This first notice of intent came on the Flat, but his first empire was over the jumps. O'Brien's first standard-bearers were the triple Cheltenham Gold Cup winner Cottage Rake (1948-50) and triple Champion Hurdle winner Hatton's Grace (1949-51), both of whom also won valuable handicaps on the Flat for their master trainer.

Then came the Grand National, with an unparalleled, unearthly three wins in three years with three horses: Early Mist, Royal Tan and Quare Times (1953-55). O'Brien, by now training at Ballydoyle in County Tipperary, harvested the Cheltenham Festival for 23 victories in all, including another Gold Cup with Knock Hard (1953). In the same year he won the Irish Derby with Chamier, a hint of what was to come. Having conquered the jumping world, O'Brien would now do the same on the Flat.

The Flat is where the money and the prestige lies, and to succeed there O'Brien had to change his outlook. He needed new owners, wealthier owners, and he found them in the US. His first major ally was John McShain, for whom he trained Ballymoss to win the Irish Derby, the King George and the Arc, and Gladness to win the Gold Cup at Royal Ascot and the valuable Ebor Handicap. O'Brien had taken the first few giant strides on his path to the top again.

Yet it might have been all over before it had hardly started. O'Brien's training licence was suspended for 12 months from May 1960 after his three-year-old colt Chamour returned a positive drug test. There was no evidence that O'Brien was responsible, but the rules at the time laid any blame solely on the trainer. To cut the story short, the case was eventually found to be of a spurious nature and O'Brien was wholly exonerated by the stewards. A year of his life had been wasted. He soon made up for it.

There is a danger of the rest of this account becoming no more than a list of horses and the races they won, in an attempt to indicate the extent of O'Brien's brilliant career. His domination of the big Flat races between 1962 and the late 1980s was almost total, and this from a number of horses in training that would be considered tiny by the standards of modern big yards. When, in 1975, he sent eight horses to Royal Ascot week and came away with seven winners, all aged three or over, he had only 13 older horses in training.

Perhaps his greatest horse was the 1970 Triple Crown winner Nijinsky, of whom O'Brien said, 'I would rate him first or second. For brilliance, Nijinsky. For toughness, Sir Ivor.' Sir Ivor won the 2,000 Guineas, Derby, Champion Stakes and Washington International in 1968.

There were also Derby winners Roberto and The Minstrel, the dual Arc winner Alleged, the unbeaten and ill-fated Derby winner Golden Fleece, Irish 2,000 Guineas and Eclipse winner Sadler's Wells, 2,000 Guineas and Irish Derby winner El Gran Senor, and Breeders' Cup Mile winner Royal Academy, to pick just a few glorious names from so many.

His alliance with football pools heir Robert Sangster helped forge the shape of modern bloodstock through their forays to the US sales to purchase the pick of American bloodlines, at sky-high prices. Sangster's partnership with John Magnier, O'Brien's son-in-law, helped to establish the foundations of Coolmore Stud, which is now arguably the greatest stallion station in the world.

His sons Charles and David grew up into trainers, with the latter saddling Secreto to beat his father's El Gran Senor in a breathless finish to the 1984 Derby. The short-head defeat cut £40 million from El Gran Senor's stud value; in a TV interview, the smiling father said, 'The money simply doesn't matter. I'm absolutely thrilled for my son.'

O'Brien's final victory at Royal Ascot came in 1993 with College Chapel, ridden by his old comrade-in-arms Lester Piggott, and the crowd around the winner's enclosure broke into spontaneous applause in recognition of the valedictory nature of this success. He retired in October 1994, his legacy immaculate, immeasurable. In 2003, he was voted the greatest figure in the history of horse racing by readers of the *Racing Post*.

Vincent O'Brien, a shy, modest, courteous gentleman, died in June 2009, at the age of 92. If the *Racing Post* held another vote, there is little doubt that O'Brien would top the poll again. Form is temporary and class is permanent, after all, but greatness is forever.

48

Phil Bull's trademark accessory. *Image © Getty*

THE TEST OF TIME

The concept of a perfect system, with which to predict the results of races and thereby win a fortune, is a universal longing. There is no such thing as a perfect system outside the realm of fiction, but one that comes as close as any and has stood the test of, well, time is the Timeform ratings system, which harnesses the evidence of the stopwatch to help assess a horse's merit.

Timeform was the invention of former schoolmaster Phil Bull, one of the great intellects in racing history, and the first edition of the seminal 'Racehorses of . . .' annual series was published in 1948, covering the previous year's horses and allotting each a rating. These ratings were, and are, produced in a thoroughly dispassionate, analytical fashion based on a statistical examination of race times, and they are respected throughout the racing world.

Bull was a multifaceted individual, a devout atheist, a fervent socialist, a white-bearded polymath with a penchant for fat cigars and champagne, an owner, a breeder, a reformer, a critic of the racing establishment and a master punter, who won millions from the bookmakers over the years. His oft-quoted opinion of racing as 'a great triviality' masked his passion for unearthing matters of great financial and statistical importance from among all that trivia.

The essence of Timeform pivots upon two factors – the time it takes a horse to run a given distance, and a rating based on that information. Bull was a time guru, and there was nothing simplistic about his reasoning. 'The time a horse takes to run a certain distance depends on many things: the conformation of the track, the state of the going, wind strength and direction, and the pace at which the race is run. Unless all these things are taken into account, the bare time itself is meaningless,' he said.

His colleague Dick Whitford, whose crucial role in the success of Timeform has been somewhat airbrushed from the pages of history, was responsible for compiling a rating for each horse that expressed its ability in pounds, a universal scale of merit, a handicap that also enables horses of different generations to be compared.

Timeform has ascribed to the 1986 champion Dancing Brave a rating of 140, the same as Sea The Stars (2009) and Vaguely Noble (1968), reckoning these three great horses of equal ability. All three are thus considered 7lb inferior to Frankel, whose rating of 147 is the highest ever issued. Over jumps, Timeform's enduring champion is Arkle, with a rating of 212. There is no direct correlation between the Flat and jump ratings; Arkle is not considered to be 65lb better than Frankel.

Other significant ratings systems are readily available; each horse in Britain has three separate ratings. There is the official rating, allotted by the BHA, which is used to determine a horse's mark for competition. There is also the Racing Post Rating (RPR), compiled by the trade daily's handicappers. The three ratings are comparable but by no means identical. The 2016 Derby winner Harzand had an official rating of 121; his RPR was 124; and his Timeform mark was 126. Different systems produce different results, and one figure is no more 'correct' than another.

Timeform is now owned by Flutter, a betting conglomerate, something unlikely to have amused the fiercely independent Bull. The scholarly, lavishly produced Timeform annuals, forthright of opinion and often keenly perceptive, are no longer printed, a victim of the move towards digital publishing, but the ratings live on.

The modern ubiquity of racehorse ratings, whether official, proprietorial, or simply cobbled together by private enthusiasts in their spare time, is derived directly from the influence of Timeform, which has become synonymous as a standard for racehorse performance, a status driven as much by Bull's forceful personality and the reverence in which he is still held as by the usefulness of the product.

Bull's role as founder of Timeform is only a part, albeit a substantial part, of his legacy to racing. But at heart he was a punter, and he would have relished the fact that his ratings system, and the imitators it has spawned, has given so many of his fellows an advantage in the eternal battle with the bookmakers. Nothing is perfect, but a winner comes close.

49

Talking the talk. Image © Getty

HE IS MOVING LIKE A TREMENDOUS MACHINE!

A picture is worth a thousand words. Well, possibly. But sometimes half a dozen words can conjure up the most beautiful picture.

In the beginning, there was no commentary, just the far-off sound of hoofbeats. Then there was the clipped, emotionless precision of the Pathé newsreels. In July 1952, the first racecourse commentary in Britain was heard at Goodwood, echoing over the South Downs. Increased television coverage brought commentary into the home, and we have listened enraptured ever since.

Commentary is prose, a functional tool that informs us about a race, but sometimes form overrides function and prose becomes poetry. The best commentators rise to great occasions, complement them with words that are absorbed into racing's consciousness. Sir Peter O'Sullevan liked the maxim 'the commentator is always half a second away from disaster'; a tightrope-walker who while he crosses the abyss occasionally dances.

There are people who can recite O'Sullevan's 1964 Cheltenham Gold Cup call in its entirety, 'this is the champion, this is the best we've seen' etc, as though it were a Shakespearean soliloquy, which it could be. O'Sullevan was the elegant, eloquent voice of the racing nation. For those of a certain age, the mare is always beginning to get up, Bustino is always fighting his way back. Peter Bromley, commentating on radio, had more to tell, his delivery a masterpiece of sound and fury, signifying everything.

Sometimes surprise suffuses the commentary, as though seeing is not believing. Sometimes the voice growls, sometimes it cracks, letting emotion seep from within. Sometimes the phraseology sounds prepared, which is unsatisfactory, making it more about the singer than the song.

A great commentary is indivisible from the race itself, part of the remembered experience. Its recall can move the listener to tears or elation by reaching deep inside and provoking an old memory, as though unexpectedly gentle fingers were plucking at the heartstrings, or lifting the hairs on the back of the neck. What follows in no particular order is a personal choice of favourites. Each will have his or her own, the soundtrack of our racing lives.

Michael O'Hehir *1967 Grand National*
They're turning now to the fence after Becher's . . . Rutherfords has been hampered, and so has Castle Falls. Rondetto has fallen. Princeful has fallen. Norther has fallen. Kirtle-Lad has fallen. The Fossa has fallen. There's a right pile-up . . . Leedsy has climbed over the fence and left his jockey there . . . and now, with all this mayhem, Foinavon has gone off on his own! He's about 100 yards in front of everything else.

Sir Peter O'Sullevan *1977 Grand National*
He's getting the most tremendous cheer from the crowd, they're willing him home now, the 12-year-old Red Rum, being preceded only by loose horses, being chased by Churchtown Boy, Eyecatcher has moved into third, The Pilgarlic fourth. They're coming to the Elbow. There's a furlong now between Red Rum and his third Grand National triumph. And he's coming up to the line, to win it like a fresh horse in great style. It's hats off and a tremendous reception – you've never heard one like it at Liverpool. Red Rum wins the National!

Chic Anderson *1973 Belmont Stakes*
Secretariat is blazing along. The first three-quarters of a mile in 1:09 and four-fifths. Secretariat is widening now! He is moving like a tremendous machine! Secretariat by 12, Secretariat by 14 lengths on the turn . . . Secretariat is all alone, Secretariat is in a position that seems impossible to catch. He's into the stretch . . . Secretariat has opened a 22-length lead. He is going to be the Triple Crown winner. Here comes Secretariat to the wire. An unbelievable, an amazing performance!

Peter Bromley *1981 Derby*
Shergar's gone two lengths clear of Silver Season, and he's opening up a lead now . . . Shergar's going for the gun, he's gone four, five, six, seven, eight lengths clear . . . Two furlongs out, the Derby is a procession, Shergar is ten lengths clear . . . There's only one horse in it, you need a telescope to see the rest, they have a furlong to go and Shergar is galloping them into the ground. Wally Swinburn looks round, he's on his own, Shergar, clear of his field, Shergar wins the Derby!

Graham Goode *1984 Whitbread Gold Cup*
It's Plundering, Lettoch, Diamond Edge rallying, Special Cargo coming with a run, and Diamond Edge is coming through, Special Cargo's finishing well . . . a three-way photo in the Whitbread!

Bill Collins *1982 Cox Plate*
Kingston Town can't win . . . My Axeman took the lead from Fearless Pride, Grosvenor coming down the outside is after them, My Axeman in front, Grosvenor and Kingston Town's flashing, he might win yet the champ, Grosvenor's got the lead, oh Kingston Town's swamping them, what a run, Kingston Town wins it.

Simon Holt *2016 Queen Mother Champion Chase*
Here's the last, he's over safely, the hill left to climb . . . This is the old Sprinter, coming up the Cheltenham hill, Sprinter Sacre by six or seven lengths, one of the great racing comebacks, the impossible dream coming true, and he regains his title!

Jim McGrath *2009 Prix de l'Arc de Triomphe*
He's getting up on the inside on Sea The Stars, he's got six or seven lengths to make up, he'll have to be a champion . . . Stacelita races into the lead, two in front . . . He is a champion I reckon, he's out after the leader, he picks up Stacelita, he powers clear . . . Sea The Stars racing

away, perfection in equine form, a horse of a lifetime, he wins the Arc by two lengths.

Tom Durkin *1987 Breeders' Cup Classic*
Judge Angelucci, Candi's Gold toward the rail, Ferdinand and Alysheba coming on the outside . . . They're less than a furlong out, Judge Angelucci desperate, Ferdinand right there, Alysheba on the outside . . . Ferdinand, Judge Angelucci, on the outside Alysheba, Ferdinand has the lead, Alysheba a final surge, the two Derby winners hit the wire together!

50

International travel is go! *Image © Getty*

ON THE MAP

What do France, Venezuela, Australia, Britain and the US have in common? Five countries, four continents, one race. Before 1952, racing was a relatively parochial sport. After 1952, it embraced a cosmopolitan outlook. The hinge that swung wide the door to global competition was the Washington DC International, a race that changed racing itself.

The inaugural running of the Washington DC International, at Laurel Park, Maryland, in October 1952, drew a field of just seven, but among them the pioneering spirit was strong. International by name, international by nature. Two horses came from Britain, one from Germany, one from Canada, three from the US, something that had never happened before. Yes, the Derby winner Papyrus had taken on Kentucky Derby winner Zev almost 30 years earlier, and the French horse Epinard had run four times in the US the following year, but neither horse had been successful and the trickle of foreign participation had dried up to nothing.

The Laurel Park contest was the visionary idea of the track's manager John D. Schapiro, who wanted to put his racecourse on the map, a map he unfolded wide. Transporting horses by aeroplane had become much more straightforward – Papyrus and Epinard travelled by boat – and Schapiro sweetened his $50,000 prize-money pot with concessions for European runners: the race would be run on turf over a mile and a half, it would be a walk-up start (starting stalls had yet to reach Europe) and the costs of transport would be met. What Schapiro needed more than anything else was an overseas winner, to promote the venture, and his prayers were answered.

Wilwyn, trained in Newmarket by John Waugh and ridden by Manny Mercer, did win; the local hope Ruhe was second, Wilwyn's compatriot Zucchero finished third and the German-trained Niederlander fourth. Flight time for the European contingent was 28 hours, with two refuelling stops, but it took them only two and a half minutes of racing to change perception forever. One racing reporter wrote that 'Schapiro had done more to promote good relations between the US and the rest of the world than all the politicians in Washington'.

Twelve months later, the French-trained Worden was successful. In 1955, El Chama took the prize back to Venezuela, and Sailor's Guide won for Australia in 1958. In between, the home team kept the spoils, a marvellously varied roll of honour that cemented the race in the international calendar, and inspired many imitations around the world.

Top-class horses such as Kelso, Sir Ivor, Run The Gantlet, Dahlia and All Along won the Washington DC International before its allure began to dwindle in the late 1980s, owing to the numerous and more valuable alternatives available to the jetsetting fraternity. By then Tolomeo and Teleprompter had won the Arlington Million for Britain, Bold Arrangement had finished runner-up in the Kentucky Derby for his bold trainer Clive Brittain, and Lashkari, Pebbles, Last Tycoon and the wonderful Miesque had hit the jackpot for Europe at the new Breeders' Cup, which did more than most to supplant Schapiro's race among the sport's priorities.

The Japan Cup, first run in 1981 and boasting a colossal prize fund, also drew competition away from the International and mirrored its impact with winners from seven countries in its first ten runnings, including Jupiter Island (also trained by Brittain) and the tough mare Stanerra, from Ireland. As the 1980s gave way to the 1990s, Hong Kong joined the club with the first editions of what have become four enormously valuable international races, with the inaugural running of the Bowl (now titled the Mile) in 1991 won by Additional Risk, trained in Ireland by Dermot Weld.

Weld was as much of a pioneer as Brittain. The previous year he had become the first European trainer to win a leg of the US Triple Crown with Belmont raider Go And Go, and two years later he would conquer the final horizon of international travel by saddling Vintage Crop to win the Melbourne Cup. In between, Leo O'Brien became the first US trainer to win a European Classic when sending over Fourstars Allstar to land the Irish 2,000 Guineas.

Horses can now travel around the world as easily as humans, and the sight of an Australian runner at Royal Ascot, an Irish horse at Sha Tin and a US runner at Meydan is commonplace. They don't go to Laurel Park any more, though.

The Washington DC International has had its name, its distance, its prestige and its importance stripped away, and what remains is a race you wouldn't cross the road for, never mind the Atlantic. But once upon a time it changed the world.

51

Arise, Sir Gordon.   Image © Alamy

WELL DONE, GORDON

The first week of June 1953 was quite a week for Gordon Richards. At its beginning, he was awarded a knighthood by the Queen for services to sport, as part of the lavish Coronation celebrations. At its end, he won the Derby for the first and only time, after decades of foiled, failed attempts. An unprecedented career had the climax it so richly deserved.

Sir Gordon Richards may well be the greatest jockey in British history, and while comparisons are always problematic his key statistical achievements are unsurpassed, and probably unsurpassable. No jockey has ridden more winners in Britain than his 4,870, or won more championships than his 26, or ridden more consecutive winners than his 12 over three days. In a golden era for jockeys, Richards far outshone them all.

He was born in May 1904, the son of a Shropshire miner, and had his first ride in October 1920, his first winner the following March. Small of stature even by the standards of jockeys, a fraction under 5ft, his capacity for hard graft and perseverance steadily paid dividends and he became champion for the first time in 1925. Richards would be champion every year until he retired, with only three exceptions – 1926, when he was stricken with tuberculosis and missed almost the entire season;

1930, when Freddie Fox pipped him by one on the final day of the season; and 1941, when a broken leg kept him on the sidelines during a truncated wartime campaign.

Such prolonged and near-absolute dominance might in other men have contributed to resentment among his fellow jockeys and ennui among the public, but Richards was universally popular. His integrity was unquestioned, his loyalty applauded, his modesty admired. He was the undisputed figurehead of racing between the wars and brought only credit upon his sport.

His sunny nature undoubtedly owed much to his natural physical advantages, for his size meant he never had to resort to starvation to make his riding weight, a purgatory that constantly beset his two rivals for the mantle of 'greatest jockey', Fred Archer and Lester Piggott, as it did jump racing's perennial champion AP McCoy. Their drawn, desiccated faces are a stark contrast to Richards's cheerful, almost chubby visage.

The comparison with McCoy is pertinent, for both jockeys were great accumulators of winners rather than renowned for big-race glory. Richards won 14 Classics, including the fillies' Triple Crown in 1942 on Sun Chariot and the 1947 2,000 Guineas on Tudor Minstrel, the best horse he ever rode, but his lasting fame rests primarily on his prodigious rate of success during a 16-year association with master trainer Fred Darling.

In 1933, he broke Archer's longstanding seasonal record with a haul of 259 winners, and in October of that year he won those dozen races in a row, starting with the last race at Nottingham, then going through the six-race card at Chepstow the following day, and the day after that winning the first five races at Chepstow before defeat on an odds-on shot brought the streak to an end. A song was hurriedly composed in his honour, entitled 'Well Done Gordon'.

'Who's the little fellow who is causing all the fuss?
Gordon Richards, Gordon Richards!
Who's the little champion who has been so good to us?
Gordon Richards, Gordon Richards!
Well done, Gordon, how you can ride,
Well done, Gordon, how you have tried [and so on]'

The little champion was indeed good to his supporters. Richards maintained a prolific strike-rate, was utterly reliable, uncommonly consistent, invariably swiftly away at the starting gate and strong in a finish despite an unconventional upright riding style. He broke his own record in 1947 when riding 269 winners, but endured particular disappointment that season when the brilliant miler Tudor Minstrel finished a non-staying fourth in the Derby at odds-on.

Richards must have believed that he would never win the Derby, the only omission in an otherwise unimpeachable career. He had been beaten in 27 Derbys when at last, on a sunny Saturday afternoon in keeping with the prevailing jubilant national mood, he drove the tall, white-faced Pinza clear of his rivals to win by four lengths, prompting widespread delight, even on the part of the Queen, who owned the runner-up Aureole. His glittering career was gloriously complete.

Richards had already planned to retire at the end of the following year, but his career came to a slightly premature conclusion in July 1954 when a horse reared and fell on him in the parade ring at Sandown, breaking his pelvis. He became a trainer, with a degree of success, and then a racing manager to prominent owners Sir Michael Sobell and Lady Beaverbrook, again with success.

Sir Gordon Richards, the only Flat jockey to be honoured with a knighthood, died in November 1986, aged 82. In that week, that joyous week in June 1953, news had also broken that Hillary and Tenzing had reached the summit of Mount Everest. By then, of course, Richards had been on top of the world for a long, long time. And he still is.

Racing has a word for it. Image © Author

THE JOLLY MADE A NOISE

'Hello, is that the owner of Blue Note? Just wanted to have a chat about tomorrow's race. Look, he blew up last time and lost a plate, but he normally jumps from fence to fence and he's been catching pigeons at home. We'll use a chalk jockey to take off seven, drop him in and ride him chilly, give him the office six out and let him make the best of his way home. He's double carpet on the morning line but the jolly made a noise last time and the faces are on, so I reckon he's nailed on for the frame. He had a blow the other morning and I just hope he doesn't get a leg between now and post-time. Understand me? Good. See you by the jamstick. Ciao!'

Jargon and slang are explicit in every walk of life, but nowhere outside racing does it seem so deliberately contrived to confuse. 'The most commonly identified purpose of jargon is to exclude outsiders from that which does not concern them,' wrote Rebecca Cassidy, Professor of Anthropology at Goldsmiths University, in her book *The Sport of Kings*.

In other words, similar to the traditional nightclub greeting: if you don't understand us, you're not coming in. Racing can ill afford such a snooty attitude. But anyway, what was that trainer on about? Where's that nonsense-sense translation guide?

'Hello, is that the owner of Blue Note? Just wanted to have a chat about tomorrow's race. Look, he got tired last time and lost a shoe, but he is usually an excellent jumper and has been working well on the gallops. We'll use an inexperienced rider for his weight allowance, ride him with restraint, ask him for an effort six fences out and see how he gets on. He's 33-1 in the early betting but the favourite may have breathing issues and those in the know have backed him, so I reckon he has an excellent chance of being in the first three. He had a workout the other morning and I just hope he doesn't pick up an injury before the race. Understand me? Well, I'm sure you do this time. See you by the winning post. Bye!'

Thankfully, only the deliberately perverse still use the old vernacular of the betting ring, a language invented specifically to bewilder outsiders with its 'jolly' and 'tips on' and 'Bismarck' and 'top of the head'. But the language used by pundits, journalists and those otherwise on the inside looking out is often equally impenetrable.

Trainers can be 'on the cold list', when they're really just out of form. Horses can run in a 'nursery', which is a handicap restricted to two-year-olds. Jockeys 'call a cab', but they're just trying to keep their balance. The best horses might get 'black-type', which is bold print used for emphasis of achievement in sales catalogues.

A tipster may 'go nap' on this horse or that; it's his best bet of the day. It might be in a 'bumper', a flat race for young and inexperienced jump horses. Let's hope it isn't 'in the van until coming off the bridle below the distance', or in the front rank until beginning to struggle a furlong and a half from the line, otherwise the 'stipes' (the assistants to the stewards) might take an interest.

Of course there is a place for jargon. Some of it is amusing, some of it can be valuable shorthand, and some of it is acceptable to cover for broad unknowns, such as 'the virus' for an unspecified respiratory illness, or 'getting his wind done' to explain a minor operation to help a horse breathe efficiently. A little bit of mystique is essential, even alluring. But too often racing jargon is used gratuitously, lazily, with intent to confuse and exclude, to emphasise the privileged position of those on the inside.

Racing is supported by an ageing constituency, and the necessity to infuse it with new blood, young racegoers who will ensure both its financial health and social relevance in years to come, is urgent. It's a reactionary sport at the best of times, doggedly resistant to change, but unless it widens its circle of insiders it is doomed, and making things easier to understand is a crucial part of that.

To do so is not to betray racing's rich heritage, or compromise its vitality, but simply to increase its accessibility. Racing shouldn't be viewed as a secret society, but an open, welcoming, inclusive one, where an outsider is not a person but just a 33-1 shot (and not double carpet).

53

Devon Loch loses the National.

THAT'S RACING

He was the horse who couldn't lose, but did. The tale of Devon Loch has been greedily absorbed by the world beyond racing, his name shorthand for a last-minute collapse, his legacy kept alive by some crackling black-and-white newsreel footage that to this day defies explanation. Devon Loch threw himself to the floor, lost the Grand National, won eternal fame.

The 1956 National was over as a contest. The well-fancied Devon Loch, owned by the Queen Mother, ridden by Dick Francis, had jumped the final fence ten lengths clear. The long run-in was perfect for a royal procession. At the microphone, Bob Danvers-Walker sets the scene. 'Into the final straight with victory in sight for Devon Loch. He's clear away from E.S.B. and Gentle Moya, only 40 yards to go, Devon Loch can't lose . . . but he's slipped, he's down . . .'

Speech failed Danvers-Walker, as it did for everyone. Devon Loch hadn't slipped, he had launched himself into the air as though attempting a jump. He sprawled on the turf, flat on his belly, legs out in front of him, Francis jolted up around his ears. The horse was immediately up on his feet, but then E.S.B. and jockey Dave Dick came galloping past to record one of the luckiest victories in sport. So much for what was seen, confirmed by the camera. What was unseen? Why had it happened?

There are as many theories about the Devon Loch incident as there are about what happened to President Kennedy in Dealey Plaza. Did the horse catch sight of the adjacent water jump in his peripheral vision and try to jump it? Was it an internal physical problem, such as heart fibrillation? Was it simply the effects of exertion, running beyond his means, for he would have broken the course record if he had completed the race normally?

Later, Francis considered it might have been due to shock at the deafening noise washing down from the grandstands. Devon Loch, who was after all running into a narrowing 'tunnel' of cheering, screaming spectators, pricked his ears and lifted his head just before he went down, looking like a horse startled by his surroundings.

Francis walked Devon Loch towards the line, but the ten-year-old was very unsteady on his feet and Francis dismounted. The heartbroken jockey was consoled by the Queen Mother with the words 'That's racing, I suppose'. Francis's theory of sudden shock at the great noise of the crowd is plausible, but George Milburn, the jockey on runner-up Gentle Moya, lent weight to the 'fatigue' theory, citing an incident at Sandown the following season when Devon Loch collapsed after another long-distance chase.

'I think it was muscular cramp, a problem that overtook him when he was getting very tired,' Milburn told Chris Pitt, author of the treasury of Grand National tales *Go Down To The Beaten*. Devon Loch never ran again; by the time of the Sandown race, Francis had also retired.

He became a columnist with the *Sunday Express*, then a writer of bestselling thrillers set mostly within racing, such as *Whip Hand*, *Nerve* and *Forfeit*, with the considerable assistance of his wife Mary. Francis's great misfortune at Aintree was, ironically, the lucky break that led to his second career, as it prompted a request for his autobiography, which would probably not have happened had he been 'just' a National-winning jockey. However, none of his novels involved anything as inexplicable as what befell Devon Loch, art unable to imitate the improbability of life.

Another case of a horse losing a race it looked certain to win occurred in the King George V Handicap at Royal Ascot in June 1988, when the clear leader Ile De Chypre suddenly veered sharply left in the last 100 yards, unseating jockey Greville Starkey.

At first the incident was passed off as just another 'that's racing' moment, but a year later it gained great notoriety when one of the defendants in a drug-smuggling trial said that he had caused Ile De Chypre to swerve by using a 'stun-gun' – disguised as a pair of binoculars – to fire a burst of high-frequency sound at the horse, thoroughly disorienting him. It is a brilliant story, would have been ideal for one of Francis's plotlines, but it is nevertheless just a story fabricated by a man in the dock hoping to divert attention from the more pressing details of his trial.

Ile De Chypre was a nervous, quirky horse, not an easy ride, and according to Tony Culhane, the fortunate winning jockey, had been giving Starkey a hard time throughout the race, trying to duck out and generally misbehaving. The simple explanations are nearly always the best, especially where horses are involved. The incident remains a memorable mystery, but only in respect of whatever foolishness Ile De Chypre had on his mind as he swerved so dramatically off course.

54

The sponsor's product.

SHIBBOLETH

There are three little words guaranteed to make any racing fan of a certain age come over a bit strange. The heart will beat faster, the knees may go weak, the stomach may turn over, the eyes will mist over into one of those thousand-yard stares. Three little words are all it takes to restore that youthful brio, that joie de vivre, that zing. Three little words: Whitbread, Mackeson, Hennessy.

Not that our racing fan is a dipsomaniac; well, not necessarily. It's simply that those three words carry a cargo of memories of the way we were, a great freight of nostalgia. Just a sponsor's name, but so much more than that.

The Whitbread Gold Cup was the first of them, the first external commercial sponsorship in racing when it was first run at Sandown in April 1957, bearing the name of brewer Bill Whitbread's family business. There had recently been races with a bookmaker's name attached, notably the Tote, but this new valuable handicap chase was the outrider for a cavalry charge of sponsors that would change the face and the financial footing of jump racing.

In its time the Whitbread was won by many of the all-time greats of jumping, Pas Seul, Arkle, Mill House, The Dikler, Desert Orchid, an end-of-season extravaganza that heralded the true annual transition from the winter game to the Flat season. It was a special race, as was the Hennessy Cognac Gold Cup at Cheltenham (soon moved to Newbury), inaugurated later that year and won by Mandarin, owned by Peggy Hennessy, whose connection to the sponsor is obvious.

Our Hennessy heroes include Arkle and Mill House again, because you can never hear too much of them, as well as Spanish Steps, Burrough Hill Lad, One Man and the mighty giant Denman. It slotted into the schedule a fortnight after the Mackeson Gold Cup at Cheltenham, created for another of Bill Whitbread's alcoholic products in 1960 and won by superstars such as Dunkirk, Half Free, Very Promising, Bradbury Star and Dublin Flyer.

These three new races helped forge a recognised pathway through the jump season, from the Mackeson and Hennessy in November, via the King George VI Chase in December, through to Cheltenham, Aintree and then the Whitbread to sign off. Mackeson was a milk stout whose popularity was fleeting, but the race that bore its name was beloved, the first big race of the jump season.

The benefits to racing were enormous. Not only did these sponsors put money into the sport, but their races provided increased opportunity for the best horses, good advertising for racing in general, and a blessed continuity for those following the action.

The first instances of race sponsorship date to the mid-1800s, when Tattersall's (see earlier chapter) backed a race at Newmarket. A little later, the owners of the Middle Park Stud and the Dewhurst Stud financed the establishment of the two-year-old races at Newmarket that still bear their name.

Long-standing sponsors include John Smith's, which name has adorned a mile-and-a-quarter handicap at York every July since 1960, making it the longest unbroken commercial deal in racing. There is no race sponsorship at Royal Ascot, but the Derby and Grand National have been sponsored since 1984. Almost everything that moves is sponsored: jockeys, trainers, horseboxes, whole race meetings.

Nothing, though, can be expected to stay the same forever. The old races still exist, but they haven't been the Whitbread since 2001, the Hennessy since 2016 or the Mackeson since 1995. All three are now sponsored by bookmakers, and while racing and its fans are grateful for the continuing investment it is disappointing that the races have lost their identities, their connection to a glorious past, our glorious past.

It must be recognised that sponsors will come and go – the Derby and the Grand National have had several sponsors apiece – especially as certain genres of advertising are no longer permitted. What is more insidious is the practice of certain sponsors to remove the familiar name of a race and replace it with their own, often for only a short-term investment anyway, thereby picking destructively away at the heritage of racing. The Bula Hurdle, named after the great and well-loved dual Champion Hurdle winner of the 1970s, is now known as the International Hurdle, a meaningless appellation.

Progress is usually accepted with a sigh and a fond backward glance, but old habits are hard to break. When the time of year comes round, there are very many within the sport who find it impossible to not speak of the race as the Mackeson, the Hennessy, the Whitbread, to the certain displeasure of the current sponsors. Recognition of the 'new' name is eventually accomplished, but like a right-handed batsman being forced to bat left-handed, the job is not done with panache.

Such usage is a shibboleth, a password to a society populated by those who have been around, paid their dues, who have a long-term emotional investment in racing. We should know better, should move on, should not stand in the way of progress. Yet the old names still call to us, resonating in the rolling landscape of the mind, like those blue remembered hills where we cannot go again.

55

Face that launched a thousand bets. Image © Getty

YOU NEVER FORGET

Where to start? The 5,000 winners, the 30 British Classics, the nine Derbys, the 11 titles? The stories, the ice-cream, the five-pound ear, Wilson Pickett? The impact, the mythology, the hero-worship, the legend? Lester Piggott defies easy categorisation, defies the laws of perspective, for the further he recedes into history, the greater his mystique appears.

Dates and times. Piggott was born in November 1935, grandson of a Grand National-winning jockey, the heir of a decorated racing dynasty. He won his first race in August 1948, aboard The Chase at Haydock, grew up as a boy wonder – even riding with success over hurdles – and as the boy became a man the wonder never went away. He won his first championship in 1960 and his last in 1982.

His nine Derbys are a record, the first coming in 1954 on the outsider Never Say Die, the last in 1983 on Teenoso. His 30 British Classics are also a record, from Never Say Die through to Rodrigo De Triano in the 2,000 Guineas in 1992. Piggott's career is easy to define in records, and if his winners worldwide are taken into account his tally exceeds that of Sir Gordon Richards.

The names of the great horses he rode are legion, would take up all the space available. Triple Crown winner Nijinsky, Derby winners Crepello, Sir Ivor, Roberto and The Minstrel, Arc winners Rheingold and Alleged, outstanding stayers Sagaro, Le Moss and Ardross, brilliant fillies Petite Etoile, Park Top and Dahlia, crack sprinters Right Boy and Moorestyle, to keep it brief.

Tall enough for a jockey at 5ft 7in, he spent practically his entire career subjecting himself to a fearsome regime of dieting and wasting, competing with his natural physical needs as effectively as he competed with his rivals on the racetrack, reputedly subsisting on cigars and ice-cream, although he wasn't quite that ascetic. He grew up with a minor speech impediment and deafness in one ear, which goes a long way towards explaining his famously uncommunicative manner, his monosyllabic approach to conversation. He was not simply being bloody-minded, although he made a point of it when it suited.

These physical issues forged his character and the flaws within it, the austerity of his lifestyle reinforced them, and his genius allowed him to exploit them. Sir Peter O'Sullevan said that Piggott's attitude resembled 'the gunfighter's delusion of being above the law', but it is also fair to say that Piggott's darker side – his ruthlessness, his miserliness, his indifference – served not to alienate him but to command respect, to foster the awe, devotion and fascination in which he was held by the racing public, who delightedly viewed these defects as tough-guy glamour, a contributory aspect of his overall allure. He was controversial, a bad boy, the antithesis of his saintly predecessor Richards, and in his great and prolonged heyday he was as big as the sport itself.

He was the first racing hero of the television age and arrived in it fully formed as an icon, making an indelible impression on this new armchair audience. Through brute strength and delicate finesse he won races other jockeys would have lost, won people money other jockeys would have lost. Put your last fiver on Lester, and he would get the job done for you. The faith he inspired in the everyday punter was extraordinary.

It was said that a jockey couldn't be confident of riding a big-race favourite until he walked into the parade ring wearing the colours, because of Piggott's persistence and skill in persuading owners and trainers to employ him instead. His big-race temperament was as ice-cold as any gunslinger, his associations with great trainers Noel

Murless, Vincent O'Brien and Henry Cecil gave him access to the best horses. A mythology grew effortlessly around him, and he revelled in it.

Everyone has a Lester story, most of them growing from the same seed of a preoccupation with money and a dry, laconic wit, some of the stories even true. One day a down-on-his-luck valet approached Piggott and muttered in his ear, 'Lester, can you lend me five pounds?' Lester shrugged. 'I can't hear you, that's my deaf ear.' The valet moved to the other ear. 'Lester, can you lend me ten pounds?' Lester shook his head. 'Try the five-pound ear again.'

After victory in the 1969 Washington DC International on Karabas, reporters who had criticised his winning ride on Sir Ivor the year before now asked him when he thought he had the race won. 'About three weeks ago,' he replied, dismissively.

He retired in 1985, trained with success for a year, and was then sensationally convicted of tax evasion, which resulted in imprisonment for 12 months, something he described in true Piggott style as 'a waste of time'. His downfall was ultimately self-inflicted; he paid his dues to the Inland Revenue with a cheque drawn on an account he had left undeclared. He was stripped of his OBE but not of his status in the eyes of his followers, his reputation trapped in an amber that gleamed unendingly in the sunshine of his former glories.

In 1990, at the age of 54, he returned to the saddle. Less than a fortnight later, in a comeback almost out-Lazarusing Lazarus, one so dramatic and improbable no Hollywood scriptwriter would have given it a second glance, he won the Breeders' Cup Mile on Royal Academy, a son of Nijinsky trained by his old ally O'Brien, past and present knitted adroitly together. 'You never forget,' he said, in that ever-imitable voice, a broad smile on his face, the world at his feet again.

In 1995 he retired again, this time for keeps. The annual awards for jockeys are called the Lesters, in his honour, and he is occasionally called for interview, to give the old answers to the old questions, reliving his past and ours once more. Where to end? It doesn't end. The myths and the legend of Lester Piggott will last forever.

56

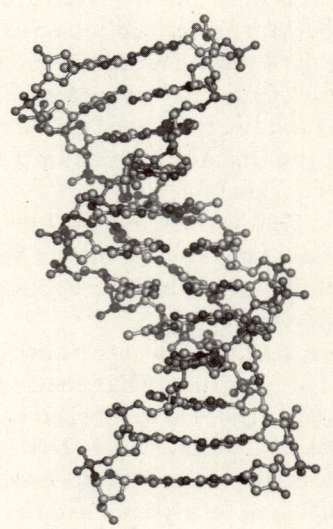

The DNA of racing.

SOMETHING ALWAYS PRESENT

It is fair to say that Canada is not one of the world's leading racing nations, but it is just as fair to say that without one of Canada's native sons the racing world would look entirely different. The country is famous for ice hockey, maple syrup and cases of crisp, cold Molson Dry, but its greatest global export by far is the influence of stallion supreme Northern Dancer.

Look at any pedigree, anywhere, and it's long odds-on that Northern Dancer's name will be there, his DNA resplendent in its ubiquity. Every one of the 18 Classic winners in Britain, Ireland, France and the US in 2020 traced back in some fashion to Northern Dancer. His influence is so pervasive among modern thoroughbreds that it might perversely be said not to be an influence at all, just something always present, like sunlight, water and hope.

The little white-faced, white-footed superhorse – he was pony-sized – was foaled in 1961, bred in Ontario by Eddie (EP) Taylor, owner of Windfields Farm. On the racetrack Northern Dancer won 14 of his 18 races and was placed in the other four, his victories including the 1964 Kentucky Derby, the Preakness Stakes and the Queen's Plate back home at Woodbine. He was thwarted in his bid for the Triple Crown when outstayed in the Belmont Stakes, taking third place.

There is fame enough there, but when Northern Dancer was sent to stud his racing career quickly became little more than an interesting footnote to his story. Such was his diminutive stature that a ramp was constructed in the breeding shed to allow him to cover mares, but they do say size doesn't matter.

His first small crop of foals included Canadian Horse of the Year Viceregal. His second crop provided the foundation for his legend and his legacy to flourish. His son Nijinsky – cleverly named, for the great Russian ballet dancer who was convinced he would be reincarnated as a racehorse – won the Triple Crown in Britain, becoming one of the all-time greats, and that colt's trainer Vincent O'Brien soon championed the Northern Dancer stock, bringing the pick of them to Europe and thence to the world.

Northern Dancer's other high-class sons and daughters included Derby winners The Minstrel and Secreto, Irish Derby winners El Gran Senor and Shareef Dancer, 2,000 Guineas winner Lomond and disqualified winner Nureyev, Irish 2,000 Guineas winner Sadler's Wells, Prix de Diane winner Northern Trick and champion sprinter Ajdal. He was champion sire in Britain and Ireland four times.

His stock were characterised by their potent blend of speed, stamina and athleticism, and as they climbed the ladder to glory so did his stud fee. By the time his stallion career came to a close in 1987, a nomination to Northern Dancer – the right to send just one mare to him – was changing hands for $1 million. At 50 nominations a season, one small horse was matching the balance sheet of a major corporation. At the sales, his offspring changed hands for many millions of dollars. On his retirement from active duty he had produced 645 foals, of which 411 were winners. It is a startling statistic.

Had this been the extent of Northern Dancer's prowess, his place in history would have been assured. However, his influence was merely in its infancy. It is one thing being a successful sire, but Northern Dancer was a colossally successful sire of sires, meaning that his legacy has become self-perpetuating, eternal. The pick of his progeny were as potent and popular as he was, and they went forth and multiplied, conquering the world.

Nijinsky, Be My Guest and Sadler's Wells were champion sires in Britain and Ireland, and the likes of Lyphard, Danzig, Northern Taste, Vice Regent, Storm Bird, Fairy King and Dixieland Band were phenomenally successful at stud worldwide. The mighty Sadler's

Wells was champion 14 times, producing a vast galaxy of superstars, even more than Northern Dancer himself, and his record-breaking stallion sons – Northern Dancer's grandsons – include the (almost) incomparable multiple champion Galileo, Montjeu, El Prado and High Chaparral.

Everything, as we saw earlier, leads back to the three founding stallions, and in particular the Darley Arabian, whose dominant line through Eclipse, Phalaris and Nearco is responsible for Northern Dancer, but the little Canadian-bred colt has founded his own dynasty, has become the most recent common ancestor of practically every thoroughbred alive.

One line among so many has had the most profound effect on the modern sport: Northern Dancer begat Sadler's Wells, who begat Galileo, who begat Australia, Frankel, Teofilo, New Approach, Nathaniel, Highland Reel and many more whose imprint on the stud book and the world's racecourses has yet to be fully divined.

Northern Dancer died in November 1990, at the age of 29. But death shall have no dominion. More than 30 years later, his sons and their sons and their sons unending are as the numberless stars in the heavens, shining from the pedigree pages like a million points of light.

57

For writing bets, and chewing.   Image © Author

LISTENING TO THE BLOWER

Those wanting to have a bet before 1 May 1961 had a number of options. Go to the racecourse, go to the greyhound track, bet over the telephone with a credit firm, use the friendly neighbourhood illegal bookmaker, with the help of bookie's runners in pubs, factories, and on street corners. Then, in a seismic shift for the betting industry and town centres alike, the betting shop was born, midwifed into existence by the Betting and Gaming Act made statute by Harold Macmillan's government.

Everything changed at a stroke. Off-course betting suddenly gained legality, accessibility and a thin veneer of respectability, although not so much that the public were allowed to see what went on in the new shops, as the law dictated that the windows and doors must be blacked out, to spare the sensitivities of Middle England.

What they would have seen is what they might have expected, albeit darkly through a thick cloud of cigarette smoke. A cashier behind a grille taking bets scribbled on pieces of paper, a list of the day's runners and riders pinned to the wall, a boardman writing up the results beamed in by the 'blower', the Exchange Telegraph, a group of men – it was always men – standing around waiting and hoping for the right result, and the floor strewn with torn-up losing slips.

Within the first month there were 7,000 shops licensed. A clause in the Act demanded that shops should neither encourage nor induce betting, with customers not intended to spend more time than strictly necessary, so the first shops were basic, functional, designed to be unwelcoming but welcoming nonetheless for the fraternity of kindred spirits who used them.

Now-familiar names appeared on the high street, Ladbrokes, Coral, Mecca, as well as very many independent concerns who have since been swallowed up by the big firms. William Hill was not convinced of the merit of betting shops and was late to the party, not opening his first shop until 1966. In the same year, betting duty was introduced at 2.5 per cent, and this rose in increments to ten per cent until it was abolished in 2001. Punters could either pay tax-on, when placing the bet, or wait and pay the tax on winnings, should there be any. It seemed foolish to wait.

Betting shops reached peak saturation in 1968, when there were more than 16,000 across Britain. Today there are fewer than half that number, following recent closures in the wake of legislation to limit the stakes on the pernicious FOBTs (fixed-odds betting terminals, casino machines) that gave shops in particular and the industry as a whole a great deal of deserved bad publicity.

The shops that remain are much more accommodating places than their 1960s incarnations, without the fug of smoke that left generations of punters unable to deny the inevitable accusation 'have you been in that bloody betting shop again?' In 1986, refreshments were permitted to be served and sporting events shown on television. The following year marked a sea-change for betting-shop punters with the introduction of live pictures from the racecourse.

Gone forever were the days of listening to a haphazard commentary on the 'blower', in which the lead could change hands several times during the final furlong and the race still be won by a horse that had never been mentioned before. Those little plastic betting-shop pens usually bore the brunt of the consequent anguish.

In 1995 the blackout was removed and shoppers could finally see in. Civilisation did not fall. Nowadays patrons have cups of coffee made for them by shop staff, the unheralded angels of the betting shop estate who despite their long hours dispense sympathy and helpful advice with a smile. One Grand National morning, the shop its once-a-year bedlam, a first-time punter was heard to ask a cashier where on the slip he should write his name and address, so his winnings could be posted to him. With a straight face, and compassion, the cashier explained his error.

The shift in betting culture to online and mobile wagering has not been kind to the shops, which despite being cleaner and brighter than ever are also generally emptier than ever. Betting shops have a bad name, which is unfair, and may even have had their day, which is regrettable. At their best, from the 1970s to the 1990s, before the computer-generated racing and the relentlessness of 'product', betting shops were a source of great camaraderie, a temporary sanctuary from the outside world, a place of shared triumph and disaster in the eternal search for a winner.

58

Racecourses under the axe.   *Image © Author*

SIC TRANSIT GLORIA MUNDI

Woore Hunt (1963). Manchester (1963). Lincoln and Lewes (1964). Bogside, Rothbury and Birmingham (1965). Sic transit gloria mundi, for the early 1960s was an era of rationalisation and closure for British racecourses, and of regret and loss for those who walked their green acres.

    Buckfastleigh, in Devon, had closed in 1960, and metropolitan Hurst Park was sold for development two years later. Much worse was to follow. In April 1963, the Horserace Betting Levy Board, established two years earlier concomitant with the legalisation of betting shops, announced plans to withdraw financial support from the end of 1966 from a dozen racecourses viewed as uneconomic. In effect, the Levy Board was condemning them, for without subsidies for maintenance and improvements the selected racecourses had little future.

    Little Woore, in Shropshire, closed almost immediately. Manchester was sold for development a few months later. A number of racecourses on the 'kill list' fought their death sentence and survived through increased public support, such as Edinburgh, Pontefract and Sedgefield, but others were not so fortunate. Rothbury, in Northumberland, had only one meeting a year so was prime for the cull. Bogside was close to Ayr, which was earmarked for investment, so the Scottish National was moved there and Bogside was sacrificed.

Lincoln was run-down and dilapidated, and the Lincolnshire Handicap, its marquee event, was transferred to Doncaster, also the recipient of the Manchester November Handicap. Lewes was relatively inaccessible and its amenities were poor. One by one they went dark, forever. Birmingham, which had not been on the list, was acquired for housing.

The closure of a racecourse is like the closure of any other sporting facility, a football ground, a cricket pitch – a crime against happiness. They are places where people went to enjoy themselves, to escape from their worries for a while, to be inspired. A sporting arena is a sacred place, full of precious memories: last-minute winners, a graceful square cut for four, a thrilling finish, close encounters with legends both two-legged and four. Take it away, and far, far more is lost than merely bricks and mortar and grass.

Since the Levy Board's axe came down there have been several more closures, Alexandra Park, Wye, Lanark, Stockton and Folkestone (which had both been on the original list), Towcester. Hereford closed in 2012 but, joyously, reopened four years later. Great Leighs was born in 2008, survived only a few months, but was reincarnated as Chelmsford City in 2015. Ffos Las, in west Wales, opened in 2009, the newest addition to the canon. The Jockey Club announced plans to close Kempton Park by 2021 so that the site could be used for housing, but the execution was stayed and Kempton continues to operate.

Although some racecourses die, they do not fade away. At Manchester, the shape of the racecourse can still be traced. At Lewes, the racecourse is still intact, and local trainers use it to work their horses. At Hurst Park, the outline of the old pre-parade ring emerged from the greensward during a heatwave in 2018, nostalgia in action, a ghost from the past walking the earth once more.

Since 1900, almost 100 racecourses (including those named above) in Britain have been closed down. At the time of writing, there are 60 racecourses in operation, if the two separate tracks at Newmarket are taken individually. Jockey Club Racecourses own 15, the Arena Racing Company operates 16, Ascot is Crown property and nearly all the others are independently owned. Jumping-only racecourses number 23, there are 20 Flat-only venues, and the rest are dual-purpose.

Occasionally acute concern arises over the future of this racecourse or that: will an independent be kept away from the grasp of developers, is a conglomerate considering streamlining its portfolio, can the British industry still support 60 racecourses when attendances are not increasing? There are no guarantees when it comes to the future of racecourses, as recent history shows. We must enjoy them all while we still can, before they pave other paradises, and put up parking lots.

59

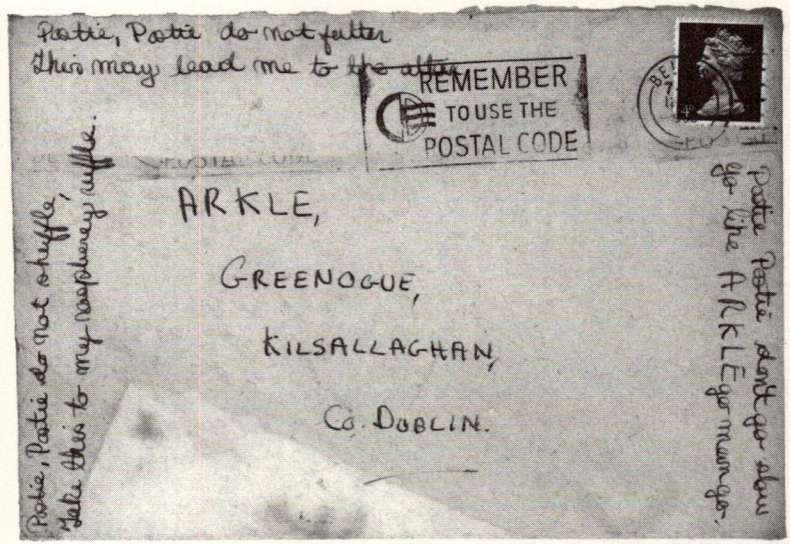

Dear Arkle... *Courtesy of Patricia Stewart*

ARKLEARKLEARKLEARKLEARKLE

Arkle was a horse. Leave it there, and you haven't gone wrong. But Arkle was more than that. He was a champion, a talisman, a national hero. Mention of his name inspired an ecstasy unparalleled in any other horse, and it still does. He was the greatest steeplechaser the world has known, and may ever know. More than 50 years after his death, he is revered, honoured, idolised, loved. Arkle was and is, while trying to not take things too far, a god of a horse.

His true worth may not be measured purely by list of races won, rivals vanquished, ratings achieved. Again, with only that to go on, you haven't gone wrong. Arkle proved himself beyond question on the racecourse, over and over again, until the rules were changed to help the other horses, until he had won everything there was to win, until his reign of glory was ended not by a lapse of form or a careless blunder but by a career-ending injury. But by that time, Arkle had risen above the merely equine. They called him 'Himself', as eloquent a term of worship as may be found in a single word.

Arkle was foaled in 1957, trained in Ireland by Tom Dreaper, ridden in his races by Pat Taaffe, owned by the immensely wealthy

Anne, Duchess of Westminster, and named after a mountain near her estate in Scotland, although Arkle was not a horse you could buy with money. 'He was a freak, an unrepeatably lucky shake of the genetic cocktail,' wrote leading turf historian John Randall. Arkle was fine enough over hurdles, better yet as a novice chaser. After that, well . . .

The 1964 Cheltenham Gold Cup was a race that brought jump racing rushing into a new era. It may be the most eagerly awaited race there has ever been. Arkle, the hope of the Irish, would take on the British champion Mill House, known as 'The Big Horse' for his size and his talent. Mill House had won the Gold Cup the previous year, had beaten Arkle in the Hennessy a few months earlier. Mill House was the best there'd been. He was odds-on to beat his three rivals. Mill House was the best there'd been. Nothing could beat Mill House.

Arkle crushed him.

The winning margin was five lengths, but it was the manner of victory that was more conclusive. The neat, well-made Arkle cruised up to the lashing, slashing Mill House at the second last, and sprinted easily away from him on the run-in. It was done. It would never be undone. Poor Mill House. Arkle had changed everything.

He also changed the way the public began to view racehorses. Arkle became public property, certainly in Ireland, where he was the source of the most fervent national pride. Ireland did not have a great deal to shout about on the world stage, but with this one short word everyone everywhere stopped to listen. Arkle belonged to the whole country.

There were sackfuls of fanmail, many of them addressed only 'Arkle, Ireland'. The postman knew the rest. There was money sent to buy Arkle carrots, requests for photographs, for cuttings of his tail, poems were written, songs were sung. Arkle's image appeared on playing cards, table mats, plates, tea-towels, postage stamps. The Guinness brewery sent him bottles of the black stuff for free, which Arkle kindly shared with his stablemates. On a wall in Dublin, someone scrawled 'Arkle for President'. It wasn't cleaned away. Arkle for President. Why not?

His impact was incalculable. One celebrated snapshot of the time involves racecourse character Twinny Byrne, whose hair had a life of its own, who was asked by a television journalist what Arkle meant to the nation. 'What's the conversation like in the pub of an evening?' Byrne wasted no time in thought. 'It's only ArkleArkleArkleArkleArkle, Arkle that's all, Arkle the whole way.'

This adulation would later find its echo in the public devotion surrounding Red Rum and Desert Orchid, the letters and the photos and the affection even from people who had only seen them on television, but there was a purity, a simplicity about the breadth and depth of feeling that Arkle engendered. Arkle was adored with a passion that would never falter. In 1966, *TV Times* magazine polled its readers on the most popular personality of the year – The Beatles were third; Bobby Moore, captain of England's World Cup winners, was second; Arkle, as ever, was first.

In December of that year, Arkle broke a pedal bone (it is in the hoof) during the King George VI Chase, and was caught close home by Dormant, and beaten. The shock of defeat, and his injury, and its implication, was like a bereavement. Letters – to a horse! But not just a horse – poured in from all corners, full of condolence, appreciation and encouragement for recovery. Arkle did recover, but he never ran again. In retirement, physical problems troubled him, and he was put down on the last day of May 1970. There could never be another.

There is a statue of Arkle at Cheltenham, and a race named after him, and a bar named after him, one of many bearing his name. His skeleton stands in the Irish Horse Museum. *The Racing Post* asked its readers to vote, and Arkle was by a wide margin their favourite horse of all time.

Arkle won three Cheltenham Gold Cups, a King George, two Hennessys, a Whitbread, an Irish National, and many more big races. Only six horses ever finished in front of him over fences. He gained many of his great victories in handicaps despite making huge weight concessions to his rivals. A rule was made in Ireland, one set of conditions for a race if Arkle ran, another if he didn't.

But this is all merely detail, no more than wrapping paper around the present. Arkle was Arkle. And they sang songs about him, and the singing will never be done.

60

Merry Christmas from the IJF. *Image © Author*

A SAFETY NET HELD BY MANY HANDS

There was a bucket going round. Some threw in silver, others pound notes, a fiver here and there. Whatever could be spared. On the label, on the bucket, were the names Tim Brookshaw and Paddy Farrell, and when people saw that, the buckets steadily filled with donations for the two terribly injured jockeys. The money has been coming ever since.

The Injured Jockeys Fund is the most uplifting example of racing helping its own. Everyone knows what risks jockeys take in the course of their job, a job that entails an ambulance following them around the racecourse, and when dreadful accidents happen the IJF is there with a financial safety net held out by many, many hands.

Tim Brookshaw was paralysed in a fall at Aintree in December 1963. Three months later, a fall in the Grand National left Paddy Farrell with a broken back. The day after the National, owner-breeder Clifford Nicholson decided to set up a fund for Farrell and Brookshaw, enlisting the help of a number of trustees including John Oaksey, whose name has come to be synonymous with the great work of the IJF through his unstinting enthusiasm and devotion to the project.

A week after the National, those buckets were carried through the Easter crowds at Southwell, Wetherby and Carlisle by jockeys who were sharing the risks with Brookshaw and Farrell, and what would soon become known as the Injured Jockeys Fund was up and running.

Almost 60 years later, the IJF has raised more than £20 million and helped more than a thousand jockeys, Flat and jumps, famous and obscure, critically injured and mercifully less so, helped them with recovery and with the means to sustain life after racing. Donations reach the IJF in many ways, charity events, bequests, personal sponsorships, although arguably the most recognised is through the sale of its Christmas cards, which appear in festive multitudes on the mantelpieces of those within the sport.

In the last dozen years three state-of-the-art rehabilitation centres have been opened to assist jockeys working to regain their health and fitness, Oaksey House in Lambourn, Jack Berry House in Malton (Berry was one of the originals with the buckets, and later a superlative trainer of sprinters and a ceaseless worker for the IJF) and Peter O'Sullevan House in Newmarket, for O'Sullevan's efforts on behalf of the IJF were no less considerable.

Outside the centres, invaluable fieldwork is performed by a dedicated team of almoners and other volunteers, who are in close contact with all those receiving assistance from the IJF and perform vital non-medical duties of care, consolation and company. Assistance is given on both reactive and proactive grounds; once a year there is a group holiday somewhere warm, which gives those who might be housebound or otherwise isolated the opportunity to renew old friendships.

The IJF's sister charity is Racing Welfare, founded in 2000 through an amalgamation of several racing charities. Its primary role is to provide support for all within the industry, doing essentially unglamorous but absolutely essential work across a constituency that embraces everyone from stable staff to ex-trainers, racecourse staff to stud employees, widows and family included.

Racing Welfare leaves no one behind, during their time in the sport and afterwards, with notable emphasis placed on mental health issues, social isolation and loneliness, as well as the provision of subsidised accommodation and 24/7 emotional support assistance. The IJF is known to all but Racing Welfare does marvellous things in relative anonymity, with offices in all the major racing centres and roving welfare officers in other parts of Britain.

The charitable impulse that began as a heartfelt reaction to the great misfortune of two jockeys has blossomed into a vast network of vital assistance, for those who risk life and limb on a daily basis and for those whose roles are less perilous. Racing can be truly proud of itself for the energy and the inventiveness and the hard work with which it has addressed the need to provide support for those who serve it.

In return, racing has the unalloyed gratitude of all those who have received help, and of all those who have contributed towards that help, whether through fundraising on a grand scale, the purchase of a dozen Christmas cards, or by a handful of change dropped into a bucket.

61

Necessary for a training licence.   Image © Author

A PRINCIPLE INVOLVED

Hell hath no fury. Her greatest victory was gained far from any racecourse, yet through this triumph she helped change racing forever. Florence Nagle trained few winners of any account, but her pioneer's place in history is assured.

Until the final third of the 20th century, the business of training horses was, if one was a woman, also a business of subterfuge and barely suppressed frustration, for the Jockey Club forbade women to hold a training licence. It was common knowledge that there were several female trainers who between them were winning plenty of races, but they were denied recognition and validation through the intransigence and hypocrisy of the governing body.

Gilles De Retz, winner of the 1956 2,000 Guineas, was trained by Helen Johnson Houghton, but the victory is credited to her assistant Charles Jerdein, for the Jockey Club was only prepared to issue a licence to a man, whether he be husband, head lad or assistant.

Auriol Sinclair won the 1958 Wokingham Handicap at Royal Ascot with Magic Boy, but the record books suggest that John Bolton was responsible. Posy Lewis trained Limonali to win the Welsh National in 1959 and 1961, but officially it was first her brother Clem Morel and then her son Ifor Lewis. The situation was the same in Ireland, where Sabia Wellesley trained winners of the 1,000 Guineas, 2,000 Guineas and the St Leger between 1947 and 1950, although the name on the licence was that of her head lad Eddie McGrath.

In Nagle's case, the licence at her West Sussex yard was held by her head lad Bill Stickley, and although she applied for a licence in her own name on an annual basis, she was annually turned down. She said that 'the only qualification for getting a training licence is a pair of trousers'.

Considering her wardrobe to be perfectly satisfactory, in 1965 she brought a High Court action against the stewards and members of the Jockey Club, seeking a ruling that she should not be barred from holding a licence on account of her gender. She was 71 and had very little to gain on a personal basis, but said, 'There was a principle involved in my fight. I am a feminist and believe that things should be decided on ability and not sex.'

Its views being exactly the reverse, the Jockey Club attempted to have this action struck out before it could be heard and briefly succeeded, but the Court of Appeal ruled unanimously in Nagle's favour, castigating the Club for its reactionary stance. Lord Justice Salmon declared that the Jockey Club's position was 'as capricious as refusing a man a licence simply because of the colour of his hair', while Lord Justice Danckwerts stated that the stewards' policy was 'arbitrary and entirely out of touch with the present state of society in Britain.'

Nagle was thus free to take her case back to the High Court, but before she could do so the Jockey Club, belatedly realising that its position was utterly indefensible, ran up the white flag and gave in to reason. In July 1966, Nagle's persistence was rewarded and she was granted a training licence in her own name. The precedent was quickly seized upon, and made commonplace.

Less than a week later, Norah Wilmot, who had trained 'anonymously' for the Queen and Queen Mother, and had won the Goodwood Cup and Doncaster Cup without the privilege of seeing her name in the record books, became the first woman to train a winner under her own name when Pat was successful at Brighton. Less than three years later, Rosemary Lomax broke the cut-glass ceiling when becoming the first woman to officially train a Royal Ascot winner, Precipice Wood – who would win Lomax the Gold Cup the following year – in the King George V Handicap.

Over the jumps, the situation was slightly different, as this branch of the sport was at the time overseen by the National Hunt Committee, which did not merge with the Jockey Club until 1968. Women had been officially permitted to train horses for hunter chases from January 1966, and two months later Jackie Brutton became the first woman to train a Cheltenham Festival winner and gain recognition for it when Snowdra Queen took the United Hunts Chase.

The list of female trainers is now a long one and getting longer, and in Britain women are regularly successful at the highest level under both codes. Jenny Pitman, Henrietta Knight and Jessica Harrington have won the Cheltenham Gold Cup; Pitman, Venetia Williams, Lucinda Russell and Sue Smith have trained Grand National winners; Katie Gaze, Jane Pilkington, Monica Dickinson, Mercy Rimell, Emma Lavelle, Lynda Ramsden, Sue Bramall and Rebecca Curtis are among the many to have trained Cheltenham Festival winners.

On the Flat, Lady Herries won the Prix du Jockey-Club with Celtic Swing, Pam Sly trained Speciosa to win the 1,000 Guineas and Laura Mongan won the St Leger with Harbour Law, while Harrington has several Group 1 races to her name, notably the Irish 1,000 Guineas. Mary Reveley trained more than 2,000 winners Flat and jumps, while a little piece of history was revisited to great satisfaction when Eve Johnson Houghton won a Group 1 at Royal Ascot in 2018; she is the grand-daughter of the aforementioned Helen Johnson Houghton. No list of successful female trainers is complete without the names of multiple Arc and Classic winner Criquette Head-Maarek and Gai Waterhouse, who has won countless Group 1s in Australia including the Melbourne Cup.

None of them have needed a pair of trousers to prove their suitability and ability to train horses. For that, they can thank the redoubtable Florence Nagle.

Music to racing's ears.   Image © Getty

FOR THOSE ABOUT TO ROCK

Racing does not feature prominently in what the old grey whistlers would call 'popular music', although Lester Piggott is lyricised by performers as diverse as Van Morrison and Chas & Dave (surely the acme of polar opposites), and the band James wrote a song called 'Sometimes (Lester Piggott)', which doesn't mention him at all.

There is also 'Bottle Of Smoke', written by those shy and retiring Pogues about a winning bet on the eponymous horse, the song basically in the form of a race report that would take a phenomenal amount of sub-editing before it could appear in, say, *Horse & Hound*. However, racing and music are found adjacent in the Venn diagram of life in respect of live concerts held at racecourses during the summer, a seemingly innocent topic that nevertheless exercises the ire of racing people more than almost any other.

The first band to appear at a British raceday may have been Sight & Sound, a local group who played at Wolverhampton on Easter Monday 1970, in an extended gap between the fourth and fifth races. Since then, when looking to boost crowds and increase turnover, racecourses have seized upon live concerts at evening meetings to cover both bases.

The last race might finish at 8.30, and then the band comes on for an hour and a half to make a night of it. Famous names are involved: Bryan Adams, Simply Red, Boyzone, UB40, Status Quo, Girls Aloud, Little Mix and Suzi Quatro, who was the first to play the July Course at Newmarket, a milestone not as glamorous as topping the bill at the Marquee or CBGBs but for those about to rock, we salute you.

It sounds simple, but of course racing makes it anything but. The majority of complaints cover two points, of which the first is easier to comprehend than the second. Booking the biggish names of rock and roll is not cheap, and when there is a live gig at the races, admission fees rise. Those who plan only to watch the horses and make a quick getaway before the music starts are therefore paying a premium for something they have no interest in.

The other issue appears to be that music nights do not attract the right sort of people. This doesn't refer to those present at the Altamont Speedway, but to people who – shock horror – aren't interested in racing but have only come for the band or the DJ. Racing is not hugely keen on new people anyway, as illustrated in the earlier chapter on jargon, but new people who don't even stand by the parade ring? Outrageous.

The indignant accusation of 'not there for the racing', as if casual football fans should be made to reel off the teamsheet of the Mighty Magyars before they are allowed into the ground, is also levelled at other attempts to appeal to those outside the inner circle, such as family days and ladies' days. These events attract larger crowds whose main focus is not on the racing programme but, strange though it seems to some, on enjoying themselves at somewhere that happens to be a racecourse.

Music nights are vital to racecourse revenue, an extra source of income that finds its way into increased prize-money and improved facilities. They do attract an audience that might not otherwise come within a mile of the track, but that is never a bad thing. Any exposure to the inside of a racecourse is valuable, and new converts may appear from unexpected places. Those who advocate singing around the bandstand at Royal Ascot are in no position to be sniffy about Tom Jones and Rick Astley playing the old hits as the sun goes down at Newmarket.

Racecourses and racing are in the entertainment business, and music nights, ladies' days and any other additional attractions are part of that remit. The atmosphere at the post-racing concert often exceeds that at the pre-concert racing, so turn it up and let people enjoy themselves. After all, rock and roll is here to stay.

63

One ... two ... a Triple Crown?

THE MAGIC NUMBER

It hasn't happened in Britain for more than 50 years. It happens in the US more often, but not often. It happens quite a lot in Japan. France? No. Ireland? Not since Val Doonican was a lad. Australia? Rarely. Germany? Just once, the same as Hong Kong.

The Triple Crown is a remarkable achievement and one that is remarkably difficult to achieve. Usually, not always, it consists of three prestigious races for three-year-olds over a variety of distances, and if any horse should sweep the series then he is raised to the most rarefied level in the sport. In Britain, the Triple Crown is the 2,000 Guineas, Derby and St Leger. In the US, it's the Kentucky Derby, Preakness and Belmont. In other jurisdictions, it is based loosely or adhesively upon the British model. There are fillies' versions of all, but in this patriarchal world they are not afforded the same open-mouthed respect as the colts' Triple Crown.

There have been 12 British Triple Crown winners but the last was Nijinsky, in 1970. Special mention should be made of the filly Oh So Sharp, who won 1,000 Guineas, Oaks and St Leger in 1985. In the US, there have been 13 in all and two this century, American Pharoah in 2015 and Justify in 2018. There are a number of reasons for the paucity of winners, differing between the two racing nations.

In Britain, the prime reason for the absence of Triple Crown winners is the St Leger, for its distance and the corollary of disfavour among breeders, who love only speed. A horse who wins the first two legs of the Triple Crown is unlikely to even attempt the St Leger, because a victory over its mile and three-quarters is kryptonite to a horse's stud value. Guineas and Derby winners Nashwan (1989) and Sea The Stars (2009) were not even entered in the St Leger.

The only attempt on the Triple Crown since 1970 was undertaken by Camelot in 2012, mainly because his owners, the Ballydoyle/Coolmore Stud empire, annually have plenty of suitable candidates for stallion duties and, practically, could take a free hit with Camelot. It didn't work anyway; he was runner-up to Encke.

In the US, the main reason is the distance of the Belmont, its mile and a half regarded as an excessive test of stamina over there, but the proximity of each race is also a factor. The US Triple Crown spans just five weeks, whereas in Britain it runs May-September and in Japan it's April-October. In the US, the Belmont is almost always the destination for a Kentucky Derby-Preakness winner, but the demands placed on stamina almost always prove too much to overcome.

Perhaps the best of all Triple Crowns was in the US in 1978, when Affirmed beat the valiant Alydar in all three legs, his margin of victory decreasing by increments from a length and a half, to a neck, to a nose in the gripping, knock-down-drag-out duel in the Belmont. Alydar is the only horse to finish runner-up in all three legs of the Triple Crown.

From time to time in Britain, columnists, pundits and marketing gurus, faced with a quiet week, hypnotised by the concept of three being the magic number, posit changes to the Triple Crown to make it more winnable. These range from reducing the distance of the St Leger to inventing a new series – say, the Eclipse, King George and Juddmonte International – that would be open to older horses too and be relatively easier to win. All these proposals miss the point entirely: that the Triple Crown should be very, very difficult to win.

Where is the prestige, the historical relevance, the achievement in winning something that has been designed to be easier to win, simply to make a few headlines? In a modern culture desperate for easy and immediate satisfaction, the fascination of what is difficult has been jettisoned. If there is a Triple Crown winner every four or five years, where's the fun in Triple Crown winners?

In Japan, there were uniquely two Triple Crown winners in 2020, the colt Contrail and the filly Daring Tact. Contrail was only the fourth since 1984 to win the colts' series, but Daring Tact was the fourth in a decade to win the distaff version. No marks for guessing which achievement was more highly esteemed.

The outpouring of joy and relief in the US when American Pharoah broke the losing streak that stretched back to Affirmed in 1978 was instructive, even down to the words of race-caller Larry Collmus, who howled delightedly 'The 37-year wait is over. American Pharoah is finally the one!' He had done that which horses do not, had become something other horses are not.

If one day a horse emulates Nijinsky, has the speed for a mile, the brilliance for a mile and a half, the endurance for a mile and three-quarters, and an owner with the inclination to try, then the achievement will electrify the sport. That's what the Triple Crown should mean. It must not be made easier, more commonplace. And maybe it will never happen again, but that's just the way it goes.

64

YEARLING, consigned by Newsells Park Stud Ltd.

Will Stand at Park Paddocks, Somerville Paddock O, Box 298

436 (WITH VAT)
A BAY FILLY (GB)
Foaled
January 23rd, 2019

	Galileo (IRE)	Sadler's Wells (USA)	Northern Dancer
			Fairy Bridge (USA)
		Urban Sea (USA)	Miswaki (USA)
			Allegretta
	Shastye (IRE)	Danehill (USA)	Danzig (USA)
	(2001)		Razyana (USA)
		Saganeca (USA)	Sagace (FR)
			Haglette (USA)

Own sister to **JAPAN (GB)**, **SECRET GESTURE (GB)**, **MOGUL (GB)**
and **SIR ISAAC NEWTON (GB)**
E.B.F. Nominated. B.C. Nominated.

1st Dam
Shastye (IRE), **won** 2 races at 3 and 4 years and £20,866 and placed 3 times including second in totesport.com Pontefract Castle Stakes, Pontefract, **L.**;
dam of **six winners** from 7 runners and 10 foals of racing age including-
JAPAN (GB) (2016 c. by Galileo (IRE)), Champion 3yr old in Europe in 2019 (9.5-10.5f.), Jt Champion 3yr old colt in England & Ireland in 2019, **won** 5 races at 2 and 3 years, 2019 at home and in France and £1,630,797 including Juddmonte International Stakes, York, **Gr.1**, Grand Prix de Paris, Parislongchamp, **Gr.1**, Beresford Stakes, Naas, **Gr.2**, King Edward VII Stakes, Ascot, **Gr.2**, placed 5 times including third in Derby Stakes, Epsom Downs, **Gr.1**, Eclipse Stakes, Sandown Park, **Gr.1**, King George VI & Queen Elizabeth Stakes, Ascot, **Gr.1** and fourth in Prix de l'Arc de Triomphe, ParisLongchamp, **Gr.1**.
SECRET GESTURE (GB) (2010 f. by Galileo (IRE)), won 4 races at 2 to 5 years and £468,862 including Middleton Stakes, York, **Gr.2**, Oaks Trial Stakes, Lingfield Park, **L.** and Warwickshire Oaks Stakes, Nottingham, **L.**, placed 9 times including second in Oaks Stakes, Epsom Downs, **Gr.1**, Preis der Diana, Dusseldorf, **Gr.1**, York Stakes, York, **Gr.2**, Middleton Stakes, York, **Gr.2**, third in Yorkshire Oaks, York, **Gr.1**, Prix Jean Romanet, Deauville, **Gr.1** and Beverly D Stakes, Arlington, **Gr.1**; dam of a winner.
MOGUL (GB) (2017 c. by Galileo (IRE)), won 3 races at 2 and 3 years, 2020 and £158,039 including Golden Fleece Stakes, Leopardstown, **Gr.2** and Gordon Stakes, Goodwood, **Gr.3**, placed twice including fourth in Vertem Futurity Trophy Stakes, Newcastle, **Gr.1**.
SIR ISAAC NEWTON (GB) (2012 c. by Galileo (IRE)), won 3 races at 3 and 4 years and £274,685 including International Stakes, Curragh, **Gr.3**, Wolferton Handicap, Ascot, **L.**, placed 10 times under both rules including third in JRA Cup, Moonee Valley, **Gr.3**, Silver Stakes, Curragh, **L.**, fourth in King George VI & Queen Elizabeth Stakes, Ascot, **Gr.1**, Juddmonte International Stakes, York, **Gr.1**, Solonaway Stakes, Leopardstown, **Gr.2**.
MAURUS (GB) (2011 g. by Medicean (GB)), won 7 races in Australia and £367,728 including Ipswich Cup, Ipswich, **L.**, Wagga Wagga Gold Cup, Wagga-Wagga, **L.**, placed 18 times including second in Premier's Cup, Doomben, **L.**, Kingston Town Stakes, Rosehill, **Gr.3**, Neville Sellwood Stakes, Rosehill, **Gr.3**, JRA Cup, Moonee Valley, **Gr.3**, Tattersalls Club Cup, Randwick, **L.**, third in A D Hollindale Stakes, Gold Coast, **Gr.2**.
Shabyt (GB) (2008 f. by Sadler's Wells (USA)), unraced; dam of 4 winners.
Shaherezada (IRE) (f. by Dutch Art (GB)), 1 race at 2 years and £19,932 and placed 4 times including second in netbet.co.uk Height of Fashion Stakes, Goodwood, **L.**

2nd Dam
SAGANECA (USA), Champion older mare in Italy in 1992, **won** 1 race at 3 years in France and £142,079 viz CIGA Prix de Royallieu, Longchamp, **Gr.2**, placed 14 times including second in Gran Premio di Milano, Milan, **Gr.1**, third in Prix des Tourelles, Longchamp, **L.**;
dam of **nine winners** from 12 runners and 15 foals of racing age including-
SAGAMIX (FR) (c. by Linamix (FR)), won 4 races at 3 years in France and £516,720 including Prix de l'Arc de Triomphe, Longchamp, **Gr.1** and Prix Niel, Longchamp, **Gr.2**, placed 4 times including third in Grand Prix de Saint-Cloud, Saint-Cloud, **Gr.1**; sire.
SAGACITY (FR) (c. by Highest Honor (FR)), won 2 races at 2 years in France and £201,638 including Criterium de Saint-Cloud, Saint-Cloud, **Gr.1**, placed second in Prix Hocquart, Longchamp, **Gr.2**, Prix du Prince d'Orange, Longchamp, **Gr.3**, Prix Exbury, Saint-Cloud, **Gr.3**, third in Prix de l'Arc de Triomphe, Longchamp, **Gr.1**; sire.
SAGE ET JOLIE (FR) (f. by Linamix (FR)), won 3 races at 3 years in France and £63,509 including Prix de Mallaret, Longchamp, **Gr.2**; dam of winners.
SAGEBURG (IRE), 4 races at 3 and 4 years in France and £258,535 including Prix d'Ispahan, Longchamp, **Gr.1**, third in Prix du Moulin de Longchamp, Longchamp, **Gr.1** and Prix Ganay - Anniversaire Air Mauritius, Longchamp, **Gr.1**; sire.
Sagalina (IRE), ran in France at 3 years; dam of winners.
SAGAWARA (GB), 2 races at 2 and 3 years in France and £165,012 including Montjeu Coolmore Prix Saint-Alary, Longchamp, **Gr.1**, placed 3 times.

The black-type of pedigree power. © *Tattersalls*

TO TEST THE BEST

For an abstract concept, at bottom no more than applying labels for the appearance of clarity, the Pattern system is often the subject of intense scrutiny. From the outside, the intellectual scuffle means no more than the rearranging of deckchairs on the *Titanic*, although as that fateful voyage took place in April there probably weren't any deckchairs anyway, but from the inside, the subject is of vital importance.

What is the Pattern? The Pattern is the overall structure of the biggest, most prestigious races, arrayed in a hierarchy so it can be seen at a glance that the Group 1 Yorkshire Oaks is a better race than the Group 2 Lancashire Oaks, possibly in some form of revenge for the Wars of the Roses, and both are better than the Group 3 Oak Tree Stakes, which is better than the Listed Cheshire Oaks.

The same principle applies around the world, although the word 'Group' is sometimes dropped in favour of 'Grade'. Over jumps, the system is confined to providing structure rather than an indication of absolute merit; all major handicaps, such as the Grand National, are Grade 3 races.

The Pattern originated from a committee comprising *eminences grise* the Duke of Norfolk, Peter Willett and Geoffrey Freer, whose report in 1965 established the need for 'a series of races over the right distances and at the right time of year to test the best horses of all ages'. Another committee identified the requisite races, and in 1971, after a false start, an integrated European Pattern (Britain, Ireland, France and Italy, with Germany joining the club a year later) took wing.

In the first year there were 243 Pattern races, 50 of them of Group 1 status. The appellations suggested a clear pathway for the best horses, like rungs on a ladder. It plainly defined quality, so that someone with no specialist knowledge could appreciate that the winner of the Group 2 Prix Hocquart has superior credentials to the winner of the Group 3 Gallinule Stakes. Horses who had won a Group 1 race would carry a penalty when running in a Group 2 race, and so on.

It was recognised as a fine solution to race classification and the ongoing pursuit of the 'improvement of the thoroughbred', but in recent years the system has become open to abuse. In a nutshell, the Pattern has been allowed to grow unconfined, prompted by commercial concerns, making prestige easier to earn and naturally cheapening it in the process.

In 2020, in Europe, there were 427 races slated for the Pattern, on the way to double the amount at its inauguration. There were 84 Group 1 races planned, an increase of two-thirds on the 1971 figure, which of course makes it easier for a horse to gain Group 1 credentials and to avoid other horses of Group 1 class. Moreover, all Group 1 races are not equal, the Man O'War Stakes is not in the same postcode of prestige as the Arc, but they have been coerced into an apparent equality through the blanket 'Group 1' tag.

This renders the mention of 'Group 1 winner' in sales catalogues – where the term 'black-type' covers Pattern results – in stallion advertisements and general conversation much less impressive than it used to be. It was harder for a horse to win a Group 3 race in 1983 than it is today, so the earlier achievement must be regarded as superior.

A random example: the outstanding champion Brigadier Gerard won seven Group 1s during his career, while the marvellous Enable won 11 while racing for two seasons more. Brigadier Gerard, whose roll of honour contains five other races that have since been elevated to Group 1 status, was rated 144 by Timeform, and Enable's highest Timeform rating was 134. Life is much easier for the best horses nowadays.

A race is now entitled to Group 1 status not because of tradition or suitability in the wider scheme, but if over a rolling three-year period it achieves an average rating of 115, computed on the performances of the first four finishers. Command of the Pattern has been lost by governing bodies and is instead being dictated in the field. The tail is wagging the dog.

The Pattern system needs thorough pruning, to remove the deadwood and return it to a position where it encourages competition among the best rather than providing a means to avoid it. That is unlikely to happen, with too many vested interests involved, and they having little desire to make life more difficult and less profitable by culling the flock of geese that lays such golden eggs.

Like an elegant shirt, tailored to fit, that is now being stretched too tightly over a bloated, unsightly frame that demands continual overfeeding, the Pattern now barely serves the purpose for which it was first intended.

65

The magnificent Mrs Shilling.   Image © Getty

A FIVE-FOOT GIRAFFE

Royal Ascot: silly hats. That is the prevailing wisdom, and the woman who did most to reinforce that image in the public consciousness was delighted by the impact she made. Gertrude Shilling added more to the gaiety of nations than would a million straight-faced models in designer couture.

After all, if you want to get ahead, get a hat. Shilling followed those instructions to the letter and became as much a part of Royal Ascot as the monarch herself. At every royal meeting from the 1960s onwards, the gossip columnists and the society diarists and the paparazzi had eyes only for her. They called her the Ascot Mascot, and the likelihood of a photo of Mrs Shilling's hat in the newspapers was the best bet of the meeting, a sure thing.

They were big, unwieldy, outrageous, attention-grabbing, all made by her milliner son David, whose imagination was only matched by his mother's chutzpah. There was the five-foot black top hat with a rabbit emerging jauntily from the top of it; a huge green apple with a four-foot arrow skewering it, an unexpected tribute to William Tell; a three-foot wide daisy with a tapering stalk running down her back; a giant football for World Cup year; a television; a vast sombrero; a five-foot giraffe; a dartboard; a colossal cup and saucer and very many more. You didn't want to be stuck behind her when a race started.

Shilling's invigorating adventure in fashion was prompted by a diagnosis of breast cancer in 1966, at which point she was given 18 months to live. Her hats were an act of defiance, two fingers up to cancer, a celebration of life, and not, as the usual sour apples presumed, a display of exhibitionism or narcissism.

In time she saw off breast cancer, became the first woman in Britain to have a breast implant, and carried on wearing her hats. Whatever one thought of her outlandish headgear, Shilling displayed far more class and decorum than porn actress Linda Lovelace, the 'star' of *Deep Throat*, who arrived at Royal Ascot in 1974 in a silver Rolls-Royce adorned with the numberplate PEN15, wearing a transparent dress with nothing on underneath. Another time, Lovelace donned full top hat and tails but neglected to wear a shirt. Perhaps she'd lost it on the favourite in the first.

The Ascot authorities, never slow to regulate their customers' attire, have formalised the dress code down to the last button, the last strap, working their way down the racecourse to the Windsor Enclosure, where simply getting dressed in the first place is probably sufficient. As ever, the small print is absorbing. In the Royal Enclosure, ladies – not women – may not wear a fascinator, although a headpiece with a base at least four inches in diameter is permitted. Someone, somewhere, will be measuring carefully. The guidelines don't mention a five-foot giraffe, which is a loophole surely worth exploring.

No one would wear it as well as Mrs Shilling, though, who wore her inimitable hats to Royal Ascot until she was well into her 80s. No dilettante she; she gave much of her time to charity and to entertaining the elderly, hopefully with glorious stories of Royal Ascot week and her son's endlessly innovative inventions, and possibly of Linda Lovelace.

She died in 1999 at the age of 89, more than 30 years after being given 18 months to live. Her legacy is the archetypal Ascot look, the one that encapsulates for so many the extravagant madness of the great race meeting. Hats off, you might say, to Mrs Shilling.

66

Kicking open the door.   Image © Edward Whitaker

ALL THESE FIRSTS

Sometimes it is more instructive to start at the end and work backwards, to see the distance travelled. Rachael Blackmore won the 2021 Grand National on Minella Times, the 11-1 shot heard 'round the world, three weeks after finishing as top jockey at the Cheltenham Festival with six winners, including the Champion Hurdle. Hollie Doyle finished in the top five of the Flat jockeys' championship in 2020. Bryony Frost won the centrepiece King George VI Chase in 2020. Back we go, boats against the current, using milestones for stepping stones.

    Before Doyle there was Hayley Turner, the first woman to ride 100 winners in a year in Britain, and Alex Greaves, the first to ride a Group 1 winner in Britain, Ya Malak in 1997. The baton passes hand to hand. Before Greaves there was Gay Kelleway, the first to ride a winner at Royal Ascot, Sprowston Boy in 1987.

    Karen Wiltshire was the first professional female jockey to win on the Flat in Britain (The Goldstone, 1978). The first to ride as a professional in Britain was Jane McDonald, in 1975. In the same year, Joanna Morgan became the first woman to ride as a professional in Ireland, the first to ride in a Classic (Riot Helmet, 1976 Irish Derby), the first to ride at Royal Ascot (Gallowshill Boy, 1978). Over the jumps, the same story was being written.

Before Frost and Blackmore there was Lizzie Kelly, the first woman to ride a Grade 1 winner over jumps in Britain and Ireland (Tea For Two, 2015), Katie Walsh, Nina Carberry and Ann Ferris, all winners of the Irish National, and Caroline Beasley, the first to ride a winner at the Cheltenham Festival (Eliogarty, 1983).

Lorna Vincent was the first professional to win over jumps (Pretty Cute, 1978), Charlotte Brew the first to ride in the Grand National (Barony Fort, 1977). Val Greaves, mother of Flat ground-breaker Alex, was the first woman to ride against professionals over jumps, a week after Diana Thorne became the first to win over jumps (Ben Ruler, 1976).

The first female jockey to win against males in Britain was Linda Goodwill, in the Lads and Lassies Handicap at Nottingham in April 1974, aboard Pee Mai. Now we have nearly reached the source, after all these firsts the first of all. In 1972, the recently enlightened Jockey Club first permitted women to ride on the Flat in Britain, although only in a series of 12 amateur races against their own sex.

The series began with the Goya Stakes at Kempton on 6 May, which attracted a field of 21, and it was won by Meriel Tufnell, riding her mother's 50-1 outsider Scorched Earth, the first woman to ride an officially recognised winner in Britain. One small victory for a woman, one giant leap for womankind. Well, perhaps. Tufnell won two more races in the series and was crowned the first female 'champion jockey', but the road ahead was long, paved with good intentions but potholed by lack of opportunity and the usual sexist attitude of the men in a man's world.

Tufnell's career subsequently took her all over Europe, notably to Sweden, where the novelty of a ladies' race had first inspired her to desert showjumping for racing, and she became the first chairwoman of the Lady Jockeys' Association. Through victory in the first officially sanctioned race for women in Britain, Tufnell's position in history is secure, but other pioneers had already begun to map this unknown territory, laying markers as they went.

In the US, Diane Crump had become the first woman to compete as a professional when partnering Bridle 'n Bit at Hialeah in February 1969, when she needed a police escort to protect her from the hostile crowd between the changing room and the parade ring. Later that month Barbara Jo Rubin won at Charles Town on a horse named Cohesion, recording the first victory for a woman at a major US racecourse. The following year Crump was the first to ride in the Kentucky Derby, finishing down the field on Fathom, and the year after that Cheryl White became the first African-American female jockey with a professional licence.

In 1973, Robyn Smith was the first to ride a stakes winner, and from her a line can be drawn to Patti Cooksey, to Julie Krone, the first woman to ride a Classic winner when victorious on Colonial Affair in the 1993 Belmont Stakes, and winner of more than 3,500 races, and on to Rosie Napravnik, who has ridden in all three Triple Crown races. In Australasia, Bev Buckingham blazed the trail for the likes of Clare Lindop, Lisa Cropp, Michelle Payne – the first woman to ride a Melbourne Cup winner (Prince Of Penzance, 2015) – and Jamie Kah.

This is a story full of firsts, of a slow, sometimes glacial succession of notable events, of milestones reached and prejudices overcome, of barriers quietly dismantled, of acceptance grudgingly granted. Female jockeys compete on a daily basis against men on level terms, but have had to prove themselves over and over again in a way that has never been expected of their male counterparts, and they keep on doing it.

From the past of Tufnell, Vincent and Morgan to the present of Blackmore, Doyle and Frost, whose great legacy to the cause is that they make such successes increasingly commonplace, steadily unremarkable. Blackmore's Aintree triumph was not as earth-shattering an event as that of Jenny Pitman almost 40 years earlier, simply because the giant strides taken by she and her fellows had made it inevitable, just a matter of time.

And from Blackmore, Doyle and Frost into the future. One day a woman will be champion jockey, will win a Classic in Britain or Ireland. One day the distinction between female and male jockeys will no longer be remarked upon, and all who ride in races will just be jockeys, somewhere past the final milestones on that potholed road. The long journey is almost over.

67

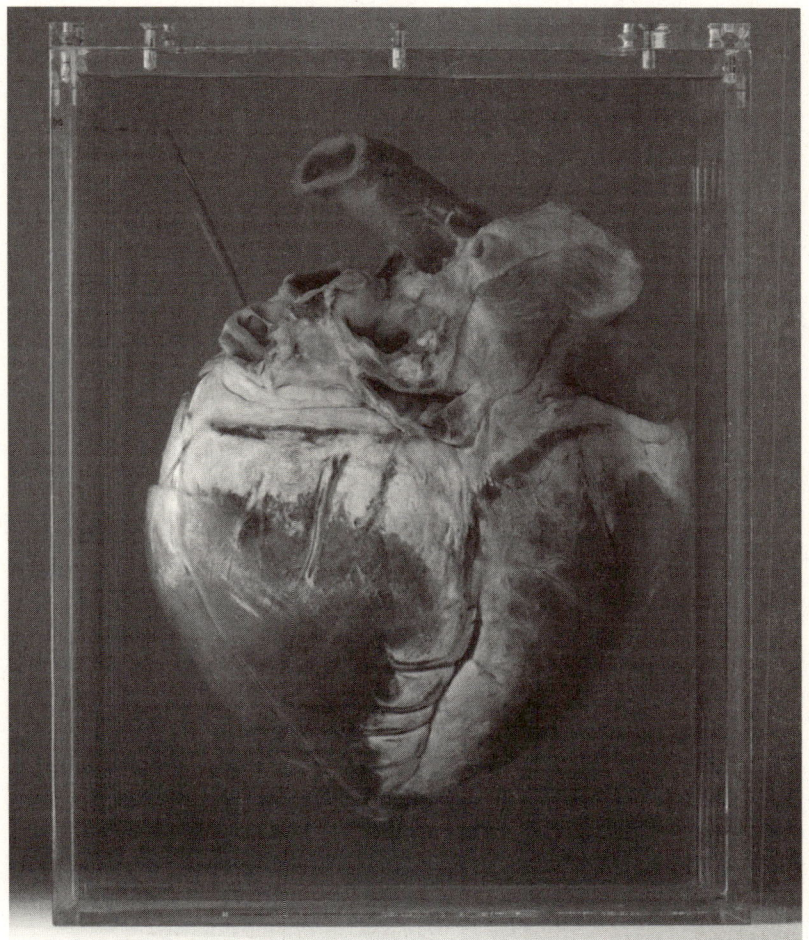

The heart of a champion.   Image © George Serras, National Museum of Australia

THE WORD MADE FLESH

What is essential is invisible to the eye. It is impossible to tell whether one horse will be able to run faster than the others simply by looking at it. Good conformation is a help, good breeding is a hint, but there are no guarantees. What is essential is its spirit, its will, its heart, and no certain value can be assigned to such qualities, unless we descend from the realm of the metaphysical.

The average horse's heart weighs 10lb (4.5kg), roughly one per cent of its bodyweight. Occasionally someone will refer to this horse or that as having a heart like a lion, although that would be a distinct disadvantage considering that a horse's heart weighs three times as much as that of a lion. So much for the average horse; there's nothing average about some horses.

The great Australian galloper Phar Lap had a heart that, once he was dead and opened, was said to weigh 14lb, a heart of (a) stone, a huge beating pump of an organ that was cited as the main physiological reason for his brilliant racetrack performances. Phar Lap's heart is on display in the National Museum of Australia in Canberra, although its authenticity is debated.

Eclipse's heart reportedly weighed the same amount, and again his outstanding performances were later attributed to this physical advantage. The top-class US horse Sham had a heart that weighed in at 18lb, according to the results of autopsy, but Sham was an unfortunate beast, born in the same year as Secretariat, destined to come off second best on the racetrack and in post-mortem. Secretariat was a giant in every conceivable way.

The son of Bold Ruler was a big red locomotive, a tremendous machine, whose wanton destruction of the clock in the 1973 Belmont Stakes was outlined in the earlier chapter on electrical timing. He had a barrel of a chest, a huge strongbox of muscle, and within it was a heart that propelled him to preternatural greatness, and which was estimated to weigh as much as 22lb. 'We were all shocked,' said veterinary professor Dr Thomas Swerczek, quoted in William Nack's book about the horse. 'Nothing I'd ever seen compared to it. It was normal, it was just larger. I think it told us why he was able to do what he did.'

What he did was the stuff of legend. Secretariat towered over the landscape, towers over it in perpetuity, the potent distillation of 250 years of breeding into the perfect specimen, the word made flesh, and that word was 'wow'.

He was voted Horse of the Year after his two-year-old campaign, a season of steadily heightening promise that was fulfilled in the most glorious manner the following year. Secretariat won the Triple Crown, beating poor big-hearted Sham in the Kentucky Derby and the Preakness and then breaking Sham's heart, his spirit, in the Belmont Stakes, which is generally agreed to be the greatest single performance of any running horse, at any time, in any place in history. It sounds a bold statement; watch the race. If the earth hadn't been round he would have run clean off the edge of it.

Secretariat won the Belmont by 31 lengths (thirty-one), without jockey Ron Turcotte touching him with the whip. He smashed the track record into little pieces, slicing almost two and a half seconds off the previous mark. Celebrated turf writer Charlie Hatton typed, with trembling hands, the words 'He could not have moved faster if he had fallen off the grandstand roof. His only point of reference is himself'. And when the day was done, and the counting over, there remained around 5,600 winning tickets on Secretariat left uncashed. People were keeping them for souvenirs. They'd already got their money's worth.

Secretariat's racing record was not perfect – he was beaten three times (and disqualified once) after the acceptable defeat on his debut – but everything else about him was. Seth Hancock, owner of the storied Claiborne Farm, where Secretariat stood as a stallion, paid him a tribute that matched in eloquence what it sought to praise.

'You want to know who Secretariat is in human terms? Just imagine the greatest athlete in the world. The greatest. Now make him six-foot-three, the perfect height. Make him real intelligent and kind. And on top of that, make him the best-lookin' guy ever to come down the pike. He was all those things as a horse.'

Secretariat was naturally voted Horse of the Year again and was retired to stud, where he was not an unqualified success, although the quality of his daughters and of their offspring ensured his name would live on in pedigrees. He died from the effects of laminitis in October 1989, whereupon the autopsy revealed his secret that to anyone who ever saw him run was no secret at all.

There are elements of horse physiognomy that are believed to imply certain characteristics. Big ears are said to suggest a generous, willing nature; a 'wall eye', one in which white can be seen around the rim of the eyeball, may indicate the opposite; a big frame, with unusually long legs, can be associated with unsoundness in wind and limb. Party Politics, winner of the 1992 Grand National, was uncommonly tall, almost 18 hands high, and bore out this theory. When he galloped he seemed to gambol, like a large Labrador puppy.

But it's what you can't see that counts. Heart of a lion? The heart of a horse is bigger, stronger. It drives him towards glory, and takes us along for the ride.

68

A rose for racing's greatest gardener.   *Image © Alamy*

WIT BY GILLETTE

He was the greatest trainer of Classic winners in Britain, but this alone does not explain the effect of Henry Cecil on racing. This complex, enigmatic, fascinating man, an aristocrat with the common touch, as happy tending to his rose garden as to his stable stars, lived his life on the redemptive rise-fall-rise narrative arc so beloved of storytellers and emerged at the end on top, the master of all he surveyed, where he belonged.

Cecil was born with a silver spoon in his mouth, later to be replaced with a cigarette, and inherited a powerful yard from his stepfather Sir Cecil Boyd-Rochfort, but his legacy was all his own work. He trained the first of more than 3,400 winners in May 1969 and sent out his first Classic winner in 1973 with Cloonagh in the Irish 1,000 Guineas, but his fortunes began truly to soar when he moved to the stables at Warren Place, just outside Newmarket, in 1977, the year after he had become champion trainer for the first time and saddled Wollow to win the 2,000 Guineas.

He would be champion ten times, would train 25 Classic winners in Britain, four Derbys, eight in the Oaks, six in the 1,000 Guineas and so on, 11 Classics in Ireland and France, and multitudes of other big-race winners, but more compelling than these exemplary statistics was the man himself, the way he trained and the way he conducted himself. His way with his horses was characterised by unlimited patience, never better illustrated than by his delicate handling of the sore-footed stayer Buckskin, whose defeat in the 1979 Gold Cup at the hands of stablemate Le Moss filled Cecil with sadness, even though he had trained the winner.

In his younger days he was an outlandish dandy of a clothes horse before graduating to his signature Hermes ties and Gucci loafers, and in his prime Cecil had a saturnine, smouldering aspect, as magnetic as any leading man. To see him holding court in the winner's enclosure, a willowy figure asking the pressmen as many questions as he was asked – 'What do you think, eh?' – head tilted to one side, fringe flopping foppishly into his eyes, lopsided grin on his face, clothes from Bond Street, wit by Gillette, was to witness a master in his merry element.

When the trophies had been collected, when the world-class self-deprecation was done, Cecil would go back to his hilltop eyrie at Warren Place and tend his garden, a quiet Eden crammed with fragrant rosebushes, pea plants that had been grown from peas found in Tutankhamun's tomb, germinating again after 3,000 years, vast beds of vegetables, a hothouse of orchids, a prehistoric tree. When night fell, he might be found in his boy's den of a study, with its shelves of lead soldiers and arcane artefacts gathered from heaven-knows-where and hoarded gleefully. If the day had brought a Group 1 winner, he would run the family standard up the flagpole in the garden; it saw plenty of use.

But after decades at the top, first slowly, then suddenly, in the way of things, it all went wrong for Cecil. Sheikh Mohammed took his horses away in 1995; Cecil's irreplaceable army of owner-breeders began literally to die out; in 2000, his twin brother David died, his marriage broke up, he was hit with a five-year drink-driving ban. The desolation in his personal life mirrored the disintegration of his career, the grinding, gradual break-up of an empire. The horses disappeared. In 1987, he trained 180 winners. In 2005, he trained 12 winners. The following year, he was diagnosed with stomach cancer. The fall from grace was absolute.

It is not whether you fall, though, but whether you give up or get up. Cecil never gave up. He got up, wore the same face in austerity as he had in prosperity, and won heartfelt admiration instead of races. Cecil had been top dog, now he was the underdog, and the British love an underdog, don't they? And soon, in the most unlikely, most uplifting, most thorough process of professional redemption imaginable, fortune's wheel began to roll back the other way.

His third marriage brought him peace, Oaks success in 2007 with Light Shift brought an extraordinary outpouring of delight at his long-awaited return to the top table, and a little later the bloodstock empire of Prince Khalid Abdullah, who had never deserted his old ally, brought him the horse of a lifetime, of any lifetime, in Frankel.

Frankel was the crowning glory of Cecil's renaissance. He was the best horse he trained, better than Derby winners Reference Point and Slip Anchor, better than the great fillies Oh So Sharp, Indian Skimmer, Diminuendo and Bosra Sham, better than the heroic stayers Ardross and Le Moss, better than Kris and Old Vic and Diesis and Royal Anthem. He was the best horse anyone has trained, but not anyone could have trained him, for he was an excitable, headstrong colt and may not have flourished without Cecil's masterly handling, his patience, his care, his innate, inimitable genius.

Yet by then Cecil's cancer had taken irreversible hold. He was dying, but the task of training Frankel kept him alive. In the winner's enclosure he now looked frail, tired, ill, and a little surprised at the waves of public adoration that crashed over him. Many trainers are admired, some are revered, but Cecil was indisputably loved. He unerringly guided Frankel through the greatness of an unbeaten career, a reflection not only of the horse's monumental ability but also of his trainer's.

Sir Henry Cecil died in June 2013. He was 70. There is a rose named after him, a white Floribunda. He would have liked that. He would also have liked, shyly, self-deprecatingly, perhaps with a lopsided smile, the fact that when he died, people who had never met him, who knew him only as a great trainer, a great man, mourned him as they would a friend.

69

Digging holes in racing's conscience.   *Image © Getty*

£4.75 A WEEK

Right, comrades, everybody out! The 1970s were a time of industrial strife, the three-day week, power cuts, strike action. The unrest spilled over into racing and manifested itself in what was described as the Battle of Newmarket in May 1975.

It does not sound like much money now, but the issue revolved around a matter of £4.75 a week. Newmarket stable staff had asked for a pay rise of 12 per cent, in those days of rampant inflation, to take their weekly pay packets up to £33.83, which was still no better than a minimum wage, and the National Trainers' Federation had dismissed it out of hand. The Transport and General Workers' Union sounded the traditional alarum, and more than 200 stable staff went on strike, although sufficient of them stayed at their posts to ensure the continued care of horses.

The militants converged on the Rowley Mile, and on 1,000 Guineas day, 1 May – International Workers' Day, aptly enough – began to fight for the cause. Horsebox windows were broken, picket lines were set up at the racecourse entrances, and before the race preceding the Classic a gang of strikers blocked the course and dragged Willie Carson from his horse Pericet.

Carson, who had hitherto supported the stable staff, changed his mind at this point, remounted and cantered back to the grandstands, where he marshalled an impromptu army of racegoers and told them that if they wanted racing to continue, they had better go and sort the strikers out. Which, with relish, they did.

The track was soon cleared, with the additional assistance of a cavalry charge from the other jockeys, and racing went ahead, the Guineas being won by Nocturnal Spree. Carson was reprimanded by the police for his actions, and the 'Battle of Newmarket' was not over.

Two days later, 2,000 Guineas morning dawned to the sight of holes dug all over the Rowley Mile, excavated by a bulldozer 'borrowed' from a nearby construction project. The holes were quickly filled in, but as the runners for the Guineas were on the point of being loaded into the stalls, around 150 strikers invaded the track and staged a sit-down protest. Several minutes and several arrests later, the course was once again cleared, the horses were assembled in a line 15 yards in front of the stalls, and the 2,000 Guineas was started by flag.

The race was won by 33-1 outsider Bolkonski from the favourite Grundy, becoming Henry Cecil's first British Classic winner. Tom Dickie, the winning groom, refused to lead his horse into the winner's enclosure, telling reporters: 'I am on strike because I am expected to support a wife and kid on the £28 I take home every week. I don't want to spend another 15 years in racing and only end up like I am now.'

Industrial action dragged on into the summer, with Royal Ascot proceeding without television coverage as the BBC's outside broadcast staff were unwilling to cross picket lines. Eventually, arbitration brought the two factions together in July and stable staff were awarded a pay increase of £4.40 a week, although goodwill was in short supply and 71 strikers were summarily sacked on their return to work. In the wake of the unrest the Stable Lads' Association was formed; it is now known as the National Association of Racing Staff.

It would take a heart of stone to not sympathise with the plight of Dickie and his cohorts, or with the stable staff in Lambourn who struck for better pay, a few more shillings a week, in May 1938 and were undermined by the use of blacklegs brought in under police escort to work at the yards. Stable staff are better served nowadays, with improved working conditions, reasonable rates of pay and widespread recognition of their efforts, but considering the fundamental role they play within the sport it would be hard to argue that they do not merit greater rewards.

70

The famed telephone box at Bellewstown. *Image © Racing Post*

A NON-EXISTENT DYING AUNT

The history of racing is richly marbled with tales of bets won or lost, big gambles gone astray, inventive wagers brought deliciously to fruition, the bookmakers howling as they grudgingly pay out a life-changing amount of money, the vicarious thrill for the bystander. The tale of Yellow Sam leads all the rest.

All the ingredients were there: a horse whose ability was probably a little better than his form suggested, a man with nerves of steel and a bagful of money, a minor race at a minor meeting, far from the long, poking nose of suspicion, and a trick, an angle, a dusting of genius. Yellow Sam, Barney Curley, Bellewstown in June 1975, big Benny O'Hanlon's dying aunt.

Curley, who died in May 2021 at the age of 81, was a legendary figure, a multi-faceted man, the mightiest warrior in the eternal battle with the bookmakers, a former Jesuit priest, a tireless campaigner and fundraiser for the Direct Aid For Africa charity, a fierce critic of racing's governance, a trainer of horses and young jockeys, a magnificent gambler. In the spring of 1975, he was low on funds, needed a winner. He asked his trainer Liam Brennan if he had a horse suitable to land a touch. Brennan did, a horse who had never won before, but might the next time.

A modest race was found, an amateur riders' hurdle at little Bellewstown, north of Dublin, and a good jockey, Michael Furlong, booked to ride. Curley had planned it all meticulously. He recruited an army of assistants to visit 300 betting shops and bet between £50 and £300 in old Irish punts on Yellow Sam, putting the money down in co-ordinated fashion 15 minutes before the race. The bookies wouldn't worry, for all they had to do was phone the racecourse and lay the money off with the on-course bookmakers. Unusually, there was only one phone box at Bellewstown races. This was Curley's crucial angle.

Twenty-five minutes before the race, one of Curley's associates, a big, burly man called Benny O'Hanlon, stood in the phone box and put a 'call' through to a non-existent hospital to enquire about a non-existent aunt who was dying. As O'Hanlon stood there, sucking on the sweets in his pocket, carrying on a one-way conversation with the dialling tone, people came to the phone box but were deterred from interfering by O'Hanlon's size and the poignant circumstances of his 'aunt'. All over Ireland, betting shop managers were on their phones, listening to the engaged tone, beginning to sweat. Yellow Sam was 20-1. When the race started, O'Hanlon put down the receiver. Job done.

It was the most brilliant coup. Yellow Sam was an easy winner. Curley, who watched the race from behind a bush in the infield to avoid making his presence known, cleared £306,000, the equivalent of £2 million today. It was a nice touch that he had to borrow a fiver for petrol to get home.

A much bigger, more straightforward gamble was landed by the five gentlemen of the Druid's Lodge Confederacy, also known as the Hermits of Salisbury Plain. So remote was their racing yard that they could plot in secrecy, while taking the precautionary measure of locking their stable lads up at night so they couldn't go out, get drunk and let slip vital information.

The kingpins of Druid's Lodge were Percy Cunliffe and William Purefoy, who placed all the bets. The horse in question was Hackler's Pride, a good three-year-old filly who was campaigned cleverly in order to be allotted a light weight for the 1903 Cambridgeshire, always one of the biggest betting races of the season. She was given 7st 1lb, and trainer Jack Fallon reckoned she had at least a stone in hand. He was right; Hackler's Pride, ridden by 15-year-old Jack Jarvis, won very comfortably.

It is estimated that the Confederates won around £250,000, which converts to the startling sum of £10 million in modern currency. The following year, Hackler's Pride won the Cambridgeshire again, and the men from Salisbury Plain won a similar amount.

So many gambles fail, so the ones that come off are worth remembering, relishing. Barry Hills won £60,000 (£1.5 million today) through backing Frankincense to win the 1968 Lincoln Handicap, which was enough to set him up as a trainer and begin a long and hugely successful career.

When Destriero won the 1991 Supreme Novices' Hurdle at the Cheltenham Festival, owner Noel Furlong landed £1.5 million in bets. Had stablemate The Illiad won the Champion Hurdle two races later, Furlong would have cleared around £5 million in singles and doubles. The Illiad had become dehydrated and finished last; what might have been.

In 1867, the victory of Hermit in the Derby made owner Henry Chaplin more than £100,000 richer in bets, and gave him glorious revenge over his former friend the Marquess of Hastings, who had stolen Chaplin's fiancee and bet heavily against the horse. Hastings was ruined, heartbroken, and died the following year at the age of 26.

Back to Curley, who was at it again in May 2010, collecting around £2 million when three of his horses, combined in trebles and accumulators, were backed at 25-1, 8-1 and 7-2 and won; had a fourth horse won, the payout would have been a record. In January 2014 he went one better, pulling off a phenomenal feat of planning and punting that involved four horses winning at three meetings to scoop a seven-figure return.

Some within racing look askance at such betting coups that often incorporate horses with poor recent form, reckoning that it looks bad for the sport and is unfair on losing punters who weren't in the know. Most, though, regard such gambles as part of the appeal of racing, something everyone would love to do if they could. The right horse, the right time, the right bet, the pleasure of being right and being paid handsomely for it.

71

Ginger, Red and the Southport surf.   Image © Getty

THE GREATEST STORY EVER TOLD

Red Rum was a one-off, a freak, an accident. Throughout his career he defied every precedent set, continually rising above unpromising surroundings like a wild rose set in stony ground. His triumphant, triumphal progress through life should not be put down to that of hope over expectation, but rather that of fantasy over reality. You couldn't have made it up.

The neat, average-sized bay horse who would win three Grand Nationals and in so doing become the most famous horse on the planet was meant to be a Flat horse, bred to stay no more than a mile, bought to be trained hard and land a gamble on his debut. He passed through more hands than a second-hand car and then found his spiritual home with a second-hand car dealer, who trained him on the local beach to mitigate the effects of what should by rights have been a career-ending injury to his foot. There has been no film dramatising the life of Red Rum, as there has been of the likes of Seabiscuit and Secretariat, probably because no audience would believe it. They called him a rags-to-riches Cinderella horse, and it was a fairy tale all right.

The most logical thing about Red Rum was his name. His sire was a good miler called Quorum, his dam was a carpet-chewing lunatic called Mared, and there in their names was his name. For all the vagaries of inheritance, he was an incredibly amenable beast, never showed a scintilla of temperament, although he always hated being clipped.

Red Rum was foaled in 1965, bought for 400 guineas as a yearling, had his first run in a five-furlong selling plate before his actual second birthday and dead-heated for first place with a horse named Curlicue, who had been born on the same farm, sold at the same sale as Red Rum. The race took place in April at Aintree. Funny how things work out.

It was a good start, especially as his owner Maurice Kingsley had had a big bet on him. Red Rum would run nine more times on the Flat, would win twice more, would even be ridden by Lester Piggott but not to victory. Then he was sold again, and again, and to cut a long and winding story short he ended up in the hands of Donald McCain, universally known as Ginger, a cheery, outspoken sort who had a second-hand car showroom in Southport and trained a few jumpers on the side, who bought Red Rum for 6,000 guineas for an octogenarian construction multi-millionaire called Noel Le Mare, an unlikely owner-trainer pairing.

The first time McCain worked Red Rum the horse was lame. He had already been diagnosed with chronic pedal osteitis in his off-fore, but McCain had not been aware. In exasperation McCain sent Red Rum walking through the surf on Southport beach, and he came back sound. So he always worked on the beach, always walked through the cold water, and his foot never troubled him again. In any other yard . . .

The 1973 Grand National was the eight-year-old Red Rum's 68th race, and most horses don't run 68 times in their entire lives. It was one of the most dramatic races ever run, with the big Australian two-mile chaser Crisp setting off at a sprinter's pace and maintaining it despite carrying 12 stone. With a mile to run he was 25 lengths clear, jumping magnificently, and looked as though he could never be caught. It would have been the greatest performance in National history, but poor Crisp was caught barely ten yards from the line, staggering with fatigue, and the horse who caught him was Red Rum. The course record went to the wind, broken by nearly 20 seconds.

Brian Fletcher rode him that day and again the following year, when Red Rum, never a bold jumper, always a clever, economical, deliberate jumper, a bright, intelligent horse, carried 12st himself and beat the dual Cheltenham Gold Cup winner L'Escargot by seven lengths. Two Grand Nationals! No horse had done that since Reynoldstown in the 1930s. No horse had ever won three.

It seemed as though no horse ever would. In 1975, the valiant L'Escargot took his revenge. In 1976, with Fletcher replaced by Tommy Stack, the huge Rag Trade had Red Rum's measure by two lengths. In 1977 . . . ah, there can't be anyone who doesn't know the story, the one that might be the greatest story ever told.

Red Rum returned to Aintree, where it had all started, for his fifth Grand National at the age of 12, with top weight of 11st 8lb and Tommy Stack to carry. His recent form had been poor, the newspaper tipsters disdained him, but his public still believed in him, making him 9-1 joint-second favourite. It was not the normal sort of National: outsider Boom Docker held an enormous lead until refusing at the first fence on the second circuit, possibly out of loneliness, and then clear leader Andy Pandy fell at Becher's Brook, and suddenly Red Rum was in front. For even in the best fairy-tales, the hero needs a little luck.

Two fences from home it was between he and Churchtown Boy, but that horse hit the fence hard, and then it was just Red Rum, the local hero, everybody's hero, this resilient, brilliant little horse, and he came galloping up to the line to win his third Grand National, making history that will never fade.

In retirement Red Rum opened betting shops, fulfilled all manner of public engagements, wore his celebrity lightly, the most famous horse in the world. He died in October 1995 at the grand age of 30, and his death led the news bulletins, a horse, imagine that, and he was buried near the winning post at Aintree, facing the finishing line.

And if you found any of that impossible to believe, no one could blame you at all.

72

The cradle of racing's super-owners.

FOUR BROTHERS

There are moments, almost always visible only in hindsight, that change the future completely, irrevocably. In racing, one of those moments occurred when four brothers from the royal family of the desert nation of Dubai decided to become involved in the sport, specifically in Britain. The changes wrought by that decision have been prodigious, profound and permanent.

The forerunner and most influential was Sheikh Mohammed bin Rashid Al Maktoum, the third of the brothers, whose interest in racing was piqued while he was studying at Cambridge and visited Newmarket, with his elder brother Sheikh Hamdan, to watch Royal Palace win the 2,000 Guineas in 1967. Ten years later, the filly Hatta opened his account as an owner when winning a maiden at Brighton.

Sheikh Hamdan's first winner was Mushref, at Redcar in July 1980, while the eldest brother, Sheikh Maktoum, had already got off the mark with Shaab, at Warwick in April 1979. The youngest of the four, Sheikh Ahmed, was the last to see his colours carried to victory but his first winner had a greater impact, Wassl winning the Group 3 Greenham Stakes at Newbury in 1983.

By then, Touching Wood had become the first Classic winner for the Maktoum brothers (1982 St Leger, owned by Sheikh Maktoum), and he was quickly followed by others, notably Ma Biche and Shadeed. At the same time, other Arab owners had made their way on to the stage. Saudi prince Khalid Abdullah, whose Juddmonte operation would grow to rival the Maktoums for quality, welcomed home his first winner in Britain, Charming Native, in May 1979.

Other less expansive but no less ambitious owners made their presence felt. The colours of Abdullah's son-in-law Fahd Salman, and his younger brother Ahmed Salman, soon became a familiar sight. Both would win the Derby, with Generous (1991) and Oath (1999). Even over the jumps, the owners' rankings were headed four times by Sheikh Ali Abu Khamsin, who owned 1983 Champion Hurdle winner Gaye Brief and winter stars Half Free and Fifty Dollars More.

Everyone was spending money in the 1980s boom, but sudden investment on the scale of the Maktoums had never been seen before. Oil had been located offshore in 1966 and Dubai was rapidly becoming an enormously wealthy state, and the purchasing power of the four sons of the emirate's ruler was practically unlimited. What they needed, what they wanted, they bought, particularly Sheikh Mohammed and Sheikh Hamdan: stud farms, horses in training, broodmares, yearlings at the sales, driving prices in the mid-1980s to stratospheric, unsustainable levels.

Inspired by the innate Arab love for the horse, beguiled by the history and tradition of British racing, and borne along by the fierce pride of making their small country a global powerhouse, the brothers steadily redrew the parameters of the sport, and their best horses became its pillars: Oh So Sharp, Pebbles, Indian Skimmer and Old Vic (Mohammed); Al Bahathri, Nashwan, Salsabil and Dayjur (Hamdan); Shareef Dancer and Green Desert (Maktoum); Mtoto (Ahmed).

In 1992, Sheikh Mohammed began the experiment that would grow into the Godolphin empire, with the development of racing in Dubai itself, through racecourses at Nad Al Sheba and then Meydan, allied to the ability to winter horses in a warm climate to accelerate their preparation for the European Classics. The first example was the filly Dayflower, and she was followed in short order by 1994 Oaks and Irish Derby winner Balanchine.

The success of the experiment has been almost unparalleled, featuring horses such as Dubai Millennium (Dubai World Cup), Daylami (Breeders' Cup Turf), Lammtarra (Derby), Sakhee (Prix de l'Arc de Triomphe), Masar (Derby) and the prepotent sire Dubawi (Irish 2,000 Guineas), and extending to two powerful stables in Newmarket and others in the US and Australia.

It is tempting but terrifying to wonder how British racing would look now, if the Maktoums had instead been consumed by another rich man's diversion. They have put into racing far more than they could ever hope to get out through prize-money and stallion fees, and their incalculable investment has led to Britain retaining its position as one of racing's superpowers.

But of course the brothers have grown old. Sheikh Maktoum died in 2006 and Sheikh Hamdan's death in March 2021 provided a poignant reminder, were one needed, that the permanence of empire is illusory. The task of maintaining the racing and breeding concerns of the four pathfinding Maktoums now falls to their children and grandchildren – Sheikh Mohammed's son Sheikh Hamdan bin Mohammed Al Maktoum has a substantial racing portfolio, while Sheikha Hissa Hamdan Al Maktoum has taken over as head of her father Sheikh Hamdan's extensive Shadwell estate – for the only thing that would have a greater effect on the sport than the family's presence, after so long, is its absence.

73

Warning: he bites. *Image © Alany*

THE ANGRY BRIGADE

Some villains wear a black hat, some carry a gun, some sit in a big chair and stroke a white cat. Others have big ears, big teeth, a long face and four legs, and are not so easy to spot.

Many horses have their quirks; some are defined by them. Occasionally the quirks are endearingly sweet, such as 1922 Derby winner Captain Cuttle being so devoted to trainer Fred Darling that he would follow him around like a dog. Occasionally the quirks are not sweet at all, but arbitrarily violent, physically threatening. Some horses belong in the hall of infamy.

Ubedizzy is the archetype, the point of reference for any late-night storytelling to curdle the blood, to bring nightmares. Ubedizzy was the recidivist's recidivist, the rogue of all rogues, a legend in his own lifetime. Oh, he had a temper. He was a good horse, a fast sprinter who finished fourth in a Nunthorpe Stakes, but his ability took a distant second place to his irascibility. His groom Andy Crook wore the scars of a thousand fraught mornings.

'He bit the end of my finger off, the ring-finger on my left hand. I'd ridden him out one morning and was taking off his tack when he lunged at me and bit my hand. You had to jump off him, not slide off, or he'd reach around and grab you. The times I used to come out of his box with a leg missing off my trousers, or my shirt torn to bits.'

Ubedizzy's innate misanthropy came to a head at Newmarket in April 1978 when, after finishing second in the Abernant Stakes, he knocked the unfortunate Martin Taylor, who had never taken him to the racecourse before, to the ground in the unsaddling enclosure, knelt on him and began to savage him. This sudden attack led to his being banned from British racing, although the more chilled-out authorities in Sweden welcomed him with open arms and he became champion sprinter there. But no horse is naturally malicious; there's always a reason.

'He had a warty growth in his armpit that was obviously quite tender,' added Crook. 'He had two girths on that day and jockey Edward Hide undid one and let it dangle while he undid the other. The dangling girth must have knocked Ubedizzy's armpit and annoyed him.'

Woe betide anyone who annoyed Ubedizzy. Other members of the Angry Brigade include Muley Edris, mentioned in an earlier chapter as the would-be assassin of Fred Archer; triple Champion Hurdle (1985-87) winner See You Then, described as 'a brute in his box, he either bit you or kicked you' by trainer Nicky Henderson; and the outstanding Flyingbolt, stablemate of Arkle, rated inferior to only 'Himself' and believed by some to have been even better than that paragon.

Flyingbolt, winner of the 1966 Champion Chase and third in the following day's Champion Hurdle, was brilliant, versatile and easily vexed. 'He was nasty, he'd bite you, it was just his temperament,' said work-rider Paddy Woods. 'He was like a man who'd injure you for fun and think nothing of it.' The children of trainer Tom Dreaper were warned to stay away from Flyingbolt, no pats or apples for that bad seed.

Others with a temper demonstrated it against their own kind, horse's inhumanity to horse. Marinsky was trained by Vincent O'Brien, but even his gentle genius couldn't mend this ill-tempered, irresolute rogue. In the 1977 Diomed Stakes at Epsom he attempted to savage Relkino three times before declining to go through with his effort, and even blinkers and a muzzle didn't stop him throwing in the towel at Royal Ascot. Marinsky did win the prestigious July Cup at Newmarket, but veered so violently left in the closing stages that the stewards had to disqualify him, and after that the Jockey Club banned him from racing.

The 1994 Gold Cup winner Arcadian Heights wore a net muzzle for the reasons that led to the famous form-book comment 'beaten when bit winner approaching final furlong'; the same year's St Leger winner Moonax tried to take a chunk out of a rival in a race in France, a propensity to violence well known to his groom Joyce Wallsgrave, who habitually wore a body protector and thick padding on her arms when dealing with her talented terror; Sir Ken, another triple Champion Hurdle winner (1952-54), reportedly fought and killed another horse when they were turned out together.

Sometimes, though, a solution is at hand. The great unbeaten St Simon, winner of the 1884 Gold Cup, was a model on the racecourse but a tartar at stud. He killed cats, assaulted grooms – one said, 'It's all very well to talk about the patience of Job, but Job never had to groom St Simon' – but his reign of terror ended when he was found to be frightened of umbrellas. In the absence of an umbrella, a bowler hat on the end of a stick was just as effective. Umbrellas? Ubedizzy would curl his lip in scorn.

74

Sha Tin rises from the sea. Image © Getty

SOMETHING OUT OF NOTHING

Faith can move mountains, they say, but so can bulldozers, manpower and ambition. All these things came together in Hong Kong in the mid-1970s to make something wonderful out of nothing much, to bring Sha Tin racecourse rising from the waves.

Racing in the colony, now the former colony, had begun with the opening in 1846 of Happy Valley, the astounding city racecourse set down among the skyscrapers on Hong Kong Island, although back then, to paraphrase the old phrase, it was all just fields.

The Royal Hong Kong Jockey Club was founded in 1884 (the 'Royal' was lost when Hong Kong returned to Chinese rule in 1997), but racing was an amateur sport and professional status was not established until 1971, which marked the opening up of the sport to overseas competitors, initially jockeys – Lester Piggott rode at an international jockeys' challenge in 1972 – and later trainers and horses. To underpin this heightened profile, the authorities embarked upon a project to double the number of racecourses available.

A site in the New Territories at Sha Tin was chosen, a little way north of the busy streets of Kowloon, but at that stage the footprint of the new racecourse was under water, beneath a slender arm of the South China Sea. In December 1973, construction started on a colossally ambitious reclamation project covering a 250-acre site, in which more than a million cubic yards of mud was removed from the shoreline and the resulting space filled with 16 million tons of material excavated from the surrounding mountains.

The project was met with opposition from local villagers, angry that the process of landfill would entail the removal of ancestral graves, and from fishermen whose catches had been affected by the work. The latter were involved in scuffles with police, but the reclamation work continued around the clock and was completed on time, and Sha Tin racecourse staged its first meeting in October 1978. The first race was won by outsider Money No Object, the perfect result for a racecourse that had cost HK$700 million to build.

Where Happy Valley is quixotic and compact, Sha Tin is more conventional, built to the global blueprint with wide, sweeping bends, a straight five-furlong course and an artificial track on the inside of the turf circuit, built to attract international competition. Now it is one of the premier racecourses in the world, with a retractable roof over the parade ring and an equine laboratory and hospital, and hosts almost all Hong Kong's major races.

The racing season in Hong Kong stretches from September to July, with meetings scheduled twice a week. Happy Valley races on Wednesday evenings while Sha Tin stages afternoon racing on Saturday or more usually Sunday. Prize-money is very high, crowds are considerable, the betting market is the strongest in the world, punters are provided with near-forensic levels of information about each horse, the biggest races have a global prestige, and the International meeting in December draws high-quality entries from around the world.

The ranks of owners and trainers are limited, for Hong Kong is a small place and the horse population is finite. Prospective owners are entered into an annual ballot to win the right to have a horse or two, while training licences are issued on a one-in-one-out basis, with numbers currently restricted to 22. Fail to win sufficient races in a season on three occasions, and you could be the one out.

Many horses from Britain and Ireland are purchased to race in Hong Kong because there is no local breeding programme, although the imports often have their names changed on arrival to suit the superstitions of owners. The 2018 Derby fifth Hazapour was rechristened Amazing One Plus; the 2020 Hong Kong Horse of the Year Exultant was known in Europe as Irishcorrespondent; and multiple

Group 1 winner Viva Pataca was called Comic Strip when trained in Britain.

In July 2018, the Hong Kong Jockey Club marked a further expansion to its estate with the opening of a training centre and racecourse at Conghua, in mainland China, approximately 200km from Sha Tin. The project was several years in construction and cost HK$3.7 billion, but this time there was no need to turn back the sea, and no mountains were moved.

75

Not for horses. *Image © Author*

THE SWEET-TOOTHED HORSE

According to the advertising jingle, a Mars a day helps you work, rest and play. According to the Jockey Club it also helps you win a hurdle race at Ascot.

No Bombs won his race at Ascot in 1979, and no one blinked. He was a talented horse. However, everyone was wide-eyed when the results of the usual post-race dope test were made public, for No Bombs tested positive for traces of caffeine and theobromine, stimulants that should not have been in his system, and he was disqualified.

Had he been doped? Was the supposedly murky world of racing reverting to type? Suspicion and accusation were rife, until the testimony of the stable lad was heard. Before the race he had been eating a Mars bar, but didn't get to finish it, for No Bombs had snatched it from his hand and wolfed it down. Half a Mars bar in the system of a half-ton horse is unlikely to have any enhancing effect on racing performance, but a positive test is a positive test and the sweet-toothed No Bombs was found his accidental place in racing history.

The history of doping is a dark chapter in racing's story. There is an obvious distinction to be made between doping to win and doping to lose, the introduction of a stimulant or a sedative, but most of the famous cases involve doping to lose. It is comparatively surer, as even with a stimulant in its system the doper cannot be certain that the horse will win the race.

The doping of horses was not even considered against the rules until 1904. The most notorious case before that date involved Daniel Dawson, who was recruited by a couple of bookmakers to 'stop' several horses and took the unsophisticated course of adding arsenic to their water, thereby stopping them permanently. He soon joined them in the hereafter; he was hanged for poisoning in 1812.

Punishments had become less irreversible by the time Bill Roper's gang cut a swathe through the country's racing stables in the early 1960s, with the unfortunate Pinturischio the most notable casualty. He had finished fourth in the 1961 2,000 Guineas and was favourite for the Derby, but at some point before his prep run at York there was a break-in at trainer Noel Murless's yard and 'Pint O'Sherry', as he was known, was 'got at'.

He missed his prep run but returned to work, and when he was seen on the gallops the dopers went back and dosed him a second time, aided by Pinturischio's lad Philip 'Snuffy' Lawler, who had been bribed. They used croton oil, an elephant laxative, and Pinturischio was never able to run again.

Roper's gang stopped many horses, but when he was finally brought to justice he was sentenced to just three years in prison. In an echo of this grisly tale, when the brilliant two-year-old Gorytus was well beaten at odds-on in the 1982 Dewhurst Stakes, it was believed that a dose of croton oil had been responsible, but jockey Willie Carson maintained that the horse was simply off colour.

As testing became more sophisticated, so did the dopers. In August and September 1990, former top jump jockey Dermot Browne doped 23 horses – the most high-profile being Bravefoot, Norwich and Timeless Times – with a syringeful of ACP (acepromazine), a fast-acting sedative, earning himself the sobriquet 'The Needleman'. The horses were injected in the hour before their races, prompting enormous concerns over racecourse security.

Browne was working for race-fixer and drug smuggler Brian Wright, known as 'The Milkman' because he always delivered. Such cosy nicknames should not ameliorate the disgraceful activities of which both were guilty. Browne and Wright were warned off for 20 years. ACP was also used to dope Viking Hoard before a race at Tramore in October 2018.

Such lawlessness is not only the province of the gutter. In April 2013, the revelation that Mahmood Al Zarooni, trainer to Sheikh Mohammed's Godolphin empire, had been administering his horses with anabolic steroids shocked the racing world. Al Zarooni was banned for eight years at a hurried assizes following the discovery that 11 horses in his yard, including Encke, who denied Camelot the Triple Crown when winning the St Leger, had been doped.

The scandal, striking at the heart of Newmarket, the spiritual home of horse racing, was earth-shattering. It later emerged that 22 of Al Zarooni's horses had tested positive for steroids, including Gold Cup runner-up Opinion Poll. Across town, eight months later, trainer Gerard Butler was disqualified for five years after nine of his horses tested positive for the steroid stanozolol.

Such incidents cause great damage to the reputation of racing, but are mercifully very rare, and when they do occur no leniency is granted to the guilty parties. Uniquely, though, one such offender got away scot-free.

Hill House, trained by Ryan Price, tested positive for the steroid cortisol after winning the 1967 Schweppes Gold Trophy at Newbury, and Price was in serious danger of losing his licence as a result. However, Hill House was then sent to the Equine Research Station in Newmarket, where it was discovered that he had a naturally occurring high level of cortisol in his body, and the case against his trainer was dismissed. Hill House was, in effect, dosing himself on a daily basis, and was allowed to continue his regime of doping.

76

Whipping up a storm. *Image © Edward Whitaker*

THE END AND THE MEANS

The subject of the whip is the most emotive in modern racing, and makes for unsatisfactory debate because the two opposing parties are so entrenched in their beliefs that accord, or even the willingness to begin the process of changing outlook, is practically impossible.

One side, the 'horsemen' within the industry, considers the whip an essential tool and a half-ton horse well able to withstand a few hearty cracks with it in the course of its six-runs-a-year job. The other, a public that has become entirely detached from the horse as an everyday object, sees only small angry men beating their noble steeds in the ugly pursuit of money. It might be viewed as a skirmish between arrogance and ignorance, and the truth, as ever, lies in between.

The pivotal moment in the whip debate may have come at Cheltenham in March 1980, when Joe Byrne and Tommy Ryan were suspended for three months for flagrantly excessive use of the whip. A review of the races in question is not particularly palatable: Byrne, aboard Batista, hits his horse around 15 times from the final flight, the majority of them full-arm heavy blows and a few down the shoulder. Ryan, riding Drumlargan, hits the same number of times, several down the side of his horse's face, abandoning the process of race-riding and letting the whip do all the work.

From this remove the suspensions barely seem long enough, although such 'energetic' whip use was not uncommon in that era. Lester Piggott beat Roberto and The Minstrel like a carpet when winning Derbys in the 1970s, and was lauded for his muscular route to victory. In Australia, jockey Mick Dittman was nicknamed 'The Enforcer' for his unsparing use of the whip and regarded as the best rider of his generation. Byrne and Ryan may have been unlucky to be singled out, but they certainly made all their own luck.

What has changed since then? The whip itself, for starters. It was of course once the long, thin, vicious instrument that people immediately think of when the word arises, but now it is shorter, wider, air-cushioned, not so much a whip as a well-padded stick. Experiments on humans holding out their hands like Tom Brown in his schooldays suggest that the modern whip causes a fraction of the discomfort of the old whip but makes more noise, the intention being to 'encourage' the horse with sound rather than fury.

There are also rules outlining the frequency of whip use. Very broadly speaking, jockeys are allowed to use the whip seven (Flat) or eight (jumps) times before the line is crossed and the stewards step in with the threat of sanctions, which means a short suspension and the possibility of a fine if the offence is deemed sufficiently serious. It should be emphasised, and cannot be emphasised enough, that real misuse of the whip, a la Byrne and Ryan, no longer occurs. Horses are struck with the whip but are never thrashed with it.

The main problems with the whip are two-fold. There can be a win-at-all-costs mentality among jockeys, almost exclusively in the biggest races, that leads them to flout the whip rules to win the valuable, prestigious race and take a fine and ban as part of the deal. If two more smacks with the whip might win the Derby, even though the threshold for whip use has been reached, human nature dictates that two more smacks will happen, the end justifying the means. The jockey's percentage will take care of the fine, a few days off is not a horrific prospect, and after all the jockey is now a Derby winner, with all the concomitant professional satisfaction and recognition.

There are frequent calls for the winner to be disqualified if the jockey has broken the whip rules, the standing sanctions clearly not a deterrent, but there are unsatisfactory corollaries to that, not least the fact that owner and trainer are not guilty of breaking the rules but are still being punished. Conversely, the disqualification of one Derby winner would be deterrent enough to ensure the rules were never broken again, but it's a big step to take.

The other main problem is immune to regulation, it being the ingrained perception that men are hitting animals in the name of sport, something that is impossible to explain away, even calmly and logically, to an audience that has no intention of listening to an opinion that contradicts their own.

The fact is inescapable: jockeys hit horses. For an increasing number, that's the end of the story, there is no distinction drawn between one smack on the rump to focus concentration and will, and a sound thrashing. But is there anything wrong with giving a horse, in the heat of competition, one smack with a padded stick behind the saddle to encourage it to do the job it was bred for, trained for?

In Norway, whips are not permitted. In Sweden, three strikes is the limit. In Germany, it is five. Jockeys maintain that they need to carry a whip for correction, if required, and that notion is impossible to contradict. Horses are animals, and cannot be talked out of dangerous situations. One sharp strike with the whip may prevent serious injury to rider and horse.

That point taken, the future of the whip in Britain – and elsewhere – depends on walking the invisible line between practice and perception. There is surely the potential to reduce the threshold to five strikes or fewer, and to increase the penalties for crossing that threshold.

Education in regard to whip use is probably a red herring. It is either accepted in some form or it isn't, a binary reality, and the devil's advocate would ask which should be educated, the pro-whip or the anti-whip faction? It still seems unlikely that use of the whip for encouragement will be banned in Britain, but 20 years down the line the conversation may have a different aspect.

77

Here lies the Golden Age.   Image © Tom Denham

LEGENDS IN THEIR LIFETIMES

There were giants upon the earth in those days. It may be fashionable to decry the 1970s as the decade that taste forgot, glam rock, punk, prawn cocktail and Liebfraumilch, but as far as two-mile hurdlers go the 1970s were a golden age the like of which will never come again.

Between 1968 and 1981, the Champion Hurdle at the Cheltenham Festival was won by just seven horses, a magnificent seven whose names blow like a summer breeze through the windmills of the mind. For sustained, repetitive, remarkable quality, there has never been a span like it in any branch of the sport.

Persian War ushered in the storm, winning three Champion Hurdles (1968-70), although if his owner Henry Alper had been even the slightest bit conventional in his dealings Persian War's life would have been much simpler. He was moved from yard to yard, but stayed with Colin Davies long enough to complete that Cheltenham hat-trick. A bid for a fourth Champion Hurdle was denied by Bula, whose trademark flying finish helped light up jump racing in those dark days of nationwide power cuts.

Bula's name means 'hello' in Fijian, but it was usually goodbye where his rivals were concerned. He showed his best when anaesthetised by the apparently nerveless Paul Kelleway at the back of the field until it seemed too late, before being jolted awake and instantly into top gear, sprinting away. His championships for trainer Fred Winter came in 1971 and 1972 and he then passed on the torch to Comedy Of Errors (trained by Fred Rimell), then Lanzarote (also trained by Winter), then Comedy Of Errors again.

Over three seasons, these two horses indulged in an absorbing, ongoing duel for the mastery, and when they had finished the score stood at 4-4. Neither horse liked Cheltenham all that much, their brilliance seeing them through, and when Comedy Of Errors wrested the Champion Hurdle back from Lanzarote in the bottomless mud of 1975 he became the first horse to regain the crown after losing it. After such a sequence of outstanding champions, an interregnum might have been expected, a natural vacancy until the next household god came along, but with no time to draw breath the next six seasons surpassed even that which had come before.

Night Nurse, a big burly bully of a horse who liked to batter the opposition into submission from the front, was the first to step forward. Described by trainer Peter Easterby as 'hard and very brave', he galloped his rivals into the ground under jockey Paddy Broderick to take the title in 1976. A year later, he took on a field that was pound-for-pound, as the boxing writers say, the finest ever assembled for the Champion Hurdle, and is still the finest.

There were ten runners in the 1977 Champion Hurdle, and seven of them would have won any championship in an era less gilded. The favourite was Bird's Nest, a riddle of a horse who ran in six Champion Hurdles without winning, the best horse never to claim the crown. His stablemate Beacon Light, Night Nurse's stablemate Sea Pigeon, third-favourite Dramatist and Irish cracks Monksfield and Master Monday completed this 'team of all the talents', and Night Nurse won the shootout after five horses jumped the second-last hurdle in unison, stretched across the track in a line of beauty that glowed through the dim light.

Runner-up was Monksfield, trained by Des McDonogh, and if Night Nurse was hard and very brave then Monksfield was very hard and impossibly brave. The little entire horse who raced with his head low and his front legs flailing wildly was often asked for his all and always gave it gladly. The following year he reached the top, beating Sea Pigeon and Night Nurse, and in 1979 he stayed there, seeing off Sea Pigeon in one of the all-time great Cheltenham finishes.

Monksfield was under pressure at the final hurdle and Sea Pigeon was cruising, but he lived for a scrap and would not knuckle under. With 100 yards to go the two were level, no quarter asked, none given, but

Monksfield's grit and guts would not be denied and the mighty little fighter clawed his way to the line in front, three-quarters of a length ahead.

Sea Pigeon, a son of the peerless Sea-Bird, was racing aristocracy who had finished seventh in the 1973 Derby and would steadily blossom into the greatest dual-purpose horse ever seen. His Flat-race pedigree had endowed him with a terrifying turn of foot, and in 1980, at the age of ten, the stiletto of his speed saw off the bludgeon of Monksfield's tenacity and there was a new champion.

Twelve months later, the old boy became the joint-oldest to win a Champion Hurdle when sprinting home like a youngster, jockey John Francome delaying his challenge until five seconds after 'too late' and Sea Pigeon going from 0-60 within three strides for a thrillingly audacious victory.

The golden age was over, but its golden glow still sustains. Persian War, Bula, Comedy Of Errors, Lanzarote, Night Nurse, Monksfield, Sea Pigeon, such names, such horses, that if the Champion Hurdle were run for a thousand years, men and women would say that this was its finest hour.

Night Nurse, probably the greatest of them all, and his scintillating stablemate Sea Pigeon lived part of their retirement together, and when Night Nurse died at the age of 27 he was buried just outside trainer Easterby's front door. Two years later Sea Pigeon, at 30, followed him into eternity, and was buried alongside his old friend, his old rival.

A plaque over them gives their names, dates and career details, all suffixed by the words 'legends in their lifetimes'. The epitaph might stand for them all, those 24-carat characters of the golden years.

78

Who wants to be a millionaire?   *Image © Getty*

SEVEN-LETTER, SEVEN-FIGURE WORD

Depending on who you listen to, money talks, or it swears, or it makes the world go around. All those character traits were in play when the first million-dollar race was conceived, a watershed moment for the sport.

Racing has always been a high-stakes game but a cool million? That was a game-changer.

In May 1981, Pleasant Colony earned his owner $317,200 when winning the Kentucky Derby, and the Aga Khan became £149,900 richer when Shergar won the Derby a month later. At an exchange rate of roughly two dollars to the pound, the races were of similar value. Tradition and heritage still led the way, and the financial rewards underlined that.

Not for much longer. In August 1981, the Arlington Million was run for the first time, a brand-new race, fresh out of the wrapper, and at a stroke the old certainties were gone. New races were minted all the time, but never before had one been designed to make such a splash. Joe Joyce, the enterprising president of Arlington Park in Chicago, wanted to put his racecourse on the world map, and what better way to do that than a brash proposition, the fabled sum of a million dollars?

The name of the race alone, that lurid seven-letter, seven-figure word, was enough to beguile its audience. The race was framed to tick the international boxes, a mile and a quarter on turf, and it drew runners from France, Britain and Ireland, all bidding for that mind-blowing $600,000 first-place prize-money, almost twice as much as any horse had won in one place before.

The big pot got the big finish it deserved, with all-American hero John Henry prevailing in a breathless finish by half a whisker from The Bart, and Madam Gay, trained by 'Pattern-race' Paul Kelleway, whose reach forever exceeded his grasp, taking third spot for Britain. The incredible John Henry would win the Million again three years later at the age of nine, but by then a million-dollar race was no longer the biggest show in town.

Currency conversions can muddy the water, so dollars have been used throughout except for conversions to sterling in the most recent examples.

In November 1984 the inauguration of Breeders' Cup day raised the ante, with five races worth a million dollars, the Breeders' Cup Turf worth $2 million, and the purse for the Classic an astonishing $3 million. In 1996 the Classic lost its status as the world's richest race with the inception of the Dubai World Cup, which offered a purse of $4 million and winner's prize of $2.4 million, Sheikh Mohammed's statement of intent to the sport.

The Dubai World Cup held its place as the world leader, with a prize fund eventually totalling $10 million, until January 2017 and the first running of the eccentrically named Pegasus World Cup at Gulfstream Park. This race had a prize fund of $12 million and a year later was worth $16 million, although its bubble would soon burst and by 2020 it was a mere also-ran with a $3 million purse, barely worth getting out of bed for.

By 2019, Sheikh Mohammed's unlimited financial muscle had pushed the Dubai World Cup back to the top of the charts, sitting pretty with $12 million, but he was swiftly outdrawn by the organisers of another new race, the nine-furlong Saudi Cup in Riyadh, which was worth $20 million (£7.5 million to the winner) when run for the first time in 2020. At the time of writing, this is the most valuable prize on offer in horse racing, although there is no knowing how long that will remain the case.

The Saudi Cup is run on an artificial surface; the most valuable prize on turf belongs to the AUS$16 million (£3.5 million to the winner) provided by The Everest, a six-furlong contest run at Randwick, Sydney. The Melbourne Cup holds second place on the turf list ahead of the Prix de l'Arc de Triomphe, Japan Cup and Dubai Sheema Classic, but prize-money in Britain is notoriously scanty in comparison with the rest of the world and the Derby has yet to offer its winner a seven-figure remuneration.

The numbers have lost their power to shock, to amaze, so blase have we become to the inflationary rewards of the sport. Remember when a million dollars was enough? Those were the days.

79

He was never seen again.

TAKEN

It is a source of regret that for all his majestic brilliance, his long summer of greatness, Shergar is most remembered for what happened away from the racecourse. For so many, the image of his unearthly ten-length victory in the 1981 Derby has been blotted out by the shadow of what befell him two years later.

The newspaper headlines, the news bulletins, the air of disbelief and outrage, those are the sharpest memories of Shergar, and afterwards the regular use of his name as a punchline. He deserved so much better than these.

Shergar (foaled 1978) showed considerable promise as a two-year-old for trainer Michael Stoute and fulfilled it with the most dazzling campaign at three, not just winning his races but dismantling his opposition: the Sandown Classic Trial by ten lengths, the Chester Vase by 12 lengths, the Derby by that mesmerising ten, the Irish Derby by four and the King George by four again. He was almost of another world, and can be forgiven his leaden fourth place in the St Leger in the context of what had come before. He retired to the Ballymany Stud of his owner the Aga Khan, near the Curragh, sired his first crop, and was ready to sire a second.

What happened next is a mixture of facts and conjecture. It is certain that in the evening of 8 February 1983, a Tuesday, Shergar was taken from Ballymany Stud by a group of armed men, loaded into a horsebox and driven away. The police were not called for another eight hours, owing to the difficulty of contacting the Aga Khan, who was in Switzerland. The police investigation would come to be ridiculed as painfully inept, with the chief investigators regarded as figures of fun for their lack of initiative.

Someone claiming to be one of the thieves had already spoken to trainer Jeremy Maxwell, who was unconnected to Shergar, informing him that a ransom must be paid for the horse's safe return. There then followed a darkly comical chain of events in which terms were negotiated through three racing journalists, including John Oaksey and Derek Thompson, who were taken to Maxwell's house for that purpose. In the early hours of Thursday morning, Thompson kept his man on the phone long enough for the call to be traced but, farcically, the technician who did the tracing had finished his shift and gone home an hour earlier.

These conversations were a diversionary tactic. On the Wednesday, the 'kidnappers' had made contact with the Aga Khan's stud manager Ghislain Drion and demanded a ransom of £2 million. The Aga Khan refused to pay any ransom, and in any case Shergar had been syndicated for stud and now had 35 owners, all of whom would have had to grant permission for a ransom to be paid.

By Friday, the 'kidnappers' were losing patience. The shareholders had demanded proof that the horse was still alive, and although a photo of Shergar was supplied, with a newspaper showing that day's date, it was not accepted as sufficient proof by the shareholders and negotiations were broken off the following day, never to be resumed. It was over.

Who took Shergar? The Provisional IRA have never admitted to involvement in the affair, and the evidence does no more than hint that way, but it is generally considered that they were responsible. The aftermath of the abduction has been strewn with hoaxes, diversions, madcap theories and fabrications, but it nevertheless seems likely that Shergar was taken to a remote location to await the outcome of ransom negotiations.

It is possible that Shergar became unruly – he was a stallion, and consequently not straightforward to manage – and was killed by his abductors when they could not cope with him. This may have happened within hours of his theft, which seems most likely, or within a day or two, or after negotiations had irretrievably broken down. His body was reportedly buried somewhere near Ballinamore, close to the border between Ireland and Northern Ireland, but no trace of it has been found.

In the near-40 years since Shergar's disappearance, there have been occasional rumours that his bones have been unearthed, or new theories propounded to clarify the events of those frantic few days. Nothing significant or useful has ever come to light.

It is time to leave Shergar now, to leave him in peace. His only crop of 35 foals produced Irish St Leger winner Authaal and Maysoon, placed in the 1,000 Guineas and Oaks, but his name has all but vanished from the pedigree pages, although it remains attached to the Shergar Cup, the international jockeys' competition held each August at Ascot.

Try to forget the circumstances of his death and remember him on that irreducible day at Epsom, when he drew further away from his Derby rivals than any horse has ever done. It was a performance that might have been even more remarkable had Walter Swinburn not eased him down in the final furlong, the race over, history in the making, Shergar's future at that point as bright as the sunlight sparkling on his jockey's silks. Let that be his legacy instead.

80

The Famous Five. *Image © Racing Post*

COME ON MY LOT!

There are several unofficial definitions of the word 'genius'. There's the one about inspiration and perspiration, and the one about the infinite capacity for taking pains, which are largely the same thing. Another definition, particular to racing people, is 'Michael Dickinson'. Many people have moments of genius, but Dickinson personified the quality.

They call Dickinson the Mad Genius, for his unorthodoxy, for his talent. This tall, boyish Yorkshireman's doctrine of painstaking preparation woven through with a natural empathy for the horse and for the business of training, fuelled by his restless energy, leavened with a light dusting of that rarest of elements – genius – brought him repeated success at the top level over jumps and on the Flat. In March 1983 he defined himself, and his career, with the most extraordinary training performance.

The story of the Famous Five is not children's fiction but racing fact. Dickinson saddled five runners in the Cheltenham Gold Cup, the most prestigious race of the season, and they finished 1-2-3-4-5. He suffered for his art, the tension of the build-up to the race pared a stone from Dickinson's already spare frame, he found sleep hard to come by and was burned out from exhaustion by raceday, but his art will hang forever on the walls of the pantheon.

Dickinson was the scion of a notable racing family. His father Tony, known as 'The Boss', and his mother Monica, 'Mrs D', held the training licence with great success before and after their son, but it was the young man's four-year tenure in the hot seat that redrew the map. His nickname? His mother called him 'Silly Boy'.

The silly boy had sent out Silver Buck and Bregawn to be first and second in the 1982 Gold Cup, and practically as soon as the ink had dried on those headlines he was planning a repeat on a much grander scale. As a man might, he talked to his wife about it. Dickinson being Dickinson, though, there was a different cast to the conversation. 'I predicted we would have the first five in the Gold Cup 12 months before the race, but only in the privacy of my car to my wife Joan,' he said. 'She probably heard the commentary for the 1983 Gold Cup 50 times before the race was even run.'

At that time, Dickinson had no more than 55 horses in his yard. For five of them to be good enough for a Gold Cup is one thing, to bring them carefully through a long season and have them at concert pitch on the day that mattered is quite another. Injuries hampered his plans, and the media attention on this young man of 33 was intense, but neither his concentration nor his confidence ever wavered.

Bregawn (ridden by Graham Bradley) was favourite in an 11-runner field; Silver Buck (Robert Earnshaw) and Wayward Lad (Jonjo O'Neill) were prominent in the betting; Captain John (David Goulding) and Ashley House (Dermot Browne) less fancied. Eerily, Dickinson's wife Joan would recall that the race played out in exactly the way those in-car commentaries suggested it would.

Dickinson watched the race on a small television near the weighing room, watched in silence until the field swept round the home turn towards the second last, until a year's tension escaped from him in one heartfelt exclamation. 'Come on, my lot!' he shouted, and on they came.

The wonderful little Bregawn made most of the running, stayed on strongly after the last to win by five lengths. Captain John, who had jumped the last alongside him, was second, followed by Wayward Lad and Silver Buck. And then everyone was looking back down the track. Where was Ashley House? Never can so much excitement have surrounded fifth place in a championship race. There he was, keeping on gamely, a long way behind but no matter. He finished fifth. Did you ever see the like?

All five were shepherded into the winner's enclosure in recognition of a feat that is unlikely to ever be equalled, let alone surpassed. That can also be said for another of Dickinson's incredible achievements, for earlier that season he had set a world record for winners trained in a day.

On 27 December 1982, Dickinson sent out 12 winners across the busy holiday programme, including first and third in the showpiece King George VI Chase at Kempton, and from his 20 runners that day only one failed to finish in the first three. The silly boy was quite a clever chap, really.

He was champion trainer three years running, his top horses including the aforementioned and also Champion Chase winners Rathgorman and Badsworth Boy, and The Mighty Mac, but in 1986 he stunned the racing world by changing focus to the Flat, becoming private trainer to Robert Sangster. The move was a disaster – his gallops had to be relaid, his horses were immature and unproven – and he was dismissed at the end of the year. His reputation suffered, but his work ethic and fierce ambition did not, and he transplanted himself to the US, where he set up as a trainer in Maryland.

Fifteen years after the Famous Five, Dickinson set the seal on his personal reinvention, his public reputation and his inimitable genius when winning the 1998 Breeders' Cup Mile with Da Hoss, who had won the race two years earlier but had only run once since, owing to chronic problems with his feet and legs. Dickinson rebuilt him, renewed him, and amazed US racing, although such feats were no surprise to those who knew him of old.

This most approachable and cheerful of trainers turned in his licence in 2007 in order to focus on his hugely successful invention Tapeta, a synthetic racing surface that carpets many of the world's major racecourses. A genius, yes, but something else, something more. Dickinson was a perfectionist, and he attained his goal.

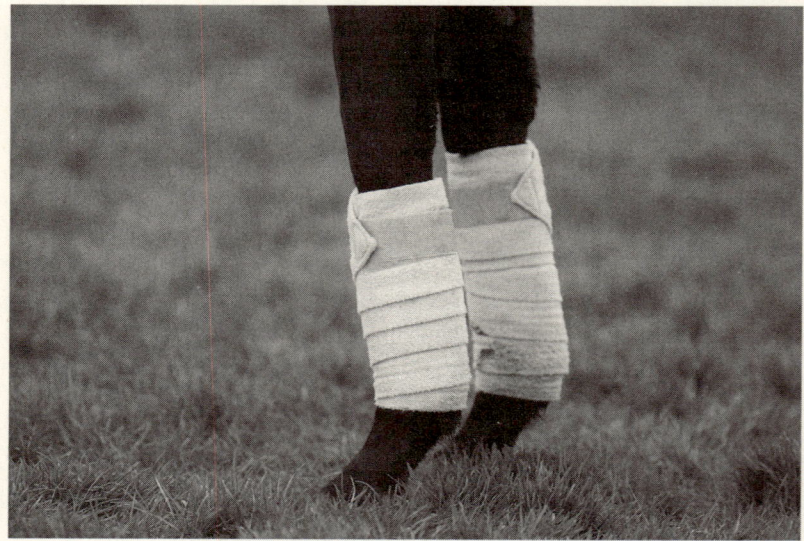
Bandages first, Queen Mother later.   Image © Racing Post

ALL ABOUT THE HORSES

By the early 1980s, everyone in racing had become used to women training racehorses. In an earlier chapter, the tale of Florence Nagle explained how it all came about. The message was still stuck inside the bubble, though, almost a secret from the outside world. It took a flashy chestnut named Corbiere and an unflashy trainer called Jenny Pitman to change perception forever.

Nagle may have unlocked the door, but Pitman threw it open. There is no better way to advertise your own abilities, and educate the ignorant about the skill and potential of your fellow women, than to stand in front of a television audience of 600 million and explain how you won the most famous race in the world, the Grand National. The message came across loud and clear.

Pitman was never afraid to voice her opinion, never known to back down from confrontation. She couldn't afford that luxury, she was a woman in a man's world, and once or twice threw a punch at a jockey to reinforce that status. By her own admission she was not as good with humans as she was with horses, but she was brilliant with horses. She trained her first winner in May 1975, spent a few years patching up the lame and halt and reinvigorating the jaded, getting herself ready should that one good horse come along. It would.

In December 1982, she trained Corbiere to win the Welsh National at Chepstow, a victory that underlined the horse's suitability for the Grand National. She knew all about the demands of that race, for her ex-husband Richard Pitman had come so close aboard the gallant Crisp ten years earlier, and she had tried her luck at Aintree already in her career, but only with outsiders. Corbiere was cut from different cloth.

He was the archetypal Pitman horse: a thorough stayer, brave and tough and durable, a type with which she would become synonymous. As it turned out, Corbiere wasn't even the best-fancied National contender trained by a woman, for Helen Hamilton saddled her own Welsh National winner in Peaty Sandy, who was a point shorter in the betting, but destiny was in Pitman's corner. On a bright, blue-skied April afternoon Corbiere raced prominently under jockey Ben De Haan, taking a clear lead at the second last and galloping on generously to see off the late challenge of Greasepaint by three-quarters of a length.

'Trailblazer?' she said in a later interview. 'I was just somebody who had to earn a living. There were plenty of flagbearers before me who showed a lot more courage and determination.'

But the significance of the result was not lost on anyone. On the way home from Aintree, she stopped at a service station and was recognised and congratulated by staff and customers, and Pitman quickly became one of the public faces of the sport, forthright, accessible, emotional, her heart in the right place, on her sleeve. Her appearances on the nation's televisions became a regular occurrence.

Corbiere would run in four more Nationals, twice finishing third, but Pitman's crowning glory was the bad-legged champion Burrough Hill Lad, who followed victory in the 1983 Welsh National with a towering performance to win the 1984 Cheltenham Gold Cup, giving her the honour of becoming the first female trainer to land jumping's two greatest prizes.

If the outstanding Burrough Hill Lad was her greatest horse, Corbiere was her bravest. Royal Athlete, who won her a second Grand National in 1995, was arguably the toughest, Pitman nursing him back to health in her patient, painstaking fashion after he had sustained a dreadful leg injury at Newbury. Four years earlier she had trained Garrison Savannah to win her another Gold Cup, this time partnered by her son Mark in a family triumph.

As for most women, respect for her achievements came grudgingly at first, then more genuinely. She had become the first top-rank female trainer, she had rocked the boat, and for many in the sport that took a little getting used to. Success breeds envy at the best of times, and some men couldn't handle being beaten at their own game, which Pitman seemed to do quite often.

She retired in 1999, with practically every major staying chase in the calendar on her roll of honour, including the King George VI Chase, the Hennessy, the Irish National and Scottish National. Few trainers, male or female, have had the empathy and affinity with the long-distance chaser that Pitman demonstrated so frequently and so effectively. For her, it was all about the horses. Nothing else, owners, other trainers, jockeys, the media, even the Queen Mother left to wait in the royal box while Pitman bandaged Burrough Hill Lad's legs after the Gold Cup, mattered as much to her.

When she started training, women didn't win big races. By the time she finished training, big-race success for women was not only accepted but expected. Pitman, an inspirational figure, led the way.

82

Caveat emptor.   Image © Alamy

NO BLOODY GOOD

Snaafi Dancer is one of the most famous horses in the racing world, but for all the wrong reasons. He fetched a world-record price as a yearling, but he couldn't run, he couldn't breed, and his name became a byword for excess and folly and schadenfreude.

His instant celebrity was purely a product of circumstance. In 1983, two racing superpowers were engaged in a duel for supremacy, old money against new money, an escalating struggle that was conducted in a blizzard of banknotes. In the green and blue corner was Robert Sangster, Vincent O'Brien and their Coolmore cohorts, in the maroon and white corner was Sheikh Mohammed, and over the course of the previous few months they had sparred with each other over the pick of the yearling crops.

The offspring of sire supreme Northern Dancer were the most valuable commodity in the sport. Prices had been driven beyond a realistic level, but this had ceased to be about simply buying horses and was now an exercise in explosive, expensive pride, all about saving face and braggadocio. So when the bay colt by Northern Dancer out of the mare My Bupers, thus a half-brother to champion US sprinter My Juliet and Group 1-placed Lyphard's Special, entered the salering at

Keeneland on a sultry July evening it was as though he was walking into a gladiatorial arena. Both sides wanted him, but more pertinently, neither side wanted the other to have him.

Bidding on Lot 308 started at $1 million. Forty-five seconds later, the previous world-record price for a yearling lay in smithereens as Colonel Dick Warden, the gentleman of the old school who advised Sheikh Mohammed, nodded his head at $4.5 million. The auctioneer knew where to look next. Joss Collins, bidding for the Sangster cartel, went blow for blow with Warden all the way up to $9 million. Warden took it to $9.6 million.

The only winner here was the vendor, Don T. Johnson, a coal-mining magnate who had struck gold when he bought My Bupers. A moment of silence, and then Collins bid $10 million, an amount so large it exceeded the capabilities of Keeneland's dot-matrix 'scoreboard'. There was barely time to draw breath before Warden raised his hand to bid $10.2 million, and Collins shook his head.

Sheikh Mohammed had won the war, but he would lose this particular battle. The colt was named Snaafi Dancer, was shipped to Britain and put in training with John Dunlop. His appearance was eagerly awaited . . . and awaited . . . and awaited.

Snaafi Dancer never raced. He couldn't run fast enough to keep himself warm; his work on the gallops was reportedly so disappointing that if he had appeared on a racecourse it might have been embarrassing. Oh, well. At least he still had the bloodline, the Northern Dancer magic to pass on to his offspring. Snaafi Dancer was practically infertile. He sired four foals, one of which won a race.

It is a hard word in black and white, but Snaafi Dancer was useless. He eventually found his way to 'retirement' in Florida, just the place for those who can't move very fast and have given up on sex.

He is no longer the highest-priced yearling in history, that place now occupied by $13.1 million colt Seattle Dancer, a son of Nijinsky bought at Keeneland two years later, this time by Sangster, who at least got a return on investment. Seattle Dancer won a Group 2 race and was Group 1-placed, and also did a fair job at stud, siring 37 stakes winners.

Yet Snaafi Dancer retains his cachet, his status as the benchmark for hubris, for those who try to buy success. The last word goes to trainer Dunlop. 'Rather a sweet little horse, but no bloody good.'

83

Racing glory at the Breeders' Cup.   Image © Getty

FANTASY RACING

The idealism of 'something for everyone' is remarkably difficult to translate into practice, but John Gaines pulled it off with a flourish when his concept of a world championship for racing grew into an end-of-year extravaganza that changed the shape of the sport.

The Breeders' Cup, or the 'Greatest Show on Earth' to its marketing department, evolved from a daydream Gaines, the heir to a dog-food fortune, had about the sort of raceday he'd like to see. It's the sort of exercise in fantasy racing that normally goes no further than the back of an envelope, but Gaines had an innovative mind and industry clout – he owned leading Kentucky stallion station Gainesway Farm – and his funding model drew the disparate strands of the racing business together.

His blueprint for the big day comprised a race each for two-year-old colts and fillies, a sprint, a mile contest on turf, a race for fillies and mares, a European-style 'long-distance' turf race and a race over the classic mile-and-a-quarter distance that would crown a true champion. Something for everyone. It would be funded by stallion owners, who would pay one annual covering fee per sire, and by breeders, who would pay a flat fee for every foal registered to the Breeders' Cup scheme. Some of that money would trickle back to the racecourses for races designated as Breeders' Cup warm-up events, and the Cup circus would travel around the premier tracks to foster a sense of belonging. Something for everyone.

The scale of the prize-money fund was the real clincher. Five of the races were worth a million dollars, the Turf $2 million and the Classic $3 million. It was billed as the $10 million raceday, a dizzying development that captivated the racing world and ensured widespread interest and support. The first Breeders' Cup, at now-defunct Hollywood Park in November 1984, was an unmitigated success. No trainer or jockey had more than one winner, the Europeans hit the board with Lashkari in the Turf, and the three-way war between Wild Again, Gate Dancer and Slew O'Gold in the Classic left the crowd spellbound. Something for everyone.

The Breeders' Cup has never looked back, although it has strayed from its original composition. It has become the natural year-end target for European horses and the coronation convention for the home team's divisional champions, and many of its races have entered the realm of legend.

There was, above all, Arazi in the 1991 Juvenile. His mid-race move, weaving through the whole field like a motorcycle despatch rider in rush hour and sprinting clear, leaving even the race-caller fumbling for words, still stretches the boundaries of belief at every repeated viewing. Personal Ensign keeping her 13-race unbeaten record intact by a nose in the 1988 Distaff; Dayjur jumping the shadow, slipping the surly bonds of earth in the 1990 Sprint; Royal Academy and Lester Piggott, the ghost from the past, in the 1990 Mile; Goldikova winning her third Mile in 2010, the only horse to complete a hat-trick in one race; High Chaparral and Johar dead-heating in the 2003 Turf.

The Classic, as befits its status, has provided so many highlights. The races of 1987, 1988 and 1989, won by Ferdinand, Alysheba and Sunday Silence, are almost unmatched in the canon for courage, drama and brilliance. The French-trained Arcangues winning at 133-1 in 1993; Cigar rounding off his perfect season in 1995; Tiznow winning twice, in 2000 and 2001, by a neck and a nose; Zenyatta missing out on a 20-race unbeaten record by a neck in 2010; American Pharaoh parlaying his Triple Crown into the Grand Slam in 2015.

The travelling show has visited a dozen racetracks, coast to coast, most often Santa Anita in California and Churchill Downs in Kentucky, but among others Woodbine in Canada, Belmont Park in New York, Lone Star Park in Texas and Gulfstream Park in Florida. Somewhere for everyone.

For all its beguiling magic, though, the Breeders' Cup has its flaws. It is a transatlantic championship rather than a worldwide affair, and the copycat usage by most European trainers of raceday medication

– permitted in the US, forbidden in Europe – in the name of a 'level playing-field' is distasteful.

Moreover, the meeting has been expanded to two days and 14 races, doubled in size with the additional races catering for divisions even within divisions, something for literally everyone. This frustratingly allows horses who might otherwise clash to be kept apart and diminishes the impact of the original idea, the half-hourly assault on the senses of truly elite competition.

But Gaines's vision is still intact, the generosity and inclusivity of his seminal idea still resonant almost four decades on. Not everything about the Breeders' Cup works perfectly, but in the mighty sum of its many parts everyone finds something to love.

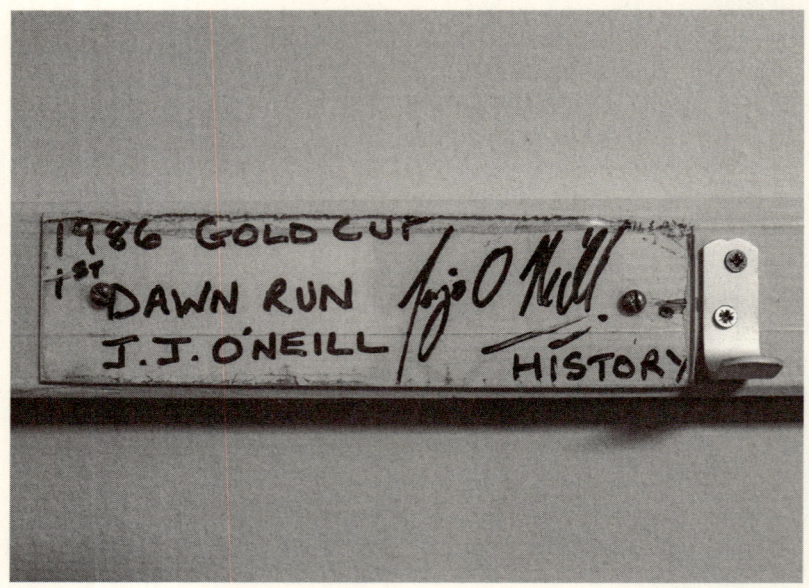

Writing racing history. *Image © Alamy*

THE MARE

There is absolutely nothing conventional about any part of the story of Dawn Run. That is both its beauty and its sorrow. It is not a long story, but what it lacks in length it makes up for in controversy, and triumph, and great glory, and is a story no one will ever tire of telling.

Dawn Run (foaled 1978) was a big mare, plain and imposing, and her sturdy frame concealed what we have learned not to call the heart of a lion. Her horse's heart was indefatigable, the most reliable thing about her, because for all her unique achievements she was certainly not a great jumper. Her technique was flawed, but it added to the excitement and reinforced her charm, and it played a leading role in the drama that surrounded her. She was owned by Charmian Hill, for whom the word 'unconventional' could have been coined.

Hill was as much a one-off as her horse. A tiny woman, sparrow-light, possessed of an indomitable personality, Hill was a formidable woman and her actions defined the career of her horse in a way matched by few owners. They called her the Galloping Granny, because she was still race-riding at the age of 63, winning a bumper on Dawn Run at Tralee in June 1982. That was her last ride; the Irish Turf Club declined to renew her licence. Her last official ride, for she still partnered her horse on the gallops.

Dawn Run was just feeling her way into a career, and the following season she ran 16 times on the Flat and over hurdles, a staggering campaign for a young horse, finishing runner-up at the Cheltenham Festival behind a good horse in Sabin Du Loir and then running twice in two days at Aintree, winning a handicap under top weight on the Friday and chasing home Champion Hurdle winner Gaye Brief 24 hours later. By then she had been ridden by four jockeys, a crucial element of the tale.

Hill never seemed satisfied with the riding of Tony Mullins, son of the mare's trainer Paddy Mullins, and although he would win more races on her than any other jockey he was overlooked on Dawn Run's two biggest days. Owners pay the bills, they make decisions, but Hill's treatment of Tony Mullins was the source of strife within the stable and without.

In the spring of 1984 Dawn Run blossomed into brilliance, winning the Irish Champion Hurdle, the Champion Hurdle itself, and later the French Champion Hurdle, a trilogy of success never achieved before or since. Jonjo O'Neill rode her at Leopardstown and Cheltenham, Mullins had his chance at Auteuil.

The demands of jumping hurdles did not test Dawn Run's technique too severely, but when she went over fences she was cavalier and not careful, a recipe for potential disaster. Injured after her successful debut, she lost a year but returned with her power and glory undimmed and was aimed at the Cheltenham Gold Cup. It was a bold plan, in general and in the specifics of Dawn Run, but that was the mare's life all over.

No horse had ever won both Champion Hurdle and Gold Cup, although many very good ones had tried. Dawn Run's claim to a place in history was not advertised by her prep run at Cheltenham, in which she blundered badly at the ditch at the top of the hill and sent poor Mullins into orbit, and once again back to the substitutes' bench. O'Neill was recalled for the Gold Cup, and Dawn Run's inexperience, sketchy jumping and inferior form suggested that she was up against it.

Yet, in a knowing nod to the unconventional, she was the favourite. Her position as market leader was underpinned by faith, hope and destiny rather than by the concrete imperatives of class and form, for she had long ago become a folk hero in Ireland. Sure, said her countless devotees, the mare can do anything. It turned out they were right.

The last two fences of the 1986 Cheltenham Gold Cup are imprinted on the collective memory. Dawn Run, who had made blunders along the way, led over the second last but was passed by the previous year's winner

Forgive'n Forget and by Wayward Lad, who went clear on the run-in. Although O'Neill switched her to the centre of the track it looked all up for the favourite, but then Wayward Lad began to tire, and Dawn Run hit her fearsome stride. The mare was beginning to get up, in the words of Peter O'Sullevan's deathless commentary, and she got up to Wayward Lad, passed him, beat him by a length. Gold Cup and Champion Hurdle. The place went wild.

A pedant would point out, quite correctly, that Dawn Run benefited from the 5lb allowance for mares that had been introduced two years earlier, and without it would have won neither Champion Hurdle nor Gold Cup. There were no pedants at Cheltenham that day.

The aftermath was as memorable as the race. Dawn Run came back to the winner's enclosure through a seemingly impenetrable wall of people, borne among them like a cork on a wave of the sea. Hill was lifted high in the air, and when O'Neill dismounted he sought out Tony Mullins and carried him on his back. There had never been a celebration like it at Cheltenham. There had never been a mare like Dawn Run.

Three months later she was dead, killed in a fall when bidding, incongruously, for another French Champion Hurdle. She was only eight. A short story, then, with an unhappy ending, but with a heroine who made it unputdownable from the first page to the last.

85

Footprints in the sand/Polytrack. Image © Racing Post

CARPET, SPANDEX AND RUBBER

Racing taking place on an artificial surface is nothing new. Horses in the US have always trained and raced on dirt, a mixture of soil, sand and clay, but it took a long time for the idea to leave its synthetic footprint on the pastures green of Britain and Ireland.

The practice of putting down woodchip or sand to make a surface that could be used for training when the usual grass gallops were too soft, too hard, too overworked – and in all weathers, say – had steadily become common, and the process reached its logical conclusion when an artificial circuit was laid down at Lingfield by pioneer and entrepreneur Ron Muddle, the father of all-weather racing in Britain. The first race on the Equitrack surface took place in October 1989 and the name in the history books is Niklas Angel, trained by Conrad Allen and ridden by Richard Quinn.

It is known as all-weather racing, although the nature of the surface can't prevent meetings being lost to fog or high winds, or five inches of snow blanketing the track. It was conceived as a method of keeping racing and, just as pertinently, the betting shops going through the winter, offering a guarantee of racecourse action and sustaining financial imperatives when all around was waterlogged or frozen.

It has played this role exceptionally well, and the all-weather estate has expanded to six Flat racecourses in Britain and one in Ireland. Jump racing was also a presence through the early days of all-weather racing, but owing to safety concerns this was discontinued in 1994. The quality of the synthetic surface has improved dramatically, with the early innovations of Equitrack and Fibresand now replaced by the proprietary brands Polytrack and Tapeta.

Polytrack is made from a blend of silica sand and recycled carpet fibres, spandex and rubber, the whole then being coated with wax. It is laid down at Lingfield, Kempton, Chelmsford City and Dundalk, as well as Cagnes-sur-Mer, Chantilly and Deauville in France. Tapeta, the invention of former trainer Michael Dickinson, consists of silica sand and fibres and is also coated in wax, and is in place at Newcastle, Wolverhampton and Southwell, as well as at Meydan in Dubai.

The proportion of all-weather fixtures has grown to more than 20 per cent (around 350) of all race meetings in Britain, and they are no longer restricted to the winter months. All-weather racing is all-year-round racing, something that has not found favour with a large constituency within the sport, given that the majority of all-weather meetings are low grade, low prize-money, low interest, low attendance fixtures, many of them staged in the evening under floodlights.

These aspects of all-weather racing have earned it a bad name, largely unjustifiably. The action may be of a moderate standard, but the races are competitive at an individual level and provide much-needed opportunities for those in the lower layers of the racing pyramid, as well as giving the nation's punters something else to bet on and thereby generating extra income for the industry. In any case, at the top end, the quality of all-weather racing has improved markedly.

Pattern races now take place on the all-weather, and in 2019 the Group 1 Vertem Futurity was run on the Tapeta at Newcastle when the original venue at Doncaster was waterlogged, the precise situation for which the implementation of synthetic surfaces was conceived. The All-Weather Championships are run at Lingfield on Good Friday, the culmination of a series of qualifying races in six categories with a prize fund of £1 million, and the number of top-class horses who have started their careers on the all-weather is considerable.

Enable, twice winner of the Prix de l'Arc de Triomphe, began her career at Newcastle, while her stablemate Jack Hobbs, winner of the Irish Derby, made his debut at Wolverhampton. The 2009 1,000 Guineas winner Ghanaati had never raced on turf before winning her Classic, having had two outings at Kempton the previous year.

It may be anathema to the purists, but all-weather racing is a necessity without which the industry's financial model would break down. It serves the grass roots of the sport admirably, if slightly ironically.

86

Gold top, of course.   Image © Getty

THE WILD ROMANCE OF LIFE

Results in the biggest races tend to prove the adage that God is on the side of the big battalions. The same names appear, the usual suspects, the power concentrated in the old familiar places. But not every time. Sometimes God rolls the dice and an unexpected number comes up, and something serendipitous happens, the sort of thing that renews our faith in the wild romance of life.

    The great Desert Orchid was odds-on favourite for the 1990 Cheltenham Gold Cup. There is no bigger race, was no bigger horse. Desert Orchid was loved more than any horse apart from maybe Arkle and Red Rum, and his animal magnetism and outstanding ability meant that he was not only likely to win the Gold Cup for the second year running, but expected to win it. At the other end of the betting market was 100-1 shot Norton's Coin, who was neither likely to win it nor expected to win it, whose journey to jump racing's mountain top was the epitome of improbability.

He shouldn't have even been in the race. Norton's Coin would have had a puncher's chance in a race the previous day, but his trainer Sirrell Griffiths forgot to enter him. The Gold Cup was all there was left, so Griffiths entered him in that, and then went back to his real job. He was a farmer from deep west Wales, had a dairy herd, a few chickens running about the place. He was a permit-holder, an amateur trainer, only allowed to train for himself and his family, and had just three horses. Before dawn on Gold Cup morning he and his sons milked the cows, and then drove the best of his horses to Cheltenham.

Odds of 100-1 are emotive. It signals to the uninitiated that here is a horse who can't possibly win, but of course that isn't true. The Grand National has had five 100-1 winners, most recently Mon Mome in 2009, most famously Foinavon in 1967, who prevailed in unforgettable fashion after the riderless Popham Down had run across the 23rd fence and caused a pile-up that brought down the entire field. Foinavon only escaped because he was so far behind that he missed the melee, was steered by rider John Buckingham through a gap in the seething mass of unseated jockeys and loose horses, and skipped away before anyone else could gather themselves sufficiently to follow him.

Odds of 100-1 are not even always indicative of lack of ability. Mon Mome shouldn't have been 100-1; he had won a good race four months earlier and been runner-up in a Welsh National. Norton's Coin shouldn't have been 100-1 either: he had been runner-up at the Festival the year before and a beaten favourite on his most recent start. Memories are short in racing. But his trainer was an anonymous dairyman from the sticks, and people like that never won the Gold Cup, and anyway, Desert Orchid was going to win. 100-1, then, offered up with scorn.

Norton's Coin, for his part, also didn't look the part. He shambled around the parade ring, prompting trainer David Nicholson, one of the big battalions, to make the observation that he 'should be in a bloody tin'. Perhaps that's when God changed His/Her mind. Some of Griffiths' friends got 200-1.

With three fences to jump, Desert Orchid was going to win. A roar from the delighted crowd. With one to jump, he wasn't. As he dropped back into third place the TV cameras fixed upon the idol, the icon, neglecting the remarkable race unfolding before an increasingly bemused audience. Norton's Coin was right there, as if by magic, which is exactly what it was, a little bit of life's magic.

He jumped the last fence alongside the third-favourite Toby Tobias and, under an energetic drive from jockey Graham McCourt, worried his game rival out of it on the run-in, winning by three-quarters of a length, a thoroughly deserving winner, no fluke at all, just a tale of the unexpected. The crowd was almost silent. The only sound was one person turning to another and saying 'Who?' They would never need to ask again. In a world of infinite possibilities, something almost impossible had happened.

Sirrell Griffiths and his family, stunned almost into shock, took Norton's Coin home again, where the village had turned out to welcome them. There was a party, and everyone stayed up all night, and in the blue-black half-light of dawn, as usual, Griffiths milked his 70 cows. Gold top, you'd say.

Norton's Coin, the 100-1 chance who looked as though he should have been in a bloody tin, who was in the race by accident, who was sired by a stallion who covered ponies for £25 and got only two winners in his life, the other in Denmark, who was trained by a dairy farmer as a hobby, who was blithely ignored by the racing world, had won the Cheltenham Gold Cup. Do you believe in miracles? Yes.

87

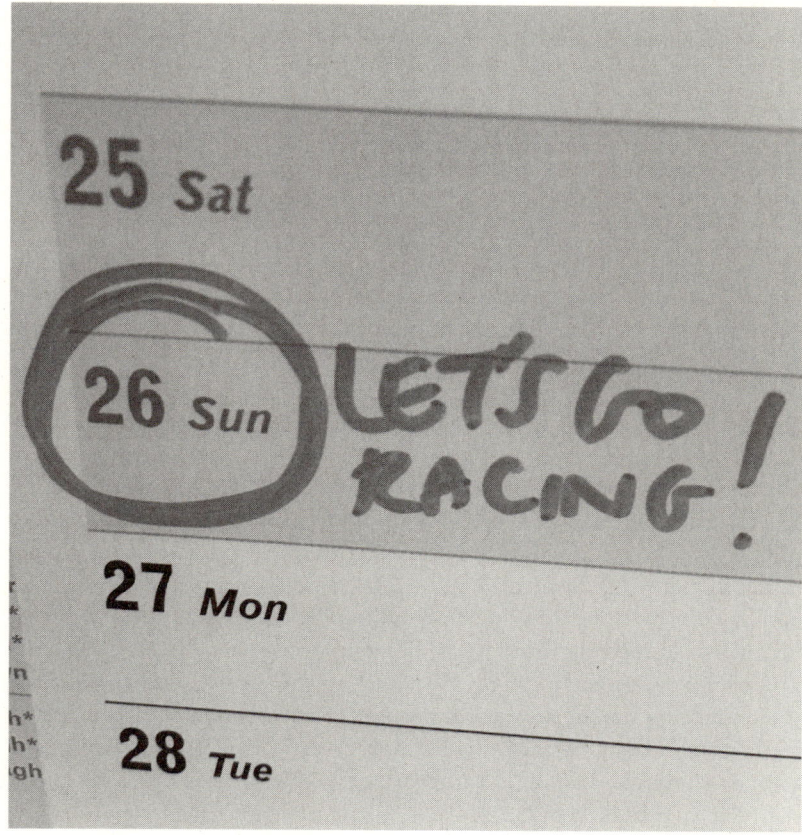

Sunday racing in Britain is born.   Image © Author

ON THE SEVENTH DAY

Never on a Sunday. At the beginning of the 1990s, that was the attitude in Britain, while the rest of the world had fun. The US, France, Italy, Ireland, Hong Kong, Australia . . . spin the globe and stop it with a finger, and it would come down on a country that staged racing on a Sunday. But not Britain.

Usually backward at coming forward, Britain had its pathway to week-round racing tied up in red tape, doomed to inaction by Acts of Parliament. There were religious and commercial objections, covered by the Sunday Observance Act, and also the Betting, Gaming and Lotteries Act, which forbade the wicked practice of having a pound each-way on a horse on a Sunday. The general public, too, plenty of whom were behind the Keep Sunday Special campaign, were in no hurry for change. For sleepy little Britain, the fantastic drowse of the afternoon Sundays dragged interminably.

Elements of the industry were also not in favour. Stable staff could envisage an extra day added to the workload without the financial rewards to go with it, and were understandably wary despite assurances from the Jockey Club, which had established a committee with the aim of introducing Sunday racing in the mid-1980s. Parliament remained unmoved by their entreaties.

At length, the evangelists for fun on Sundays, the seventh-day adventurists, took a radical approach and the first Sunday meeting in Britain was scheduled to take place at Doncaster in July 1992. The Bishop of Doncaster gave an address before the first race, a sanction that went some way towards appeasing those whose objections were based on religious grounds, and more than 23,000 crammed into the Town Moor to watch a little piece of history being made.

The first race was won by Savoyard, trained by Michael Jarvis and ridden by Walter Swinburn, but as betting on a Sunday remained illegal, there were no on-course bookmakers and no odds were returned. It would be three years before the law was changed to allow betting shops to open and on-course bookmakers to shout the odds on Sundays; the first Sunday meeting with betting was at Newmarket in May 1995, one of a dozen scheduled that year.

Britain had finally caught up with the rest of the world, and now there is racing on the seventh day every week, with every racecourse in the country owning at least one Sunday fixture. Still, though, the British attitude to Sunday racing is half-hearted, as though it is tolerated rather than encouraged.

In the rest of Europe, Sunday is the big day for the biggest races, the Prix de l'Arc de Triomphe, the Irish Gold Cup, the Deutsches Derby, the Premio Parioli, a showpiece day. The majority of Sundays in Britain play host to mundane fare, with the notable exceptions of the 1,000 Guineas at Newmarket in May and the Greatwood Hurdle at Cheltenham in November.

Sundays, in all walks of life, are not what they used to be, but the fact remains that Sunday is still generally one of the two days available for racing to chase the leisure market, and the suspicion remains that racing is underselling itself with its seeming reluctance to revisit the fixture list and, to borrow an idea, Make Sunday Special. The drawbacks are known, but the advantages are unexplored.

It has been documented that racecourses find it hard to attract corporate hospitality at weekends, and the issue of screening big Sunday cards on terrestrial television is also a stumbling block. For many racecourses, Sunday is seen as a day to bring families to the sport, and families could not care less whether they are watching low-grade handicaps or Group 1 races as long as their two-pound each-way bets are reasonably successful and the children are happy – so why stage big races on Sundays? Sundays are a day to play safe rather than be ambitious.

Perhaps it would be interesting, in high summer, to maximise public appeal, to alter the parameters of the big festival meetings, Glorious Goodwood, the York Ebor meeting, the Newmarket July festival, so that they cover both days of the weekend. As an experiment, it would surely be worth trying. From never on a Sunday to always on a Sunday has been done once; why not again?

88

The red flag of chaos. Image © Racing Post

INTO THE VOID

It was a disgrace. A shambles. Lift the thesaurus from the shelf and choose a description. A farce. An embarrassment. A calamity. A humiliation. It was the 1993 Grand National, the 'race that never was'.

What took place at Aintree on that sorry Saturday still has the capacity to send a shudder lurching down the spine. The record books state simply 'void race', a short, clinical summary of the day British racing disappeared into the void.

Things started badly. They got no better, but the start finished the race off. As the 39 runners for the Grand National paraded, a small group of animal rights protestors trespassed on to the course by the first fence and had to be removed by security staff, delaying the start, plucking at the nerves. When the horses finally reached the starting place, starter Keith Brown, officiating at his final National, lined them up and sent them on their way. This is where the problems began.

The starting gate itself was not fit for purpose. Brown pushed down on a lever that was attached to the tape, which lacked any elasticity or tension and did not spring up efficiently. The jockeys had lined up their horses right against the tape, so when it went up it became entangled around several runners, preventing them from breaking away with the rest of the field. False start.

Brown waved his red flag to indicate to his assistant Ken Evans, standing further down the track, that it was a false start, and Evans brandished his flag to indicate the same to the jockeys, who pulled up their horses before they had gone very far. The recall procedure had worked. A bit of a cock-up, but no harm done.

So the same process was repeated. The horses were close enough to the starting tape, which swayed pathetically in the breeze like a poorly strung clothesline, to put their heads over it. There was a lot of noise from the adjacent crowd. Some of the horses were beginning to boil over. Brown could be heard calling to jockeys 'keep their heads back'. They didn't. Brown shouldn't have pulled the lever but, in such a febrile atmosphere, no one was making good decisions, and he started the race. As the tape went up, it again became tangled in horses and jockeys.

Even at this point the situation could have been saved. Brown waved his red flag to signal to Evans that it was a false start, except that his flag was furled, and from Evans's perspective must have been impossible to see. The message didn't get through. Evans didn't wave his flag. And the National field galloped towards the first fence and jumped it. The race was on. Except it wasn't.

Brown had signalled a false start. The starter's decision was final. The race was void, as BBC commentators Peter O'Sullevan, John Hanmer and Jim McGrath repeatedly informed viewers. Yet the horses galloped on, their jockeys unaware. Back at the start, the useless starting tape was still wound around Richard Dunwoody's neck as he sat on Wont Be Gone Long, one of nine horses who had never left the starting gate.

The crowd, who had heard over the public address system that another false start had occurred, began to jeer. As the field passed the grandstands for the first time, a man waving a red flag stood on the course in a futile bid to halt the race. Some jockeys pulled up their horses, but some may have thought that those waving flags were demonstrators, or thought that 'this is the National, keep going and sort it out later'. Whatever the reason, a dozen or so horses went off on the second circuit.

Seven horses eventually finished the race, with 50-1 shot Esha Ness, trained by Jenny Pitman, crossing the line first ahead of Cahervillahow and Romany King. If 'winning' jockey John White had been blissfully unaware of any problems during the race, he could not have mistaken the hail of derision from the crowd as he crossed the line as anything other than confirmation that he had not won, that this was not a race, but the race that never was.

Blame blew around Aintree like torn-up betting slips. The buck stopped with Brown, who later admitted that the events of that crazy afternoon had ruined his life, but he had nevertheless called a false start and waved his flag, albeit unconvincingly. The focus then turned to flagman Evans, who didn't wave his flag at all, because he hadn't seen Brown's flag. Evans was at the bottom of the ladder, a part-timer earning £28 for his day's work, so he was an easy target for the embarrassed grandees of the Jockey Club and was treated very unfairly by the official report.

The real problem lay with the starting procedure, and the antiquated, faulty nature of the starting apparatus. Lack of investment and a failure to embrace change were the real issues here, and the Jockey Club was as culpable as anyone else. There was an accident waiting to happen, and it happened on Grand National day. After the horses had bolted, assessments were made to the nature of the National start and remedial measures were implemented, including a sturdier starting tape.

Murphy's Law held sway that afternoon. If it could go wrong, it did. Human error, mechanical error, a perfect storm that blew up in racing's face. No horses or jockeys were hurt. Small mercies, and all that.

89

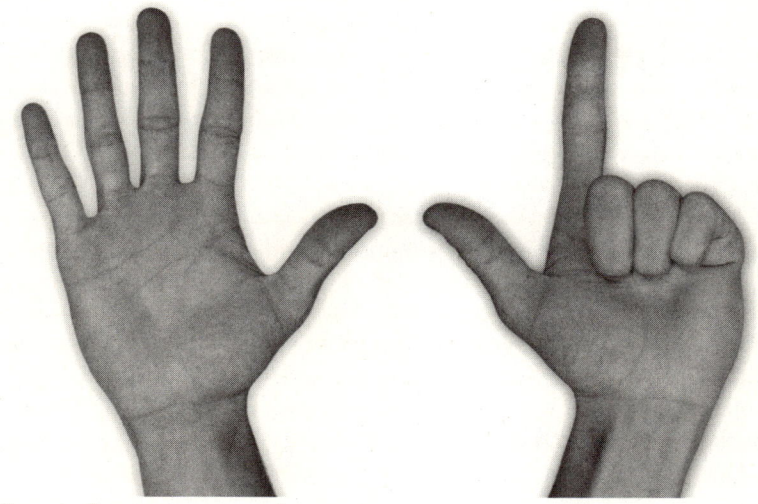

Four... five... six... seven!

A YOUNG ITALIAN JOCKEY

Naming the members of the Magnificent Seven is a common quiz question. Yul Brynner, Steve McQueen, Charles Bronson . . . wait. The other Magnificent Seven? Wall Street, Diffident, Mark Of Esteem, Decorated Hero, Fatefully, Lochangel and Fujiyama Crest.

The events of 28 September 1996 changed lives. At the end of the day some bookmakers had gone out of business, and some punters would never have to work again. Racegoers at Ascot had witnessed something they would never, could never forget, and a young Italian jockey named Lanfranco Dettori had become the biggest name in the sport, a position he would never relinquish. There were seven races at Ascot that afternoon, and Frankie Dettori rode all seven winners.

Once upon a time Sir Gordon Richards won 12 consecutive races, including six on one day, but those victories were gained in minor company at provincial Chepstow, not on one of the biggest days of the season at Britain's premier Flat racecourse. Dettori's feat was unprecedented, almost inconceivable. Magnificent, you might say.

A glance at the racecard that morning revealed that Dettori was likely to have a good day. He was on a few favourites, a couple more with good chances. The only one that couldn't really be fancied was his final ride, a handicapper with top weight. Casual punters all over Britain, looking for a Saturday flutter with an edge, struck combination bets on Dettori's mounts, some of them, all of them, small stakes. Because you never know.

Dettori won the first three races, including the showpiece Group 1 Queen Elizabeth II Stakes, but it wasn't a big surprise. Trebles are common. Then he won the fourth race, and the dynamic changed instantly. Bookmakers began to reckon up liabilities, journalists began to wonder about rewrites. Among the Ascot crowd, there was the dawning awareness that something unusual was happening.

A fifth winner. A sixth winner. Fever pitch. It is no exaggeration to state that the level of anticipation as Dettori walked into the parade ring to get up on Fujiyama Crest had risen beyond comparison, off the scale. In the morning, Fujiyama Crest had been 14-1. The bookmakers had already sustained huge losses, but in an attempt to mitigate further financial misery they were sending sackfuls of money into the on-course market to bring down the horse's starting price, and the 14-1 shot was now the 2-1 favourite.

Dettori was already very well known, very well loved, for his chirpy personality, his Italian good looks, his brilliance in the saddle. He was first jockey to Sheikh Mohammed's uber-powerful Godolphin stable, he was the reigning champion jockey, he was a winner. Now, as he cantered Fujiyama Crest to the start, the whole grandstand rose to applaud him. As he passed the post in front on the first circuit, applause broke out again. It was a two-mile race, and with every passing furlong the delirium ratcheted up a notch.

As the field turned into Ascot's short straight, Dettori was still in front, the crowd willing him home. Then Northern Fleet came out of the chasing pack, Pat Eddery riding for his life. Eddery was an all-time great jockey, a tough, unsentimental fellow, and he would have spoiled the Dettori party and not blinked. The whole world telescoped to two horses, running. Northern Fleet got to Fujiyama Crest's quarters, his girth, his neck . . . and then time and space ran out, and Fujiyama Crest passed the post in front. Seven winners for Dettori. A day like no other.

Ascot exploded with joy. There was a headlong sprint to the winner's enclosure where Dettori, half-mad with delight, howled and screamed, performed his trademark flying dismount, ran around with a bottle of champagne spraying the crowd. The journalists went to their rewrites with a will. The bookmakers swallowed hard, and began the reckoning. It later emerged that a few people had left the racecourse before the last race to beat the traffic, which is akin to turning off the television ten seconds before Neil Armstrong emerged from the lunar module.

It was reported that Dettori's seven winners cost the bookmaking fraternity £40 million, all those small-stake accumulators paying out life-changing sums, although the publicity they received in the process eased the pain. Their nemesis was instantly transformed from *a* jockey to *the* jockey, renowned far beyond racing's garden wall, his life never quite his own ever again but his celebrity boundless. For all the immense and prolonged success in his long and glorious career, that day, those seven winners, defined him as a person and as a jockey.

Fujiyama Crest had run the race of his life, coaxed and practically carried to victory by his inspired rider. He did nothing of any account after that, but when he retired he went to live with Dettori, seeing out his days in the lap of luxury, payback for his part in the most extraordinary day.

In October 2012, Richard Hughes rode seven winners from eight rides at Windsor, finishing third on his other mount, but that remarkable achievement had a fraction of the impact felt through Dettori's seven-timer. That unparalleled impact might be best assessed by the fact that an hour after that tumultuous final race, three hardened old-school journalists, looking at each other with a wild surmise, muttering about how they didn't really do this sort of thing, were still waiting patiently outside the weighing room for the great man's autograph.

90

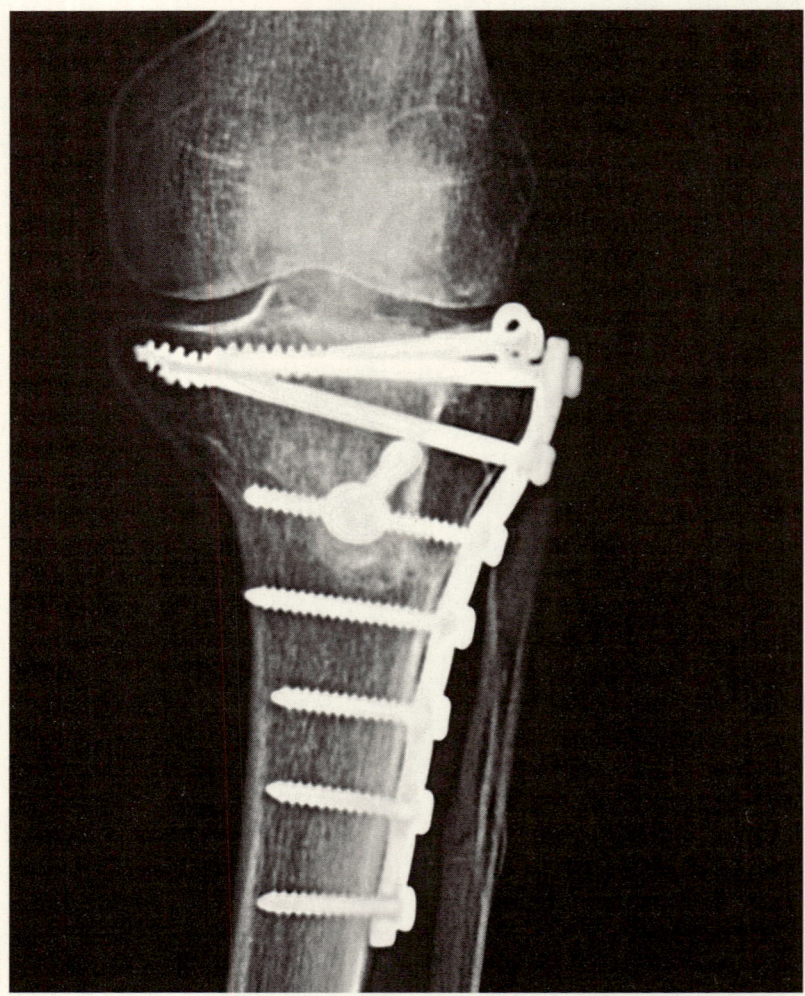

Not quite unbreakable.   *Image © Getty*

THE GREAT ACCUMULATOR

Man as machine. The career of AP McCoy, two decades spent relentlessly conquering armies of statistics, was characterised by defiance as much as brilliance, grit as much as glory, doing daily battle with his body and his will as well as with the opposition and the history books.

At the end of it all there was nothing and no one he hadn't outdone, this awe-inspiring freak of a jockey, a human number-generator, but sometimes his domination seemed to cost him more than he gained. Being a top sportsman is hard work, and where McCoy was concerned it really looked like it. The iron man from Moneyglass in Northern Ireland won 20 consecutive jump championships (1996-2015), which isn't a misprint, posted a record 4,348 winners over jumps, including one seasonal harvest of 289 winners and eight others of more than 200, and won practically every big race in the calendar, although his share of the biggest was less impressive than many of his comrades.

When in March 1997 he did the Champion Hurdle-Cheltenham Gold Cup double on Make A Stand and Mr Mulligan, it might have marked the beginning of a career similar to that of his friend Ruby Walsh, one as studded with big-race prestige as a bun with currants, but he won only one more Gold Cup and two more Champion Hurdles, one Champion Chase, one King George. McCoy's game was numbers, his role instead the Great Accumulator, quantity over quality, and there has never been anyone better at it.

Anthony Peter McCoy – he began as Tony, steadily became AP, but for family and friends it's Anthony – rode his first winner over jumps on Riszard at Gowran Park in April 1994, although he had ridden his first winner of nine on the Flat more than two years earlier. He moved to Britain for the 1994-95 campaign and ended it as champion conditional, and the following season won the first of those 20 titles. McCoy was never not champion, never anything less, but the internal and external pressures that come with that status left their mark.

McCoy has a dry, wry, lugubrious wit in his calmer moments, but when he was riding he rarely looked as though he was enjoying himself, even when the winners were flowing. He treated victory with the offhandedness of a winetaster, rolling it around his mouth for a second and then spitting it out, all the emphasis on the next winner, never the one at hand. This was in part the mentality of a great champion, no complacency allowed, constant focus, but partly because he was generally in discomfort.

His medical book contained a list of injuries that might be associated with a stuntman rather than a jockey. McCoy always considered himself unbreakable, but was referring to his spirit rather than his skeleton. He may not have broken every bone in his body, but he made a fair stab at it, and usually dragged himself off the injury list ahead of schedule because there was a winner in the offing. Memorably, he was kicked squarely in the face by a horse called Mr Watson at Wetherby, breaking two teeth and needing 23 stitches to hold his face together, but there was a sure thing running the next day at Ascot and there was no time for time off. McCoy rode at Ascot, and won. As he told his ghostwriter, 'getting injured doesn't mess with your head in the same way as getting beaten does'.

There was also the constant battle with the scales, the meagre diet, the daily hunger, the heartbreakingly hot baths to sweat off a pound or two. More than most, McCoy suffered for his art.

Yet what art. McCoy was the St Jude of racing, the patron saint of lost causes, for his strength in the face of pain and hunger also manifested itself in the refusal to concede defeat. Perhaps the most famous example of that was aboard Wichita Lineman in a handicap at the Cheltenham Festival, when he had 11 horses in front of him with two to jump, six lengths to make up on the run-in, yet somehow lifted his mount into the lead in the last two strides. He was seen wearing a grin after that tour de force, and he may even have been in tears after Don't Push It had helped him to his long-awaited and only Grand National win in 2010, but we won't tell anyone.

McCoy's career was neatly divided into two, with the first half spent as stable jockey to Martin Pipe, a similarly statistical freak, and the second half as retained jockey to leading owner JP McManus, whose string of horses is numbered in the hundreds. Along the way he partnered some top-class horses – Best Mate, Master Minded, Denman, Big Buck's – but they were never his rides on a permanent basis, just spares, their greatest victories gained for other jockeys.

He always said he would retire if he couldn't be champion, but when he bowed out in April 2015 he was still champion, and would have been as long as he kept riding. McCoy was to his sport what Gordon Richards was to his, the undisputed leader, one of the very few all-time greats. He embodied all the qualities of the supreme champion, and proved it every time he pulled a set of silks over his half-starved, broken body, counting on yet another winner to blot out the pain.

91

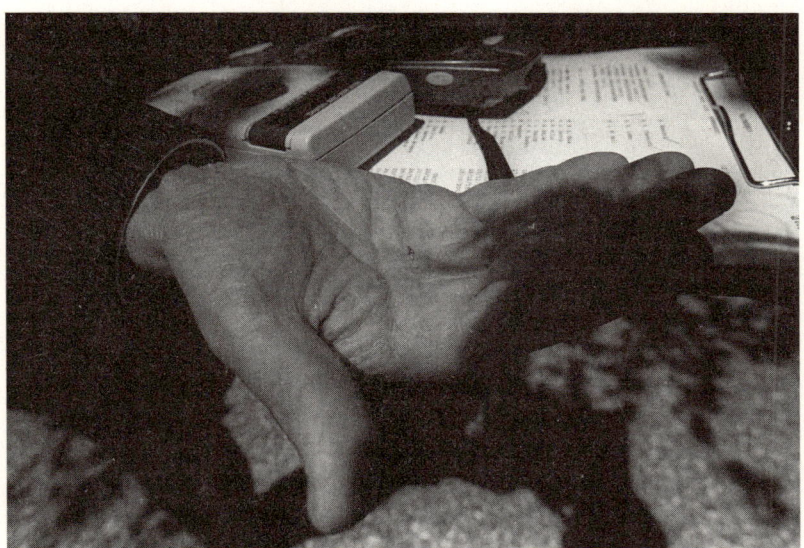

Microchips with everything. Image © Racing Post

UNDER THE SKIN

To stretch a point, a racehorse is no more than a big expensive pet, so like any other pet each one is fitted with a microchip to aid its identification. It being vital that a horse purported to be X is actually X and not masquerading as Y, the microchip is the front-line weapon against identity theft.

In an earlier chapter, it was noted that the *General Stud Book* defines what it means to be a thoroughbred. Take a horse at random: Breton Banquet. His existence is recorded in the *GSB*, proving he is a thoroughbred. That's his birth certificate. He has an equine passport issued by Weatherbys, in which his individual markings are recorded, such as a blaze, a star, white feet, any whorls of hair in his coat, anything that differentiates him from the norm, as well as a medical record of vaccinations, operations etc. That's his NHS file, and it goes with him wherever he goes, to the races, to a different yard, for life.

Breton Banquet also has a microchip secreted under the skin on the left side of his neck, and this can be read with an electronic device on arrival at the racecourse and again when leaving the stable yard en route to the parade ring, and the number checked against the database. That's his ID, his driving licence, his photocard, his point-of-race credentials.

Microchips were introduced in Britain and Ireland in 1999, and are in use throughout the world. Another means of identification, especially in the US and Canada, is a reference number tattooed on the inside of the upper lip. In Australia, to be accepted into the *Stud Book*, a thoroughbred must be freeze-branded on its left front shoulder with a mix of letters and numbers, enabling ready verification.

A microchip will also identify a horse should it be found somewhere abandoned, ill-treated or starving. This is mercifully very rare, but can sadly happen to the best of horses. Supreme Glory, runner-up in the 2003 Grand National, was found neglected in a field – through no fault of his 'racing' owner – and was rescued and rehabilitated and rehomed.

No system is perfect, and there have been cases of mix-ups at the racecourse when one horse is confused for another. At Yarmouth in July 2017, two horses trained by Charlie McBride had their microchips scanned and checked on arrival, but not when leaving the stable yard pre-race, and the three-year-old Millie's Kiss ran in and won a two-year-old race instead of her stablemate Mandarin Princess. An identical blunder occurred at Southwell in January 2018, when African Trader and Scribner Creek, both five-year-old geldings trained by Ivan Furtado, ran in the wrong races because they had been scanned but not identified correctly by a racecourse integrity officer.

The dual method of checking a microchip – on arrival and pre-race – is still as foolproof a procedure as can be practised on a busy raceday. The pre-race check should ideally be done as close to the race as possible, after the horse has been saddled and the jockey on its back, which would have prevented an embarrassing situation for all-time great trainer Aidan O'Brien at Newmarket in October 2020.

Mother Earth and Snowfall, both trained by O'Brien and running in the Group 1 Fillies' Mile, were identified correctly on arrival and as they entered the pre-parade ring, but the trainer's representative put Mother Earth's saddle on Snowfall and vice versa. Mother Earth's jockey rode Snowfall, Snowfall's jockey rode Mother Earth; an innocent mistake, but O'Brien, who was not at Newmarket, was fined £4,000 for failing to ensure his employee could identify each horse. Human error, the one thing technological advances can do nothing about.

92

You bet it's a game-changer.   Image © Getty

DIGITAL REVOLUTION

There may be nothing new under the sun. The concept of the betting exchange, billed as the internet-era alternative to traditional bookmakers, has its roots in the Tattersalls Rooms of the Georgian age, in which men-about-town made and laid wagers among themselves over a pot of hot coffee.

In 1999, Andrew Black and Edward Wray revisited and reinvented the idea, imagining an online marketplace where punters could set their own prices and bet with each other, possibly while drinking coffee. They called their innovation Betfair, and the first market on which bets were made was the 2000 Oaks, won by the favourite Love Divine. It was a small step – there was only £1,476 matched on that initial market – but a giant leap for betting, a digital revolution, not so much a breath of fresh air as a huge gulp of pure oxygen.

Black and Wray did not possess a unique vision, there were other betting exchanges scrapping for a foothold in the turn-of-the-century online landscape, but Betfair quickly became the market leader and evolved into a colossus, absorbing its main rival Flutter and rampaging through the betting world to the dismay and hostility of the industry's big names such as Ladbrokes and William Hill.

A betting exchange follows the model of a stock exchange, allowing customers both to make bets and to lay bets, with the host taking a small percentage of commission from winnings. John Smith doesn't think Happy

Jack will win the 2.30 at Plumpton, so he offers 4-1 (decimal odds of 5) where the traditional bookmaker is offering 7-2. Sally Green fancies Happy Jack, so she backs him at Smith's 4-1.

There are tens of thousands of John Smiths and hundreds of thousands of Sally Greens, all betting anonymously with each other at the click of a button in a market of constant and fierce fluidity, with the groundbreaking facility to bet right up to the final strides of a race, with in-running markets accounting for around 15 per cent of the total volume matched. In-running betting introduced the notion of the 1.01 (1-100 in old money) horse, the clear leader who couldn't be beaten, but sometimes was. Devon Loch would have been 1.01 in-running.

John Smith has no licence, no overheads, no staff, no shareholders and no corporate responsibility, so he is free to offer inflated odds to attract all the Sally Greens, who don't care about John Smith's situation as long as he has enough money in his account to cover their bets, which he does. This aspect of an unconstrained free market worried the big bookmakers, as did the fact that their market share was being eroded by Betfair and by the Betdaq exchange, and it does lead directly to the main objection levelled at the exchanges.

Bookmakers are regulated. Exchanges are regulated. John Smith isn't. Perhaps John Smith is an owner, a trainer, a jockey, a stable lad, and he knows that Happy Jack is definitely not going to win, so he can anonymously lay the horse with impunity.

The ability of an unlicensed individual to lay a horse is at the foundation of very many race-fixing scandals; although betting exchanges have a memorandum of understanding with the governing body, to enable access to the records of their clients in such circumstances, it doesn't stop the fix, it only enables the post-fix investigation of the individuals involved.

Betting exchanges in general and Betfair in particular – Betfair merged with bookmaker Paddy Power in 2016, and later rebranded as Flutter Entertainment – are no longer the plucky little start-ups, the cool kid in town, and are simply corporate bookmaking behemoths, joining the Establishment alongside the firms they once sought to supplant. The effect their introduction had, though, the waves they made, was as dramatic as anything ever seen before.

The emergence of the exchanges changed the dynamic, offering punters a choice they never knew existed, a choice they never knew they wanted. An old-fashioned, very simple idea, combined with new vision and complex technology, has altered the perception and the reality of the betting industry forever.

93

Born in a barn. *Image © Racing Post*

A TWINKLE IN HER EYE

In the spring, a young man's fancy lightly turns to thoughts of love. How quaint. In the spring, a stallion's fancy lightly turns to thoughts of sex, and plenty of it, the sap not the only thing rising.

The bloodstock industry is a billion-dollar concern, all predicated upon the fact that when a daddy horse and a mummy horse love each other very much, they . . . no, we're all adults here. When a stallion and a broodmare are brought together in the covering shed the act itself is perfunctory, brief, emotionless and watched by several people to make sure all is satisfactory. When each thrust can be priced in the thousands, there is no room for mistakes.

The covering season begins in mid-February and can last until June. The mare's gestation period is roughly 11 months, and the ideal is for a foal to be born as close as possible to, but after, January 1, because a January foal has a three-month advantage of maturity and strength over his April counterpart that can be significant at the sales and in the early stages of his career. A 31 December foal is a terrible blunder, for it will officially be a yearling within 24 hours. On such occasions there may be a 'delay' in recording the birth.

It used to be the case that stallions would visit mares, making the tour of stud farms like a sailor on shore leave, but now it is the mare who invariably makes the journey, brought in to be covered, often with a foal at foot, before being taken home again with a twinkle in her eye. A stallion might cover four or five mares a day; that isn't a twinkle in his eye, it's the dull gleam of fatigue.

In the old days, stallions were strictly restricted to 40 mares, but when the bloodstock boom of the mid-1980s swept away all the received wisdoms, market forces began to dictate how busy a stallion would be. The busiest stallion in Britain and Ireland in 2020 was the jump sire Maxios, who covered 298 mares; the hardest-working (well, they *call* it work) Flat sire was Churchill, with 250 mares. Some stallions shuttle to Australia and New Zealand to perform two covering seasons a year.

With in-breeding being a central tenet of the industry, there are concerns that too much input from too few sires will further decrease the options for breeders, but the introduction of a stallion cap would inevitably be challenged on grounds of restraint of trade. The topic of artificial insemination is occasionally addressed, but although AI is permitted in Arab racing and in sport horses, the International Stud Book Committee is unwilling to sanction anything other than 'natural cover'.

Covering fees range from a few hundred pounds to the private 'if you have to ask, you can't afford it' cost of sending a mare to superstars such as the late, great, perennial champion sire Galileo. Those sending a mare to Frankel will pay £175,000; crack sprinter and sire of sprinters Showcasing is priced at £45,000; Sottsass, winner of the 2020 Prix de l'Arc de Triomphe, started his second career at a fee of 30,000 euro. There is a price for every pocket: Maxios has a 7,000 euro price-tag, if he can fit you in.

This may seem all about the stallions, and of course it takes two, but broodmares can only have one foal a year, and thus the impact of a stallion on the breed is more considerable. Mention should nevertheless be made of Hasili, a remarkable mare who produced five individual Group/Grade 1 winners, a world record she shares with New Zealand mare Eight Carat. The mare Windmill Girl foaled two Derby winners in Blakeney and Morston, a feat matched by Urban Sea, dam of the aforementioned Galileo and of Sea The Stars.

In a sphere in thrall to the fickleness of fashion, the old adage 'breed the best to the best and hope for the best' is as good a proposition as anything, especially the last four words. A different method was adopted by Chevalier Edoardo Ginistrelli, who noticed that his mare Signorina neighed to the unheralded stallion Chaleureux whenever she passed his field. Ginistrelli became convinced that the two horses were in love, and arranged a mating based on what he called 'the boundless laws of sympathy and love'.

The result of this sentimental union was Signorinetta, who won the Derby and the Oaks in 1908. In an industry that is obsessed with sex, it's nice to know that sometimes love is all you need.

94

Maybe not the retiring type. Image © Alamy

A FULL AND FULFILLING LIFE

From one end of the process to the other, birth to retirement. Like dogs, like any animal, horses are for life, not just for the short segment of it spent galloping round a big field with the noise of the crowd in their ears. Sooner or later, the familiar names disappear from the racecard, and when one stable door closes, another must open somewhere else.

The horses mentioned in the previous chapter, the stallions, the broodmares, we know what becomes of them. They're all right, always will be. What of the moderate gelding, the slow old steeplechaser, the injury-prone sprinter? When their names are forgotten, does the rest of them get forgotten too?

Help is at hand. In 2000, British racing's governing body set up the welfare and aftercare charity organisation Retraining of Racehorses (RoR;

ror.org.uk), to act as a safety net for those who leave the system, roughly 3,000 horses a year. Horses have tremendous capacity, are incredibly versatile, and the RoR scheme, like a job centre, helps to steer them into a new career that might last 20 years or more. The charity is funded partly by contributions from within the industry, notably owners, whence it comes through a deduction from entry fees.

Horses who have retired from racing can do almost anything next: point-to-pointing, eventing, showjumping, dressage, showing, polo, horseball, any equine discipline imaginable all the way down to being a hack or a companion horse. The crux of the matter is education, the re-education of the horse, which is generally straightforward, and the education of owners to appreciate that their horse has plenty of options at the end of its career, and to understand they have a responsibility to their horse to ensure its ongoing health and happiness, which is more problematic.

Some of the major owners have large estates where their old-timers live the life of Riley. Jockey Richard Johnson gave Looks Like Trouble, on whom he won the 2000 Cheltenham Gold Cup, a home for life. Many trainers are proactive in finding new homes and careers for their retirees, and as the message reaches a wider audience the opportunities increase.

To reinforce the concept, at major race meetings there are often parades of retired racehorses, many with hallowed names such as Cheltenham Gold Cup winner Coneygree, multiple Grade 1 winner Cue Card, and Grand National winner Pineau De Re. Also on display are others who are only household names in their own homes, with information provided about their new careers and the wealth of possibilities available for others like them.

There are also rehabilitation and rehoming centres around Britain – such as the British Thoroughbred Retraining Centre in Lancashire – that take in retired horses and prepare them for the next step. Of course a small percentage of horses are unsuitable, for physical or mental reasons, to be rehomed, and these remain at the centres as flagship horses for publicity purposes. At Greatwood, in Wiltshire, retired racehorses play a role in educating disadvantaged children and young adults with special educational needs.

Old Friends farm in Kentucky was founded in 2003 and is home to more than 200 retired and rescued racehorses, and it draws around 20,000 visitors a year who go to see Classic winners such as Silver Charm, Sarava and Birdstone, as well as gallant obscurities who have been gathered in this luxurious safety net. In Australia there is Living Legends, a similar visitor destination near Melbourne that is home to many Melbourne Cup winners, including Brew and Efficient, and champions from Hong Kong such as Silent Witness and Bullish Luck.

Perhaps the finest example of any racehorse in retirement was the 1992 Melbourne Cup winner Subzero, who spent his life after racing as a much-loved, snowy white ambassador for his sport and for his fellow retirees. Subbie had his own product line of t-shirts and hats, made television appearances, visited children in hospital, went to schools and colleges and retirement homes simply to give people the opportunity to meet a horse, and raised money for equine charities. He died at the age of 32 in August 2020, a people's horse like no other, a legend in his own long lifetime.

With increased funding and greater education for owners both present and future, many more horses will be able to have a full and fulfilling life after they retire from the racecourse. Not every racehorse can be a Subbie, but every racehorse can be something other than a racehorse.

95

Billesdon Brook and her owners. *Image © Racing Post*

MY HORSE

There have been so many alterations to the racing landscape between the start of this book and this chapter, and one of the most uplifting has been the emergence of a new constituency of owners. Racehorse ownership used to be the province of the peerage, the landed gentry and the business tycoon, but now it is readily available to the retired accountant, the shop owner and the school dinner-lady.

This has become possible through the rise in popularity and accessibility of racing clubs and syndicates, both in Britain and Ireland and worldwide. For a modest outlay, anyone can own a small part of a racehorse and glean a huge amount of enjoyment from it. Even the ownership of what is often described as 'a few hairs of the tail' entitles a part-owner or shareholder to regard Lucky Boy as 'my horse' and immerse themselves in the same proprietorial emotions as do the Aga Khan or Michael Tabor.

The differences between syndicates and racing clubs are broadly related to size and involvement. A syndicate is often composed of a group of friends, or employees at a small business, or pub regulars, say perhaps a dozen or 20, and the group (or one of the group) owns the horse outright, pays equal shares for its training and keep, and assists with making decisions about its career.

A racing club can embrace thousands of people who pay a relatively nominal amount for a year's membership, with a lucky few having their names drawn in a ballot to attend the races as owners each time one of the club's horses runs, but who don't actually own the horse or make any decisions in regard to its career. It all depends on the depth of one's pocket and the desired level of involvement.

Both types of ownership have had exceptional success. In 2005 alone Motivator, owned by the Royal Ascot Racing Club, won the Derby; the marvellous mare Soviet Song won the Group 1 Falmouth Stakes for the Elite Racing Club; and Makybe Diva won the Cox Plate and her third Melbourne Cup for the Emily Krstina syndicate run by Tony Santic.

Other notable partnership-owned horses include Harbinger, winner of the 2010 King George VI & Queen Elizabeth Diamond Stakes for one of the many Highclere Thoroughbreds syndicates; 2013 champion two-year-old Toormore, who raced for one of the Middleham Park Racing syndicates; 2011 Champion Hurdle winner Rock On Ruby, owned by the Festival Goers syndicate; and 1998 Grand National winner Earth Summit, owned by the six-strong Summit Partnership.

Syndicate ownership is at its strongest in Australia, where practically every big-race winner has multiple owners with shares of varying size. She Will Reign, bought for AUS$20,000 and winner of the AUS$3.5 million Group 1 Golden Slipper, had 22 owners: builder, salesman, five former rugby league team-mates, housewife, carpenter, three coalminers, podiatrist, retiree, teacher, landscaper, hospital worker, two businessmen, ice-cream factory worker, nurse and family carer, just a bunch of ordinary Aussies all of whom had their name printed in the racecard, adding to the cachet of ownership, something that is regrettably not available to syndicate members in Britain and Ireland.

That wouldn't have been easy in the US, where 2020 Kentucky Derby and Breeders' Cup Classic winner Authentic had 5,314 owners. The website myracehorse.com owned 12.5 per cent of the colt, and micro-shares of that 12.5 per cent were sold at a rate of $206 for 0.001 per cent. That minuscule amount is not even a hair of his tail, it barely equates to a drop of blood, yet tell that to the 5,000 enthusiasts who can say that their horse won the two biggest races in America.

It's sometimes called the Sport of Kings, but it's also the sport of an increasing number of those, like the She Will Reign collective, who thought that the sport would never have room for them, and racing is so much the better for it. But becoming an owner through a syndicate or a racing club should not be seen as a means of making money, especially so in a racing club. That is not what is being sold.

What is being sold is inclusivity, the right to be on the inside looking out for once, the right to lie awake round midnight, unable to sleep for excitement because your horse has a favourite's chance in tomorrow's big race. It is the selling of a dream, of something beyond price, especially as the dream might one day come true.

96

Betting tickets of a bygone era.   Image © Alamy

NOISE, COLOUR AND INTRIGUE

The betting ring, located in the mid-range Tattersalls enclosure at British and Irish racecourses, is a riot of noise, colour and intrigue, one of the chief attractions of a day at the races, a place of honour and rough-edged glamour, the very essence of the game.

Well, that's what it used to be like during its glory years of the 20th century, when the ring was full of larger-than-life characters among bookmakers and punters alike, when money flowed through it like a great green river of readies. Today, in a very few instances – the Cheltenham Festival, Royal Ascot, the big summer meetings – the betting ring still retains the gamy flavour of yesteryear. At all other times it is a perfunctory place, shorn of purpose and relevance, the on-course market worn down by technology and changing culture. The betting ring has lost its soul.

There is a time-honoured image of the good old days: the 'rails' bookmakers at one end, with their boards displaying the prices on the rail dividing Tattersalls from Members, generally representatives of major firms such as Joe Coral and William Hill; the majority of bookmakers in the centre of the enclosure, standing at their pitches shouting the odds, 'take the 11-8', encouraging their punters, putting on a show; the small-time operators further down the enclosure or in the Silver Ring, dealing in the shillings and pence that gave that area its name. Among them all, men standing on boxes wearing white gloves and moving their hands like mime artists, tic-tac men, sending news of changes in odds around the ring in an instant.

A punter would approach a bookmaker, examine the prices on his board, ask for a tenner to win five on 5-1 chance Lucky Boy. The bookie would drop the tenner into his capacious satchel, brimming excitingly with banknotes of all denominations, and give the punter a little piece of pasteboard with a number on it, the number written down in a ledger by the bookie's clerk. If Lucky Boy won, the punter would return with the pasteboard ticket, the bookie would check the number with his clerk, tear up the ticket, reach into his satchel with a thrilling rustle and pay up. Usually, Lucky Boy lost, and the punter tore up his own ticket.

And it was not just a man's world. Helen Vernet became the first woman to take bets in 1918, after she became aware that many women wished to bet only in small sums, which some bookmakers were reluctant to accept. She was unlicensed and was soon warned off, but was then employed by Ladbrokes, for whom she worked for many years.

The first bookmaker is believed to be Harry Ogden, who set up business in Newmarket at the end of the 18th century. Before that, bets were made between individuals at the racecourse or at specified places such as Tattersalls' Rooms, the irony being that betting between individuals now takes place on online exchanges such as Betfair and Betdaq, which has dramatically reduced the significance of the modern betting ring. What goes around, comes around.

In the ring's heyday, the bookmakers set their own prices according to their opinion, so punters could trot around the pitches looking for 5-1 where everyone else had 4-1. Supreme operators such as William Hill himself, and later the flamboyant self-publicist John Banks, and later still the less flamboyant Freddie Williams, laid vast sums and paid out with a smile. But as bookmakers' boards evolved from chalk to magic marker to dot matrix, as the pasteboard was replaced by a paper receipt, this individuality dwindled along with the custom.

Punters could bet in betting shops, then they could bet online, then they could bet on their phones. Why wander through the betting jungle when you can get the same odds, or better odds, on your phone without leaving your armchair? Now it is common to see every bookie's board showing identical prices, with such little liquidity in the market that bets are immediately laid off into the exchanges to minimise liabilities. The on-course market used to be stronger than off-course, now it is much weaker, and the old saw about never seeing a poor bookie is no longer true.

There was once a need to bet with on-course bookmakers, now there is no need. Racecourses are less interesting places as a result, and racing is the poorer. A busy, vibrant, strong betting ring at every racecourse, every day, would be of immense benefit to the entire industry, but it would be very unwise to bet on that ever happening again.

97

Walking stick, GoingStick. Image © *Edward Whitaker*

PENETRATION AND SHEAR

The appliance of science has transformed vast tracts of racing, but in certain areas the simplicity of its agricultural origins are still visible. The condition of the ground, the greensward upon which all the flashy million-pound colts and much-loved jumping stalwarts leave an impression, in more ways than one, is a case in point.

The terms used in Britain are common parlance – hard, firm, good to firm, good, good to soft, soft, heavy, along with the Irish variant 'yielding', which equates to good to soft – and notable for their lack of nuance, although portmanteau constructions such as good, good to soft in places widen the scope for variety. Moreover, these values are considered and confirmed by something as arbitrary as a clerk of the course shoving his walking stick into the sod and making a subjective analysis of his findings. This, of course, applies only to racing on turf. On the all-weather, the going is invariably given as 'standard', although in extreme circumstances it can also be 'fast' or 'slow'.

This system has prevailed over the centuries because the official description of the 'going' has never been required to be overly precise.

An educated guess, backed up by experience and instinct, has always been regarded as sufficient, especially as every racecourse and every clerk's interpretation of its condition is different. What Mr Jones reckons at Ludlow may differ markedly from Mrs Smith's opinion at Wincanton, even though Miss Brown might consider the two identical. If it's good for the goose, say, it might be good to firm for the gander.

Such subjectivity reigned as though by divine right until March 2007, when something that vaguely resembled a walking stick was introduced to complement the actual walking stick. The GoingStick, an implement much more advanced than its name suggests, was developed to bring a numerical certainty to the process, to be used as an objective assessment of the ground alongside the clerk's subjective opinion, a belt and braces approach, the harmonisation of ancient and modern.

The GoingStick measures two elements of turf resistance: the downward penetration, how much force it takes to push the tip into the ground, and the shear, the force required to pull the tip back to an angle of 45 degrees, which is intended to replicate the action of a horse's hoof.

The results are recorded electronically, to be downloaded and published as required. Six readings are taken at any given point on the racecourse – three penetration, three shear – and readings are drawn from no fewer than 30 points, providing at least 180 measurements from which an overall going report can be compiled. The scale ranges from 0.1, which would imply ground so soft as to be more like quicksand, to 15, which implies ground so hard as to resemble concrete. In general, readings fall between three and 12.

The theory is immaculate, but the practice is prone to flaws. The overall picture is clouded by the different composition of the ground at individual racecourses, and by one set of calibrations being used for Flat racing and one for the jumps. The GoingStick is also user-specific, its readings dependent to a degree on something as basic as how forcefully the clerk pushes it into the ground, and given that many clerks are responsible for a single course (some may cover two or possibly three racecourses) then the machine must also be regarded as course-specific.

Objectivity is thus a relatively elusive concept, although the precise figures obtained from the GoingStick do provide a solid basis for comparison over a period of time at a given racecourse, even if results do not translate perfectly between different racecourses. The march of technology in this field has therefore not been foot-perfect, and consequently the old ways have not been superseded. The clerk's walking-stick verdict is still the one used by pundits and punters for a ready description of the going on a particular day.

Another objective method of ascertaining the nature of the ground is by the clock, with the time of each race often a reliable guide when used in comparison to previous races over the same distance. For the most subjective assessment, though, simply consult the winning jockey. Whatever the weather, whatever the underfoot conditions, he or she will say that the ground is perfect.

98

Scarves are not just for warmth.   Image © Getty

SHOW RATHER THAN TELL

Devotion used to be a less demonstrative act. The heart was not worn on the sleeve, or anywhere else. If the heart had its way at all, it was restricted to a photograph clipped from the newspaper and tucked into a wallet, a purse, or stuck to the bedroom wall like an icon.

Arkle changed that game, as he changed them all. There was Arkle memorabilia, then that cottage industry expanded with all those t-shirts and tea-towels declaring love for Red Rum. A grainy black-and-white photo wouldn't cut it any more. And now, with the modern trend for leaving no nuance of the personality unadvertised, racecourses have become partisan arenas in which adherence to this horse or that is made blatant, support as obvious as though it were the home end at Selhurst Park or the Millennium Stadium.

Scarves, as in football or rugby, are the perfect banner. Sensibly warm, luridly coloured, clearly visible. If someone is wearing a pink scarf with lime green spots, in the process wrecking the look of his presumably carefully chosen raceday outfit, it is plain that he is a fan of Champion Hurdle winners Faugheen or Annie Power. A red and blue scarf indicates affection for the great dual Champion Chase winner Sprinter Sacre, orange and black for King George winner Thistlecrack. Green, pink and white is

Frankel or Enable, although the fad is generally for jump horses, given warmth considerations. Red, purple and gold, like a Roman emperor, for Cheltenham Gold Cup winner Native River.

It started – or if it didn't start, it quickly reached top gear – with the rivalry between Paul Nicholls-trained stablemates Kauto Star and Denman, who shared three Cheltenham Gold Cups (2007-09). It was almost explicit that you had to be for one or the other, like totalitarianism or democracy, a Kauto man or a Denman fan, and the marketing machine of Great British Racing took full advantage, producing scarves, badges, rosettes, and all kinds of excelsior. It helped that the two horses had slightly different personalities – Kauto Star was more versatile, more brilliant, while Denman was a no-nonsense relentless galloper – and the two factions developed an amiable cod-animosity.

This woolly flurry of fervour reached its peak in 2010, when Kauto Star was bidding for a third Gold Cup and Denman a second, but their bubbles were burst in bathetic style by Imperial Commander, whose supporters wore black and white scarves. Now it is possible to note how long someone has been enamoured of racing by the vintage of his or her scarf, in the same way that a pair of binoculars festooned with cardboard admission badges used to be the unmistakable mark of an old hand, or merely someone who had an issue with throwing things away.

Owners in a syndicate wear scarves or ties matching their jockey's silks, and racegoers sport scarves bearing the corporate colours and logo of the leading betting exchange that have been given away free as a gimmick. It is harmless fun, a throwback to antique times of coats-of-arms, to when peers of the realm chose racing colours based on their own personal livery, and an easy source of revenue with a wide market. Leading Flat trainers wear baseball caps adorned with the name of the next big stallion sensation, a new one every year, the failures relegated to the darkest corner of the tack room.

Expressing where alliances lie, and the depth of those alliances, used to be reliant on a word in the right place, but now it is so much more convenient to show rather than tell, show your devotion, show your connection, show you belong. Sleeves are old hat; wear your heart around your neck.

99

The number of a beast. Image © Alamy

ALONE AT THE SUMMIT

It has taken approximately 350 years of thoroughbred breeding to produce the perfect specimen, or what is reckoned the perfect specimen, a horse so good he could not be beaten, capable of performances so remarkable that even the stone-hearted number-crunchers of the sport would push their calculators aside, stand up and cheer.

This is the best we've seen, to appropriate Peter O'Sullevan's description of Arkle, whose position at the peak of jump racing is taken as read. On the Flat, the picture is not quite as clear, given its global parameters, but his equivalent is almost certainly a horse named Frankel, and lucky are those born at the right time in those three and a half centuries to witness his greatness.

Frankel (foaled 2008) is a son of the prepotent overlord of bloodstock Galileo, from a female line that also traces back through Northern Dancer.

He was trained by Sir Henry Cecil, bred and owned by Prince Khalid Abdullah, and was given his name in recognition of the prince's chief US trainer Bobby Frankel, who died in 2009. The name was being kept for a good horse, a fitting tribute to the man, and no racing man could have been better memorialised.

The burly colt with four white feet was crowned champion two-year-old, winning all his four races. To be champion two-year-old means little on a broader scale, though, like being a 16-year-old footballing prodigy. It is an indication of potential, nothing more, and very many are the champion two-year-olds who failed to live up to their billing and have been forgotten. Frankel did not just live up to that billing, he exceeded it in the same fashion as he outstripped every horse who went against him.

His extraordinary performance in the 2011 2,000 Guineas at Newmarket laid the foundations for what was to come and fixed his greatness in amber for perpetuity. It was his Secretariat moment: by halfway, he was so far clear of his pursuers that the race was no longer a race but merely an exhibition of pure brilliance. He won by six lengths, having been 15 clear at one stage.

Frankel's talent was showcased above all by the appearance of barely restrained power, a bull of a horse, held on tight reins by jockey Tom Queally but seemingly always on the point of breaking free. He was indeed a headstrong colt, and during the early stages of his development there were concerns that his character might prevent his undoubted ability being channelled in the right direction, yet he was managed so superbly by Cecil and his staff that his temperament was tamed without affecting his natural desire to run.

Frankel then won the Sussex Stakes by five lengths and the Queen Elizabeth II Stakes by four, confirming himself as one of the greats. The following season, strengthened by maturity and experience, surrounded at every step by an almost physical aura of majesty, he produced what has been rated as the single greatest performance on a British racecourse, on any racecourse.

In the Queen Anne Stakes over a mile at Royal Ascot, after being shepherded through the first half-mile by his usual pacemaker and three-parts brother (by Galileo's sire Sadler's Wells, same dam) Bullet Train, Frankel was pulled out to deliver a challenge two furlongs from home and produced such a devastating change of pace that Queally may have sustained whiplash. He sprinted away from a high-class field, every stride emphasising his superiority, passing the post 11 lengths clear of his habitual whipping boy Excelebration, himself a three-time Group

1 winner. Now he was no longer one of the greats, but was separate from them, alone at the summit, the greatest.

The style and substance of that victory led Timeform to anoint him with a rating of 147, the highest on record, a mark two pounds higher than the outstanding French colt Sea-Bird. This was practically heresy, but it was greeted with widespread acceptance, no quibbling from an outraged old guard, just a tacit acknowledgement, almost a shrug, as though to say 'well, what else can you do?'

The rest of Frankel's career passed in a blaze of sustained glory, ridiculously sublime, reinforced by the affection in which the racing public held his trainer. In different circumstances Frankel would have been admired and revered, but his connection to Cecil meant that he was also loved. On his last two starts he stepped up to a mile and a quarter with no flickering of his eternal flame, the same result time and time again, 14 races, 14 wins, ten Group 1s, and that rating of 147 standing out like the Hollywood sign.

Frankel was campaigned conservatively, he never raced outside Britain, he was kept to a mile for the majority of his career, he was odds-on for every race bar his debut. He was never truly taken out of his vast comfort zone, but there is no reason to believe he could not have coped with anything asked of him. To criticise him is pointless; no one cavils at Shakespeare because he never wrote a novel, or doubts Bradman because he wasn't much of a bowler.

It is in our nature to compare. Is it right to say Frankel is the best ever? Better than Sea-Bird, Secretariat, Ribot, Brigadier Gerard, Dancing Brave, Phar Lap, Man O'War, Citation, Mill Reef? Better than all these different, magnificent horses whose deeds will never fade?

Yes, very probably. He is rated so, and it might well be said that Frankel was better at doing what he did than any horse ever foaled. To watch him race was to be serially astounded, recurrently awestruck, our emotion backed up by the cold hard figures that told us we could believe what we saw. One day there may be a better horse. But this is the best we've seen.

100

How to bet in 2021.   Image © Author

JUST THE GLORY OF A HORSE

We can be as remote as the stars, and still share the same heaven. Racing has always been a hands-on affair, but today it can all be done with the tips of the fingers, though the connections made through 500 years still bind us tightly, still hold us in thrall. Technology has moved us forward, but we look backwards even as we reach out to the future.

    The smallness of a mobile phone now gives us the whole world. We read the *Racing Post* at the touch of an app where once we rustled through the pages of *The Sporting Life*; we ponder a tipster's online selection where once we listened gleefully to Prince Monolulu; we make a bet with a click here, a click there, the same thought processes in play as for our ancestors in the Tattersall's Rooms, or for our grandfathers seeking out the bookies' runner, just a different physical process; we watch a race on a tiny screen, without the sun on our faces.

There is more information available than at any other time. We can know almost everything about a horse with the same tap of a finger, read the latest news about its trainer or jockey. Eclipse was no more than an artist's impression, drawn from life but somehow lacking in it, but we see Frankel move, stretch out, muscles rippling, just the glory of a horse at a time when horses are otherwise no longer a part of our daily lives. Yet their glory sustains, and sustains us.

Owners can see their horses at exercise without leaving the office, videos of the gallops clicked directly to their phones, no need to stand in the cold wondering which one is your horse, the only thing missing the camaraderie of the dawn mornings, but the rest of the syndicate is on a WhatsApp group so the chat, the excitement, the togetherness is still intact.

Trainers can buy a horse without feeling its legs or looking into the deep well of its eyes, looking for that which Vincent O'Brien described as 'talking to me'. Another click, this time on the name of Richard Tattersall; bought. Jockeys can view past performances of their next mount, board a plane and fly 10,000 miles, get off the plane, get on the horse, win the race. Journalists can write the race report and transmit it with yet another click, no more fuzzy phone lines and a bored copytaker who asks 'how are you spelling Piggott?'

And yet, and yet. The horses we see at the racecourse have the blood of the Darley Arabian coursing through their veins, the dusty fingerprints of history all over their glossy hides. When they run, they elicit comparison with their peers but also with horses whose bones were picked clean centuries ago, yet who retain their great lives in the collective memory. Eclipse, Kincsem, Arkle, Secretariat, Nijinsky, Night Nurse, their influence as strong now as it was then.

They are ridden by jockeys who owe their style to Tod Sloan, jockeys who wear little coats of many colours that the peers and princes of the pre-Industrial age would recognise. Their chances are assessed by pundits who gleaned their racing education from Phil Bull, they carry saddles containing the weights Admiral Rous would have assigned them, and when they race they do it for prizes of silver and gold, as they did so long ago.

Perhaps one or two of them are owned by the Queen, whose line of royal succession has little to do with Charles II, but whose sentiments are shared with that merry monarch. Somewhere in the crowd, although not one as large as that seen at Epsom on sepia-tinted Derby days, are women wearing hats that owe their creation to the legacy of Gertrude Shilling, standing next to men warmed by a pre-race glass of what was once the sponsor's product.

Then two horses draw clear of the field and those watching them shout with excitement like they did hundreds of years ago, and when with unending grace and courage and will one outruns the other, it reaches the winning post first, the same marker that has served this purpose since time out of mind.

The thread of life unravels, drawing one foot into the future while tethering the other to the past. What we are now is because of what we were, the echoes of history as loud as hoofbeats on turf, the heartbeat rhythm of our racing lives.

BIBLIOGRAPHY

Racing Post cuttings library.

John Randall & Tony Morris, *A Century Of Champions* (Portway Press, 1999).

Wray Vamplew & Joyce Kay, *Encyclopedia of British Horseracing* (Routledge, 2005).

John Welcome, *The Cheltenham Gold Cup* (Pelham Books, 1984).

Jacqueline O'Brien & Ivor Herbert, *Vincent O'Brien, The Official Biography* (Bantam Press, 2005).

Michael Tanner, *The Champion Hurdle* (Mainstream, 2002).

Sean Magee, *Great Races* (Anaya Publishers, 1990).

Chris Pitt, *A Long Time Gone* (Portway Press, 2006).

Ivor Herbert & Patricia Smyly, *The Winter Kings* (Pelham Books, 1989).

Richard Austen, *At The Festival* (SportsBooks, 2015).

Sean Magee, *Arkle* (Racing Post, 2005).

Ivor Herbert, *Red Rum* (Aurum Press, 2005).

John Hughes & Peter Watson, *Long Live The National* (Michael Joseph, 1983).

Chris Pitt, *Go Down To The Beaten* (Racing Post, 2011).

Rebecca Cassidy, *The Sport Of Kings* (Cambridge University Press, 2002).

William Nack, *Secretariat* (Blue Door, 2010).

Laura Hillenbrand, *Seabiscuit* (Fourth Estate, 2002).

100 Greatest Races (Racing Post, 2005).

The Benson & Hedges Book of Racing Colours (Weather Oak Press, 1973).

The internet.